Living in
LONDON

A practical guide

TENTH EDITION

Written and published by The Junior League of London

Registered Charity No. 1103298

This edition first published in 2006 by The Junior League of London, 9 Fitzmaurice Place, London, W1J 5JD; www.jll.org.uk.

Design by Neal Cobourne

10th edition. First published in 1981.

The authors and publishers have made every effort to ensure the accuracy of the information in this book at the time of going to press. However, they cannot accept any responsibility for any loss, injury or inconvenience resulting from the use of information contained in this guide. Please help us keep this guide up to date. We have done our best to ensure that the information in this guide is correct at the time of going to press, but places and facilities are constantly changing and standards and prices fluctuate. We would be delighted to receive any comments concerning existing entries or omissions.

Output by Acorn Photoset, London
Printed & bound in Great Britain by Cambrian Printers Ltd, Aberystwyth, Wales.

A catalogue record of this book is available from the British Library.

ISBN 0-9525195-4-2

ABOUT THE JUNIOR LEAGUE OF LONDON

The Junior League is an organisation of women committed to promoting voluntary service, developing the potential of women and improving the community through the effective action and leadership of trained volunteers. The organisation has been operating in London since 1979.

ACKNOWLEDGEMENTS

Editing this book was a daunting task and never would have been possible without the valuable insight, recommendations and continuous support of the entire 2005/06 Living in London Committee: Hallie Ambler, Lesley Bisesi, Anne Hammerstein, Michelle Hogan, Jill Hurst, Ashley Lilly, Jennifer Nutbrown, Corey Papps, Sarah Solmssen and Brandy Treadway, and some very special friends: Robin Kanarek, Andrea Kantor, Tracy Longhurst, Anni Marjoram and Chris Mohrmann.

We must extend a heartfelt thank you to Sally Keck and all of the students at Colville Primary School for creating all of the fantastic artwork contained in this book. Many thanks also to the countless Junior League of London members who provided all of the reference material within this guide.

Special thanks to all of our corporate and personal sponsors whose financial assistance allow the proceeds of this book to go directly to charity.

Sincerely,
The co-editors of the 10th edition: Lisa Hill & Jenny Noe-Nordberg

INDIVIDUAL SPONSORS

GOLD SPONSORS

Anne and Ronald Thompson

Karen & Geordie Young

BRONZE PATRON

Credit Suisse First Boston

FRIENDS OF LIVING IN LONDON

Hallie & Bruce Ambler

Aundrea & Jim Amine

Sheila Bajaj

Caroline Beery

Heidi Black

Helen Bruckman

Ersel Buckley Sharp

Joan Buerk

Tiffany Burnette

Brittan & Rob Chepak

Pamela Creel

Jennifer Crowl

Jacqueline de Sanctis

Amy Duckett

Abigail Durban

Beth & Jonathan Franklin

Eileen Glynn

Anne Hammerstein

Lisa & Brett Hill

Caroline John

Ashley & Craig Klaasmeyer

Marie Kluth

Kevin & My Phuong Lecocq

Susan Lenora

Betsy Ludwig Abdallah

Paula & Dermot McNulty

Liz & Tom Murley

Sara Niedringhaus

Markus & Jenny Noé-Nordberg

Mary Perrotta

Jennifer Rigby Morrison

Ann M. Riker

Sarah Solmssen

Susan Shea-Gerson

Sarah Solmssen

Laura Sukawaty

Melissa Taylor

Sudie Throdahl

Jennifer Tonkel

Brandy Treadway

Adriana Vargas

Nancy & Neil Weidner

George & Patti White

CORPORATE SPONSORS

ACS INTERNATIONAL SCHOOLS

Cobham Egham Hillingdon

The American School in London

HUMPHRYS' EDUCATION LTD

Contents

CONTENTS

"*Living in London* was written by people, who, like you, were new to London and now have a full appreciation of what the city has to offer. It is full of personal recommendations and advice from volunteers whose shared experiences will ease your transition and make discovering London enjoyable. It also contains a wealth of practical advice on a range of issues from the health service and the education system to the hidden corners of the city. *Living in London* is an invaluable resource guide put together by The Junior League of London.

I hope you enjoy your stay in London and learn to relish the diversity of this our great world city."

Ken Livingstone
Mayor of London

Preface

WELCOME TO LONDON!

A vibrant city of world-class culture, history, and diversity awaits you. London is truly magnificent; and despite what many might think, a lot has changed since the Romans founded "Londinium" in the year 43 AD. And as hosts of the 2012 Olympics, the best is yet to come.

London is truly a multicultural city...where people from every country around the world are made to feel at home.

Despite the excitement, moving to London can be challenging. It is a large, complex and sometimes, bewildering city. It takes time to understand its complexities, identify its charms and discover its hidden secrets. Getting accustomed to little differences plays a key role in making one feel at home.

The Junior League of London is a self-funding, UK registered charity that works to improve the lives of families in need in London. Using art as its medium, the League provides meaningful and dynamic programmes that positively impact the lives of London's most disadvantaged children. By purchasing this guide, you have already made a valuable contribution to your new community.

Relish in London and all of its offerings...as Samuel Johnson, the English Poet (1709-1784) said: *"When a man is tired of London, he is tired of life; for there is in London, all that life can afford."*

Drawn by Oceone

Moving

CONTENTS

IMMIGRATION

You must ensure that you have permission from the British Government before moving to the United Kingdom. Depending on your nationality and the purpose and length of your stay in the UK, you may need to obtain a visa before entering the country. Please note that most people travelling to the UK for more than six months must now obtain entry clearance before travelling. Immigration into the UK is under the jurisdiction of the **Home Office's Immigration and Nationality Directorate (IND)**. Details, application forms and instructions for applying to live and/or work in the UK can be found at www.ind.homeoffice.gov.uk. If you do not arrive in the UK under the correct category, you may not be allowed to enter or you may be deported. It is imperative to organise the process correctly before moving.

Information about immigration is often the subject of rumour so be sure that you get advice from a reliable source. If you are moving in connection with a job, the Human Resources department often organises the process for you. If you need independent advice, be wary. If your adviser is not a lawyer, solicitor, barrister or legal executive, you should ask if they are "OISC authorised". A list of OISC-authorised advisers is available from **The Office of the Immigration Services Commissioner** at 020 7211 1500 (www. oisc.gov.uk). In addition, you may wish to contact the **British Consulate** or **Diplomatic Post** closest to where you live for advice. **The Foreign and Commonwealth Office** (www.fco.gov.uk) lists all diplomatic missions. Embassies also often have lists of attorneys practicing in the UK who can assist with immigration matters.

> *Did you know?...The permission from the British Government to stay in the country is called your "leave to remain".*

WORK PERMIT HOLDERS AND THEIR FAMILIES

Most people moving to the UK come under the work permit scheme. The employing company must apply for the work permit prior to your arrival through the **Work Permits** (UK) division of the IND. Allow at least two months before the date you need to begin work in the UK for the application process. The permit applies specifically to the job and to the individual. Once the application has been approved, a work permit is issued and sent to you. If your work permit is valid for more than six months, you must apply for a visa in your home country before travelling to the UK. The **British Consulate** or **Diplomatic Post** will stamp a visa certificate into your passport or travel document. The visa certificate must be presented to the immigration authorities upon entry into the UK. Allow at least one month to apply for your visa. You will be required to show your stamped passport each time you enter or leave the UK and may be asked to confirm your work status. Visit the **Home Office**'s visa website (www.ukvisas.gov.uk) for more information and online visa applications (www.visa4uk.fco.gov.uk).

Spouses, dependants and children of overseas nationals who hold a work permit can apply for a visa at a **British Consulate** or **Diplomatic Post** before moving to the UK. A same-sex partner who can demonstrate that he or she has been in a relationship akin to marriage for at least two years can also obtain entry clearance. For specific advice about immigration to the UK as a same-sex partner, visit the website of the **UK Lesbian & Gay Immigration Group** (formerly the Stonewall Immigration Group) at www.uklgig.org.uk. The application should be done after the spouse or partner's work permit is approved and allow at least one month to apply.

Spouses, dependants and same-sex partners of work permit holders with correct entry clearance can work in the UK without being issued a work permit.

REGISTRATION WITH THE OVERSEAS VISITORS RECORDS OFFICE

A limited number of non-EEA nationals are required to register with the police. **The Immigration Office** will put a stamp in your passport when you arrive in the UK if you are required to register and you and members of your family residing with you in the UK must register with the **Overseas Visitors Records Office (OVRO)** within seven days of your arrival in the country. Children under the age of 16 do not need to register. You should contact your local police station for information about where you need to register. You will have to pay a registration fee.

You will be given a green booklet (certificate) called a "Police Registration Certificate" that you must produce within 24 hours, if asked to do so by the police or immigration officers. It is best to always carry this certificate with you while in Great Britain. The certificate will also make re-entry into the UK easier when you travel abroad on trips lasting less than two months. The certificate should be submitted to the Immigration Office on departure if travelling abroad for more than two months.

Any change of address or name change must be given to the OVRO within seven days. When a child turns 16 years of age, he or she must register with the OVRO only if a stamp requiring registration is endorsed in his or her passport.

EXTENSIONS OF STAY; CHANGE OF EMPLOYMENT

The endorsement, stamp or certificate in your passport indicates how long you have leave to remain in the United Kingdom. In order to stay longer, your employer must apply to Work Permits (UK) for an extension (within two months of the expiry of your stay).

A work permit is issued for a particular position. If your employment ends, your work permit is no longer valid and you should make arrangements to leave the UK within a reasonable amount of time. If you switch employers, your new employer must apply for a work permit before you begin working. A work permit cannot be "rolled-over" into another job. Please note that it is simpler to get a work permit for an employee if he or she has had one before.

After five years of residence in the UK, a work permit holder and his or her dependants may apply for Indefinite Leave to Remain, permanent residence status, which will lift the need for a work permit and entitle the holder to certain public benefits. However, be aware that lengthy delays are probable, and it is not at all unusual to wait longer than six months for the **Home Office**'s decision. It may be possible to expedite the process by applying in person at the Home Office, Immigration and Nationality Department, Lunar House, 40 Wellesley Road, Croydon, Surrey, CR9 2BY; 0870 606 7766, or by hiring the services of a solicitor or lawyer. Before going to the Home Office in person, be prepared to spend the entire day there and ensure that you have all the correct information with you.

EEA NATIONALS AND THEIR FAMILIES

A national of a member state of the **European Economic Area** (EEA) or Switzerland is free to enter the UK to work and live. No prior permission is required and no work permit is needed for employment, but you may need to register under the **Worker Registration Scheme**. Visit www.workingintheuk.gov.uk for more information.

EEA nationals exercising their rights of free movement are entitled to bring their dependants with them to the UK, even if they are non-EEA nationals. Non-EEA family members require entry clearance in the form of a family permit, which must be obtained before entering the country. The non-EEA dependants of an EEA national may stay in the UK so long as the EEA national spouse is exercising his or her treaty rights by working in the UK. After living in the UK for five years, the non-EEA national is entitled to apply for permanent residence status (Indefinite Leave to Remain) (see "*Extensions of Stay*" above).

If you are a citizen of the EEA, you can apply for a resident's permit when you arrive in the UK. The application is made to the **Home Office** (see above) on form ECC1. You will need to submit a passport for yourself and each family member or national identity documents and two passport-sized photographs of yourself and any of your dependants over the age of 16. The Home Office may take 6 – 12 months to process your application. Therefore, if you are a frequent traveller, be sure to make the application using your national identity card or a notarised photocopy of your passport.

OTHER IMMIGRATION CATEGORIES

There are many other categories under which people can live in the UK, including: British ancestry, working-holiday makers, students, independent means, innovators, highly skilled migrant workers, investors and sole representatives of an overseas firm. For details about any of these schemes, go to the Home Office website at www.ukvisas.gov.uk and look over the visa forms at www.visa4uk.fco.gov.uk. The Home Office also has information about working in the UK at www.workingintheuk.gov.uk. Please note that most of these categories are paper intensive and require you to apply at a British Consulate or Diplomatic Post before arriving in the UK. Be sure to reserve plenty of time to gather all supporting evidence and documents and have your application reviewed. Again, your local British Consulate or Diplomatic Post will be able to advise you on these schemes.

CLIMATE AND WEATHER

Weather in London is unpredictable; however, extreme conditions are rare. The average temperature varies from a low of 0°C (32°F) to a high of 24°C (about 75°F). July is the warmest month and January is the coldest month. One common climate condition is a very soft drizzle, so carrying an umbrella or rain hat is a good idea.

Temperatures are usually reported in Celsius. An approximate conversion from Celsius to Fahrenheit is to double the Celsius and add 30.

Celsius (Centigrade)		Fahrenheit	Celsius (Centigrade)		Fahrenheit
-3°C	=	26.6°F	20	=	68.0
-1	=	30.2	25	=	77.0
0	=	32.0 (freezing point)	30	=	86.0
1	=	33.8	37	=	98.6 (average human body
5	=	41.0			temperature)
10	=	50.0	100	=	212 (boiling
15	=	59.0			point)

WHAT TO BRING AND WHAT NOT TO BRING

What to bring when you move to London is an individual decision and should be based on the anticipated length of time you will reside in the UK. It will also depend upon your housing — whether furnished or unfurnished, house or flat.

WHAT TO BRING

The following items may not be readily available or easily replaced in the UK. If they are available in the UK, they may be considerably more expensive than they are abroad.

Personal Items

- Eyeglasses, contact lenses and related products.

- Special cosmetics and beauty products, particularly dermatologist-recommended ones.

- Medical prescriptions may be branded differently. Ask your doctor or pharmacist for the name of the underlying compound to ensure that you receive the same medicine when you refill your prescriptions in the UK.

• Any over-the-counter medicine that you particularly like. See *Chapter 8: Children* for a listing of equivalent children's medicines and products available in the UK.

For the Home

• European and English beds and bedding vary greatly in size from those sold elsewhere, particularly the United States, and are relatively expensive. If you bring your beds, bring the appropriate bedding.

• British recipes use imperial and metric measurements, and some UK measuring utensils differ in size from those sold elsewhere. To ensure that you can make your recipes in the UK, you may wish to bring a set of measuring cups and spoons along with your favourite cookbooks.

For Cooking Tips

• See *Chapter 10: Cooking, Food and Drink.*

Miscellaneous

• Children's games, sports equipment (baseballs, softballs, bats, footballs, basketballs and bicycles).

• Special decorations for various holidays you celebrate throughout the year.

WHAT NOT TO BRING

• Cordless telephones

- Light bulbs (except appliance bulbs — see the sections on electricity below for an explanation of electrical differences)

- Christmas tree lights

- Electric clocks (if moving from the Americas or Japan)

- Liquor/Spirits (excluding wine), except duty-free allowances

- Cigarettes, except duty-free allowances

- Perfumes, except duty-free allowances

- Paints, cleaning agents or other combustible or flammable items

- Plants and bulbs

- Meat, fruits and vegetables

- Certain fish and eggs

- Most animals and all birds (except pets — see "Bringing Your Pet to the UK" below)

- Items made from protected species, including reptile leather, ivory and fur skins.

HM Revenue and Customs has information regarding what not to bring and frequently asked questions on their website at www.hmrc.gov.uk.

Did you know?...The laws regarding firearms being brought into Great Britain for sports purposes and/or decorative sports equipment are extremely restrictive. You are advised to check the current law when you move. Applications and more information are available at www. met.police.uk/firearms-enquiries/ index.htm.

ELECTRICAL DIFFERENCES

Deciding on which electrical appliances and equipment to bring to the UK or leave home can be confusing, especially if you are relocating from North America. British (and most of Europe's) electrical current is 220/240 volts and 50 Hz (frequency or cycles per second) while the North American current is 110 volts and 60 Hz (frequency or cycles per second). Understanding which voltage and frequency is compatible with your electrical devices will facilitate your decision-making. Some devices, if designed for several voltages, can be used directly in the UK with a plug adaptor. Others can be used with a voltage transformer, and some cannot be used at all. Given the expense of adaptors and transformers, and the shortage of space in most British flats, you may find it easier to purchase smaller appliances after settling into your new home.

For a list of plugs, voltages and frequencies for each country, go to www. answers.com and search "list of plugs, voltages and frequencies".

ADAPTORS

Most UK plugs have three square prongs. Electrical devices that do not need voltage transformers can be used with a plug adaptor or the non-UK plug can be replaced with a UK plug. While the latter option is cheaper, be sure to ask an electrician or local hardware store if you are unsure of how to replace the plugs.

TRANSFORMERS

In general, most non-European electrical goods are incompatible with UK electrical supply because of the voltage difference (220/240V for UK versus 110V for North America, for example). This means that if you try to use them in the UK, they will burn out. You can get them to work if you use a transformer, which is a plug-in device that will convert 220/240V to 110V. Transformers are available in shops in London and the surrounding area. Transformers are sized from 30 watts to 1,500 watts and are priced according to their wattage (starting at approximately £15). A hair dryer or electric curler will require up to a 250-watt transformer. A blender or food processor will require up to a 500-watt transformer, while a refrigerator will require up to a 1,500-watt transformer.

Transformers, depending on the size, can be used to power several appliances so you do not necessarily need one transformer for each device. However, they are bulky and heavy and therefore not very portable.

DUAL-VOLTAGE APPLIANCES

Some appliances, such as home computers, printers, video recorders, televisions and stereos, are dual voltage and can function on 120V or 240V. The appliance may automatically adjust to the correct voltage or a switch on the appliance may need to be adjusted. Check your appliances for this feature because it will allow you to use it in the UK without a transformer.

APPLIANCES INCOMPATIBLE WITH THE FREQUENCY

The electrical supply in most of the world, including the UK, is 50 Hz, while it is 60 Hz in North America and parts of South America and Japan. This frequency difference comes into play in motorised appliances, where the speed of the motor is important. There is no simple device that will convert 50 Hz to 60 Hz, so any device with a motor will run at a bit more than 80 per cent of its normal speed when it is run on a transformer. For hair dryers, fans, washers, blenders, refrigerators and dryers that might not be a problem. For analogue clocks, it is a problem.

In using certain devices with motors, like video recorders, personal computers and audio equipment, the frequency difference is not an issue because the electrical current is automatically converted to Direct Current in the machine so the device will run at the right speed, independent of frequency.

SPECIFIC APPLIANCES

Refrigerators

A refrigerator can be run on an appropriate-size transformer to convert to UK voltage. North American refrigerators (110V, 60 Hz) may be purchased in the UK, but they are very expensive. If you are renting and wish to have a large refrigerator, make sure that there is space in the kitchen to accommodate one since British refrigerators are often small.

Washing Machines and Electric Dryers

A washer can be run on an appropriate-size transformer to convert to UK voltage. The dryer will probably be 240V and may work without a transformer, but the machine should only be installed by a qualified electrician. North American washers and dryers are larger than UK appliances and may not fit in your particular house or flat. If you wish to have larger appliances, be sure that you have adequate space for them.

Did you know?...If you are interested in buying American appliances during your stay in the UK, try American Appliances at 020 8505 5616 (www. americanappliances.com).

Gas dryers can be used in the UK if your flat or house is serviced with gas, but they will need a transformer for the motor and may need a different pressure regulator for the gas.

Televisions, Video Recorders and DVDs

It may be wise to sell these appliances before moving and buy new or used ones when you arrive. While TVs, video recorders and DVDs purchased abroad can be run in the UK with a transformer, they have limited use because of the differences in broadcasting standards. The TV will not pick up British stations, by antenna or cable, unless it is a "multi system" TV, equipped with a switch for the PAL system, which is the UK standard. Similarly, American video recorders will not play British videos unless it is a "multi-system" machine equipped with a switch for the PAL system.

Did you know?... DVDs are coded differently for different regions of the world. For example, North America is coded as Zone 1, Europe and Japan are coded as Zone 2 and South America is coded as Zone 4. If you are bringing your DVDs, make sure the DVD player you purchase can play DVDs from the appropriate zone. Likewise, do not buy DVDs in the UK and expect to be able to play them when you return home.

Telephones

Do not bring cordless telephones.

Some telephones may be used in the UK after purchasing an adaptor, although the price of an adaptor may be more expensive than the price of a new phone. Otherwise telephones are not compatible with the UK system.

Computers

Most computers are dual voltage and can function as either 120V or 240V by the flick of a switch. However, your computer accessories (e.g., speakers and printers) may not be. Contact customer service or review your user manuals for verification. If they are not dual voltage, your computer, monitor and printer will run on a transformer in the UK. Bring your surge protector or purchase one when you arrive in the UK.

Lamps

All lamps (except those using halogen or fluorescent bulbs) can be used in the UK if they are used with an adaptor or are fitted with UK plugs. 110V light bulbs will explode if used in the UK because of the voltage difference, so you may need to leave your light bulbs at home. The ballast in halogen lamps must be changed and may be difficult to find.

Miscellaneous Electrical Information

Some electrical appliances purchased in the UK do not come with socket outlet plugs. Attaching a plug is an easy procedure, but keep a store of plugs with both 3 amp and 13 amp fuses. Different appliances require different fuses, so be sure to have the correct fuse for each appliance. If your appliance fails to work, check the fuse and plug before calling the electrician. Obviously, all electrical appliances are potential fire hazards and should be used with caution. Always consult an electrician if you are not absolutely certain how an appliance should be correctly operated.

If you have electrical appliances that require appliance bulbs, such as sewing machines, refrigerators and freezers, bring the bulbs with you.

Wall outlets in a flat or house may not be of a uniform size. For this reason, when you shop for plug adaptors, appliances or electrical items, check the outlets in the room where the appliance/adaptor will be used. While the 13 amp square, three-prong pin plugs are becoming standard, you may also find 2 amp, 5 amp and 15 amp round-pin plugs.

For your electrical questions and needs, contact Ryness Electrical Supplies at 020 7278 8993 (www.ryness.co.uk). They have branches throughout London.

> *Did you know?... If you plan to rent accommodation, keep in mind that most flats and houses come furnished with basic appliances.*

SHIPPING HOUSEHOLD EFFECTS

Deciding which household effects to take with you depends on many factors, including the anticipated length of your stay and the type of accommodation to be maintained. A total move can take several months to arrange while a temporary or short-term move can happen almost immediately. If possible, try to schedule a house-hunting trip to view different types of properties before you move. UK housing typically has little storage space both inside (e.g., closets) and outside (e.g., garages). Storage centres are often expensive so you should think about how your household effects will fit into you new home.

Start by making lists:

What is going with you on the airplane?

What is needed soon after you arrive (if you are going into temporary housing, it may be necessary to bring these items with you as excess baggage or via an air shipment)?

What is being shipped in a container via sea/air?

What is going into storage?

Things to give away?

Things to sell?

Things to discard?

Once you have finally made all of these decisions, it is a good idea to have the lists duplicated. There is nothing more frustrating than misplacing your only copy of one of these important lists.

MOVING

> *Did you know?...It is important to remember when choosing items to bring that many flats are converted 19th century houses. They are very beautiful; however, the hallways and doors can be very narrow and may not accommodate large pieces of furniture.*

When selecting a moving company, choose a reputable one. Investigate the company's performance record and check references. Go over all items in detail with the moving company's representative and have everything in writing. Get more than one estimate. Do not choose a firm simply because it is the cheapest; it may turn out to be a 'penny wise, pound foolish' decision. If you are moving abroad for work, your company may have a list of preferred carriers. Do not be afraid to ask questions about the process and make sure that you receive copies of all important documents.

You may have the option of shipping your goods via air and/or sea. Air shipments normally take one to two weeks and are usually the most expensive. Sea shipments will likely be in a container and normally arrive within four to six weeks. If you are moving abroad for work, your company may specify a certain size container. Be sure that you ask about the specifics before scheduling the estimates.

If you are shipping via sea, you should know which ship is going to carry your container and when it is scheduled to depart for and arrive in England. Upon arrival, your moving company should make arrangements with **HM Revenue and Customs** and the British removal company that will transfer your shipment from the port to your home. It can take a few days or a couple of weeks to clear customs. Be sure that you have the appropriate contact information for all steps of the journey.

You should be knowledgeable about the moving and removal companies' loss and damage protection policies — read all of the small print on any contract. It is essential to have insurance. Your local homeowners' policy stops covering your belongings when they leave port so be sure to know the scope and coverage of the insurance for the shipment. It might be wise to check with one or more private insurance companies instead of relying on the moving company's insurance programme.

For insurance purposes it is necessary to have an itemised inventory. This list might be done by categories, such as furniture, silver, paintings and accessories, or room by room. Pick the system that best suits your needs and remember to value all items at replacement value. It is a good idea to have everything appraised and to record everything with photographs.

Make several copies of the inventory. One copy has to go to the insuring company, which may be the moving company or an insurance agent. Take more than one copy with you when the shipment arrives in England. This inventory list makes it easy to record any possible damage which might require repair and an insurance claim. If possible, be present when your goods are unpacked at your home. Bring up any insurance claims quickly since most policies do not permit claims after a certain amount of time has passed.

PACKING YOUR HOUSEHOLD

Make sure your specifications and instructions are being carried out to your satisfaction. Ensure that each and every box is labelled with its contents and destination (even the room).

If you are doing any of the packing or unpacking, check for insurance coverage. Usually breakables are covered only when packed and unpacked by the moving company. The shipping charges normally include all packing and unpacking.

PACKING YOUR LUGGAGE FOR THE PLANE

Some items that might go into your luggage are: a sewing kit, a small first-aid kit, umbrella, address book, extra pair of glasses, extra prescriptions, small toolkit, carrying bag for groceries or laundry, baby buggy, books, some old clothes for cleaning or painting and comfortable shoes. Do not ship jewellery — carry it with you.

Take copies of any important legal documents with you. First and foremost, make a full copy of your passport and any visa or work permit information. Additionally, you should have copies of any wills, insurance policies, rental contracts on properties and investments, and a list of current charge accounts with their account numbers. Make sure a trusted friend or attorney knows the whereabouts of the originals. You may also want to carry copies of family medical records with you.

CUSTOMS AND VAT

The British Government allows importing of all household or personal effects duty free if they have been owned six months prior to the date of entry into the UK. Proof of purchase must be available on items less than six months old. Certain other household items may be dutiable. There are also special regulations regarding the importing of inherited goods and antiques into Great Britain. In addition, excise taxes are payable on certain items, such as liquor and cigarettes.

If possible, have a file with a copy of the bill of sale for every valuable item, such as cameras, watches, jewellery, silver, major appliances, etc. If you do not have these bills of sale, an alternative is a copy of an old insurance policy that itemises these articles. Carry these documents with you; do not ship them.

All items that are not at least six months old are subject to duty charges and VAT (Value Added Tax – currently 17.5% on most goods). Check with your moving company or the closest British Consulate regarding which items may be subject to duty and excise tax plus VAT, as the customs and duty charges can vary depending on the item in question.

For additional information, contact **General Enquiries, HM Revenue and Customs**, 0845 010 9000; www.hmrc.gov.uk.

BRINGING YOUR PET TO THE UK

While Great Britain still requires a six-month quarantine for domestic pets, it is now possible to bring pets into the country without quarantine under the Pet Travel Scheme.

For a more complete listing of quarantine kennels and the current quarantine requirements, contact the **Department of Environment, Food and Rural Affairs (DEFRA)**, 0845 933 5577; www.defra.gov.uk. Kennel recommendations can also be found in *Chapter 11: Services*.

The Pet Travel Scheme applies only to certain types of domestic animals arriving from certain countries. If you are planning to take your pets to the UK through the scheme, begin the process approximately eight months before you expect to move to ensure that your pet will not have to spend any time in quarantine. The scheme requires a substantial amount of paperwork and coordination with both your local veterinarian and the local agricultural authority in your home country. **DEFRA** has extensive information about the Pet Travel Scheme and the EU pet passport, including forms and checklists, on their website at www.defra.gov.uk/animalh/quarantine/index.htm.

A brief outline of the necessary steps are:

• You must microchip your pet and verify that the microchip can be read by standard scanners.

• After the microchip has been fitted, your pet must be vaccinated against rabies and a blood test must be sent to an EU-approved laboratory. If the test is successful, then your pet will be able to enter the UK at least six months after the date of the test result. If you enter the country before then, your pet must go into quarantine until the expiry of this six-month period.

• Immediately before entering the UK, your pet must receive a tick and tapeworm treatment and all paperwork must be correctly completed.

• As well as complying with the pet travel scheme, you must arrange for your pet's transportation. The scheme requires that your pet enter the country using an approved transport company and route (a list of which can be found on **DEFRA**'s website). You must purchase a carrier for your pet that meets the airline's kennel guidelines and labelling requirements (this information is usually available on each airline's website; kennels can be purchased from the airline or a pet supply store).

• Most airlines also require a certificate of acclimation from your veterinarian and a statement regarding food and water from the pet owner. The certificate of acclimation states that your pet can fly at certain temperatures. It can only be obtained 24-48 hours before departure. This certificate can be problematic if you are travelling during very high or very low temperatures.

• You must complete a customs form for your pet and ensure that it will clear customs upon arrival in the UK. Most airlines require a broker to clear pets through customs and often can provide these services if asked. If they cannot, then call customs or **DEFRA** to get more information. Note that is essential to clarify your point of entry (e.g., Heathrow, Gatwick or other UK airport) to ensure the broker is at the airport where you will arrive.

Travelling with a pet can be very expensive. The price of your pet's ticket will depend on the size of its carrier and can often exceed the price of your ticket. Your approved carrier may require you to travel on the same flight as your pet. However, pets are normally flown as cargo and it may not be possible to book their tickets more than a couple days in advance of the flight. If so, you should have flexible reservations so that you can change your flight date without being penalised.

While it is possible for you to navigate the Pet Travel Scheme on your own, several companies offer services that make it easier for you.

Air Animal Pet Movers, +1 800 635 3448; www.airanimal.com.

Pet Relocation, +1 877 PET MOVE; www.petrelocation.com.

Passport for Pets, 0800 137 321; www.passportforpets.co.uk.

If your business is handling your moving arrangements, inquire about their resources and make sure that the costs of your pet's move will also be covered.

In the event that your pet must be quarantined in the UK, arrangements for boarding kennels must be made and confirmed by letter before you leave your home. Allow four to six weeks to complete all associated paperwork and keep in mind that the most accessible kennels may have waiting lists.

> Did you know?...Penalties for smuggling animals are severe. Such an offence will result in a heavy fine, a prison sentence for yourself or the destruction of the animal.

ARRIVAL AT THE AIRPORT

There are five airports in London, but you will most likely arrive at Heathrow or Gatwick. It is a long walk from the gates to **Immigration and Customs Control**. Therefore, if you require a wheelchair, are travelling with a newborn infant or have medical problems, you should pre-arrange special assistance with your airline.

If you are a non-EU passport holder, you will submit a completed British "landing card" given to you on the flight, at the Immigration Desk (Passport Control). The officer may ask to see your travel documents or work permit so that he or she can stamp your passport accordingly. He or she may ask you a few questions regarding the reasons for your entrance into the country. After you are through Passport Control, check the electronic board to find out the area for your flight's baggage claim. In the UK, and in many other European international airports, luggage pushcarts are free of charge. If some or all of your luggage does not arrive, contact a representative of your airline before leaving the airport.

CUSTOMS

If you have nothing to declare and are arriving from a non-EU country, proceed through the area marked with the green sign. If you are arriving from another EU country, proceed through the area marked with the blue sign.

If you have items to declare, you must go to the area marked with the red sign. The customs inspector will probably ask you a few questions and may ask to see these items. You are required to pay any duty or tax at the time the belongings are brought into the country so be sure to travel with UK currency. Foreign currency or travellers cheques can be cashed at the airport banks. There are also Automatic Teller Machines (ATMs) available in most airports that will automatically dispense UK currency. It is often cheaper, and easier, to use ATMs. Check with your bank beforehand regarding your PIN number and whether you will incur any fees for using foreign ATMs.

MOVING WITHIN LONDON

Moving within London can sometimes be as big a production as moving to the UK. Some things to remember are:

- If you need to secure parking for unloading or loading a lorry or van, contact your Council at least two weeks ahead of time. Your Council will block parking spaces for you for free, or for a small fee.

- Transfer your TV licence to your new home; www.tvlicensing.co.uk. Cancel all direct debits for services to your former home.

- Try to set up services (e.g., cable and telephone) before you move into your new home.

- **Royal Mail** (www.royalmail.com) offers a Redirection Service (mail forwarding). For a fee, they will forward all of your mail from any UK address — including magazines and packages — to your new address in the UK or abroad for up to two years. Any local post office will have the requisite forms for you to fill out.

- When hiring a moving company, be sure to check references and inquire about insurance limits. Many moving companies will move boxes that you have packed yourself, which can be less expensive than purchasing a full moving service. Prices are sometimes lower if you move during the week rather than on a weekend.

Housing

What makes London such a wonderfully livable city is that it is made up of many small "villages", each with its own particular charm. Deciding on the best location for you and your family is difficult only because the choices are so great. You must consider a number of factors: the high cost of certain areas; proximity to work and schools (or easy transportation to them); convenience of shopping facilities; and atmosphere. If it is at all possible, any house-hunting trip should begin with a day spent driving around the city, taking in the flavour and overall feel of each area. If you are new to the London area, find an experienced guide to take you around the city. Your relocation / estate agent, black cab or minicab companies are good sources (there are also some recommendations in *Chapter 11: Services*). By the time your tour ends, your list of areas in which to search may be considerably shorter than it was earlier. Those few hours can save you days of wasted time and energy, not to mention frayed nerves.

The first decision to make is whether you want to live in Central London,

2

in one of the suburban communities of Greater London, or in the country.

Another factor to consider is in which area of London you want to live in. London stretches across some 30 miles and is divided into 32 areas, each with its own council providing local public services such as street cleaning, social housing, libraries and parking. To pay for these services, each area sets its own level of local "council tax", which can vary significantly even between neighbouring areas. For example, the City of Westminster and Wandsworth have very low council tax rates, while Islington, Camden and Kensington / Chelsea have much higher council tax rates. There are also differences in the quality of services, particularly in the state schools, which are mostly run by each council.

Parking within London can be challenging and violators will receive a fine or worse — have their vehicle "clamped" or towed. Certain London neighbourhoods (notably the City of Westminster, Kensington and Chelsea) only offer metered parking to visitors. Other areas offer visitor passes to residents that can be used on an hourly basis or for an entire day. If you own a car, you must purchase a resident's parking permit from your local council which allows you to park in designated residential areas.

The following brief descriptions of some popular areas in London may be of assistance.

LONDON NEIGHBORHOODS

Central London (SW and W post codes)

The communities of Central London are expensive but convenient for shops, theatres, restaurants, clubs and public transportation. These areas have a high proportion of international residents.

Belgravia (SW1)

Near Buckingham Palace and Hyde Park, this area consists of magnificent Regency squares, late Georgian terraces and mews houses. Some of the larger houses are now used as embassies and consulates; others have been divided into flats. Belgravia is one of the more expensive and desirable areas

2

of London, and as in Mayfair, supermarkets are limited in size and therefore, provide a limited selection of goods. This area is served by Victoria and Sloane Square tube stations.

Chelsea (SW3 and SW10)

South of Knightsbridge, South Kensington and bordering the Thames river, Chelsea features a range of mostly low-rise period buildings, including Victorian cottages and mansion blocks. Sloane Square and the King's Road are convenient for shopping, although the latter's reputation as one of London's trendiest areas is now more tradition than fact. Chelsea also boasts many cosy local pubs and restaurants, as well as excellent antique shops and markets. The area is not well served by public transport as there is no tube station beyond Sloane Square.

Kensington (W8)

South and west of Kensington Gardens, Kensington features tree-lined residential streets and squares — a mixture of Georgian and Victorian terraced houses, red-brick mansion blocks and elegant villas. Kensington High Street and Notting Hill Gate offer convenient shopping and access to public transport. There are also numerous cinemas, restaurants and pubs in the area.

Knightsbridge (SW1, SW3 and SW7)

Bordering Hyde Park to the south, this expensive area features Victorian terraces and squares, cobbled mews and red-brick Victorian mansion blocks. Once part of a forest on the outskirts of London, Knightsbridge today is home to Harrods and other fine stores, making it one of the world's most famous shopping destinations. The tube station is on the Piccadilly line, serving the West End and Heathrow.

Maida Vale (W9)

Maida Vale has a rich supply of flats of various sizes and types. The area's wide streets are lined with large terraced houses and red-brick mansion blocks, often with access to large private gardens, including some with

2

tennis courts. The area surrounding the Grand Union Canal, known as "Little Venice", has many large stucco houses, some of which remain single-family homes while others have been converted into flats.

Marylebone (W1)

North of Oxford Street and south of Marylebone Road, this area has many 18th century streets and squares, mews houses and portered Edwardian mansion blocks. It is convenient for the West End shops, and has excellent public transport links to the City and to nearly all of London's mainline rail stations. Marylebone High Street has become a fashionable spot for shopping and dining. Regent's Park is nearby.

Mayfair (W1)

Bordered by Hyde Park, Oxford Street, Regent Street and Piccadilly, Mayfair has been a fashionable central neighbourhood since the 1700s. Many of the large Georgian houses have been divided into flats or have been converted into luxury hotels and offices. There is a good supply of flats in large, well-maintained mansion blocks. The area is limited for grocery shopping (the local custom of daily shopping still prevails); however, it is well situated for many of the finest clubs, restaurants, antique shops and designer boutiques.

Pimlico (SW1)

South of Victoria Station, bordering the Thames, this area has lovely white stucco squares and terraces. Its quietness owes much to the complicated one-way street system. Pimlico is a more affordable alternative to its neighbouring communities of Belgravia and Chelsea, and is popular with members of Parliament and other government workers based in Westminster.

South Kensington (SW3, SW5 and SW7)

South Kensington's streets feature large terraced houses, many converted into flats, often with access to private garden squares. One of the most central residential areas in London, South Kensington benefits from plentiful tube and bus services providing easy access to the West End, the City and Heathrow Airport. The area is also home to four of the capital's major museums, as well as the **Lycée Français**, which attracts many French families to the area.

West London (W and SW post codes)

In addition to the west / central neighbourhoods listed below, going westward from Knightsbridge are the residential areas of Brook Green, Chiswick, Hammersmith, West Kensington and Shepherds Bush. These contain tree-lined streets with large houses, many of which have been converted into flats. These neighbourhoods are well served by public transport with the Central, Piccadilly and District lines. It is also on the right side of London for a quick journey on the M4 motorway to Heathrow Airport. With riverside walks, pubs and excellent facilities for shopping, leisure and health, this area is ideal for families planning to settle in London for a considerable amount of time.

Bayswater and Paddington (W2)

West of Marble Arch and to the north of Hyde Park, this area has modern blocks of flats, as well as some squares mostly rebuilt after the war. It is convenient for Oxford Street shopping and Mayfair, and is considerably cheaper than neighbouring Notting Hill. Paddington is nearby, which has benefited from wide-scale development and urban regeneration of the Paddington Basin, as well as the new Heathrow rail link. It also has some very pretty period cottages and magnificent stucco terraces.

Fulham (SW6)

Just west of Chelsea, Fulham has a number of large parks. It is home to many young British professionals and their families, as well as increasing numbers of expatriates who are attracted by the larger private gardens and better value for money. The typical Fulham street is lined with two- and three-storey Victorian terraced houses, many of which have been converted into flats. Several large mansion blocks are located near the river.

2

Holland Park (W14)

Surrounding Holland Park, this area features leafy streets and some of the largest detached and semi-detached houses in London. The area also offers a good supply of flats in large mansion blocks and converted Victorian houses. It is convenient to the shopping and entertainment facilities of Kensington High Street and Notting Hill Gate, and there is easy access to the West End and the City by public transport.

Notting Hill (W11)

Just north of Kensington, Notting Hill has large houses, often with good-sized private or communal gardens, and easy access to the West End and the City by public transport. The area is close to both Holland Park and Kensington Gardens, and has a large variety of local restaurants, trendy shops, bars and antique shops. Notting Hill is home to the Portobello Road Market on Fridays and Saturdays and hosts the largest annual street party and carnival in Europe, held normally over the last weekend in August.

North London (N and NW post codes)

Hampstead (NW3)

Hampstead offers the quaint ambiance of an English village while affording the convenience of being close to Central London. The High Street is dominated by exclusive boutiques, cafes and restaurants. Its winding, hilly streets feature brick townhouses and large detached houses, many of which have been converted into flats. It is adjacent to Hampstead Heath, which has many walking paths, large ponds for swimming and fishing, art shows and outdoor concerts in the summer at Kenwood House, one of the most glorious country houses in London.

Hampstead Garden Suburb (NW11)

North of Hampstead, this area is definitely a suburban enclave. It features cottages and beautiful four, five and six bedroom homes, many stately Georgian and ambassadorial types, with well-manicured gardens. It has two small but varied shopping areas. Many homes back onto Hampstead Heath;

however, in some parts, it is necessary to have a car.

Highgate (N6)

Northeast of Hampstead Heath, Highgate Village is quietly residential with a definite country atmosphere. It has a golf club and many homes, both old and new, with large gardens. Parking and driving are quite easy.

Islington (N1)

East of Regent's Park, Islington is a friendly, lively place with modern terraced houses, Victorian villas and smartly restored Georgian squares. Camden Passage, noted for its antique shops and market, is there, and the area enjoys easy access to the City and the West End. The restaurants and bars along Upper Street are the centre of the area's vibrant night life.

Regent's Park (NW1)

The elegant residential area around Regent's Park is most famous for its Nash terraces overlooking the park. Its impressive homes include Winfield House, the residence of the American Ambassador. Modern blocks of flats, the London Zoo and the Open Air Theatre all add to its diversity.

St. Johns Wood (NW8)

Northwest of Regent's Park and suburban in feeling, St. Johns Wood has many large detached and semi-detached houses as well as large blocks of flats with good views over the park. The American School in London is located here.

Swiss Cottage (NW3)

North of St. John's Wood, Swiss Cottage offers large blocks of flats, low terraced houses and modern townhouses with a cosmopolitan flavour. The heart of Swiss Cottage is dominated by a large public leisure centre attached to the main library.

East London (E post codes)

East of Tower Hill is a newly developed area — Wapping and the Docklands. Housing is mainly either warehouses (which have been converted in the last 10 years to a very high standard) or new developments (which often have river views). Some residences have off-street parking, 24-hour porters, indoor swimming pools and other fitness facilities. Transport is improving and the Docklands Light Railway runs a service between Tower Hill, Bank, Beckton, Stratford, Greenwich and Island Gardens stations. Canary Wharf, in the heart of the Docklands, is the new home to a number of banks and other financial institutions, which has made East London particularly appealing to young professional couples. In this up-and-coming area, new shops and restaurants are opening all the time.

South London (SE and SW post codes)
Battersea (SW8 and SW11)

On the south side of the Thames across from Chelsea Harbour, Battersea is dominated by Battersea Park and the now-derelict Battersea Power Station. Battersea is cheaper than living north of the river, with many brick Victorian mansion blocks and larger late Victorian properties. With excellent facilities for shopping, parking, education, health and sports, it is very popular with young Londoners due to its parks and bar and restaurant scene.

Clapham (SW4 and SW9)

Always popular with families, this area surrounds Clapham Common, and features large Victorian family properties on tree-lined streets with on-street parking. Clapham's three tube stations are served by the Northern line, making this a recommended location for young City professionals who are looking to buy rather than rent.

Putney (SW15)

Along the south bank of the Thames, Putney has a chain of attractive open spaces with extensive sporting grounds, especially rowing clubs. It contains the oldest high-rise flats in London as well as many two-storey homes with gardens. There is a busy and convenient street for shopping as well as the Putney Exchange, an enclosed shopping mall. Putney has main line trai and bus links to Central London as well as a tube station (which is not particularly close to the area's residential neighbourhoods).

Shad Thames (SE1)

This riverside neighbourhood stretches east from Tower Bridge. The area boasts a high concentration of warehouse conversions and newly constructed apartment complexes. It is also home to the Design Museum, and there is a Friday antique market within the nearby Bermondsey Market. There are numerous restaurants, specialty food shops, clothing stores and bookshops. Its location provides easy access to the City and the Docklands.

GREATER LONDON

More and more newcomers to London are moving to communities farther from the centre. These communities are often less expensive, and are generally regarded as good places to bring up families. Typically, the homes have larger gardens, there is less crime and the schools are better. Most have every type of housing, from rows of brick terrace houses to tall stately Georgian terraces to large detached houses.

The disadvantages to these communities are the longer commutes to Central London and the City, and the necessity for a car in most locations. However, express trains can make it faster to commute from towns in Greater London than from sections of Chelsea so it is worth checking out the transportation links.

Barnes (SW13)

Located west of Putney, on the Thames, this area features low terraced houses from the late Victorian and Edwardian eras. It has a wonderful "wilderness" common, sporting grounds and a swan pond. Barnes offers bus and train transportation, but not a tube station.

2

Richmond (TW10)

Southwest of Barnes, Richmond is a lovely suburban village with large houses and beautiful gardens. Its many parks add a delightful country atmosphere and it is home to the botanical Kew Gardens. Richmond Park comprises 2,000 acres of parkland, and Richmond Green is often the setting for cricket matches.

Wimbledon (SW19)

Wimbledon, famous for the tennis tournament held here every summer, is located eight miles southwest of Central London. Wimbledon has a suburban atmosphere, with Wimbledon Common comprising 1,200 acres of land for riders, walkers and picnickers. The village has a wide range of shopping and the train and tube station offers convenient transportation to London. Centre Court is a new shopping complex next to the station.

Other equally charming areas worth considering are Blackheath (SE3), Dulwich (SE21), Kew (TW9), Greenwich (SE10) and Wandsworth (SW18).

> Did you know?...The term "High Street" refers to the main street of an area or town. There is usually a selection of shops, restaurants, pubs and banks located on the High Street.

Living in the Country

Within commuting distance of London are some wonderful suburban communities with large houses and enormous gardens. There is no question that one can find almost palatial splendour in the rural areas for what one has to pay for a house in London. Yet, again, the commute into London must be considered, although trains can offer several options.

Surrey, south of London, encompasses many charming villages — Cobham, Esher, Walton-on-Thames, Weybridge, West Byfleet and many others — all with good public transport into London. The **American Community Schools (ACS)**, the **TASIS England American School** and **Marymount International Schools** are also located in Surrey.

Northwest of Central London are the communities of Wembley, Harrow, Pinner and Ruislip. These areas are popular for their suburban atmosphere and more garden-for-the-money value. They primarily contain semi-detached and small detached houses.

Further northwest are the communities of Northwood, Chorleywood, Moor Park and Watford — all with large houses and gardens. These areas are convenient to the London Orbital (M25) and the many suburban superstores.

INSTRUCTIONS FOR RENTING AND BUYING PROPERTY

Once you have narrowed down your list of areas, there are other crucial issues to consider, depending on whether you are going to rent or buy a home in London. Indeed, once you are established in London, you may see what a unique and exciting investment opportunity London can offer.

RENTING/LETTING PROPERTY

Estate agencies located in a High Street will normally only carry listings for that particular neighbourhood. The decentralised nature of the rental market can make it difficult to look for property if you haven't narrowed your search. A good starting point is the website **www.primelocation.com**, which lists properties to buy or rent in London and the rest of the UK.

The UK rental market can move quickly and many times properties are not on the market more than one month before their availability date. As a result, it is not beneficial to house-hunt too far in advance. You may want to consider moving into temporary housing first and then taking time to find your permanent home.

Renters should be aware of the Housing Act 1988, which regulates your right to extend your tenancy and the landlord's right to repossess the property or increase the rent. Your solicitor (lawyer) or relocation agent can explain this in detail. You should not sign a tenancy agreement or lease without first having it approved by a solicitor familiar with such documents. Your company may have an in-house lawyer who can do this for you, or you can contact the **Law Society** (main office located at 113 Chancery Lane, WC2A 1PL; 020 7242 1222; www.lawsociety.org.uk) for names of firms specialising in such work.

2

There are two important aspects of the housing market that you may encounter:

> • Many rentals are fully furnished (including dishes, sheets, towels, etc), which can make your move very straightforward. You only need to bring your clothes, the children's toys and other personal items. But sometimes the furnishings may not be of a very high quality. It may be possible to negotiate with the owner to remove the furnishings and move in your own, provided you are prepared to pay for the storage costs. If you find you need additional storage for furniture that will not fit into your house or flat, see *Chapter 11: Services* for self-storage locations.

> • Some rentals are only available as a "company let", which means that the lease is made out to your corporation and must be signed by the Managing Director or his/her appointee. The company therefore guarantees the tenancy.

Did you know?...Single occupants receive a 25% discount on council tax. Students also receive a discount.

COUNCIL TAX

Council tax is a local tax set by each local council to help pay for local services such as rubbish collection and street cleaning. There will be one bill per dwelling to be paid by the resident or by the owner (where the property is untenanted). The amount paid will be based on the value of the dwelling.

DEFINING YOUR RENTAL CHECKLIST

For happy renting, it is important to get the legal and practical aspects right. Negotiation is all about striking a balance between your needs and requirements and those of the landlord. Here are a few tips.

Read the Small Print

There are three main types of tenancy agreements: an *Assured Shorthold Tenancy (AST)* for rents up to £25,000; a *Standard Tenancy Agreement* for rents above £25,000; and a *Company Tenancy Agreement*, where the company is the tenant and you are the "permitted occupier". Although the wording is very similar, you should watch out for the following:

- Do you have a break clause? Job mobility makes it sensible to be able to terminate early and this is usually granted subject to a minimum tenure of six months. Read the language carefully regarding the notice period to see if the lease permits termination at six months or permits you to give notice of termination at six months. In the latter case, termination will occur at seven or eight months depending on the required notice period.

- Do you have an option to renew? You may want an option to extend for a second or third year.

- What is the level of annual rent increase? It is likely to be no less than the Retail Price Index (inflation) but a minimum of either 3% or 5%. A maximum percentage can also be negotiated.

Be Prepared

- Rent is expressed on a "per week" basis. As there are 52 weeks in a year, your monthly rent is equivalent to 4.3 weeks — not four weeks.

- The deposit required against dilapidations is normally six weeks. If pets are allowed, this may go up to eight weeks. It may not be returned until you have proved you have settled your utility bills.

- If you are asked for a holding deposit to secure a tenancy, make sure it is refundable against the full deposit.

- Sort out your "wish list" at the negotiation stage (e.g., linens or a microwave). It is difficult to go back to the landlord later.

2

• There may be additional charges for related matters, such as drawing up tenancy agreements and check-ins.

Best Practice

• Set up a direct debit to pay the rent. You are obliged to pay on time.

• You have no legal right to withhold rent, whatever your grievance, so discuss any problems with your agent.

• Ensure your check-in is conducted by an independent inventory clerk, as this will form the basis of the dilapidation charges.

• Take care with picture hooks or you may end up "redecorating" (repainting). Review the terms of your tenancy agreement to make sure you are complying with any specific requirements.

• Make sure the utilities (gas, water, electricity, telephone, television licence and council tax) are transferred into your name at the onset and out of your name when you leave.

• Get to know your managing agents and be realistic about what they can achieve — that way you will get the best out of them. It is rare in the UK for a tenant to talk directly to the landlord during negotiations. The normal process is for the tenant to talk to his or her agent, who then talks with the landlord's agent, who then talks with the landlord.

• Protect your belongings with tenant's contents insurance. Normally, the landlord insures the property and its contents (if furnished) and the tenant is responsible for his or her own belongings. Insurance quotes can be lower if certain security devices such as locks and security alarms are installed. If possible, obtain an insurance

2

quote before finalising the tenancy agreement so that you can request that the landlord install the proper devices. If your London office cannot recommend an insurance broker, you might telephone the **British Insurance Brokers Association** on 0870 950 1790, for a recommendation.

• Always get your property professionally cleaned when you leave. Domestic cleaning is no substitute. Ensure that your tenancy agreement includes the requirement that the property be professionally cleaned before you move in.

Know Your Neighbourhood

• Proximity to schools/parks/playgrounds.

• Proximity to amenities (shops, restaurants and pubs).

• Is there a local supermarket?

• Proximity to the bus, tube and/or train — is there an easy link to work?

• Availability of on-street or off-street parking.

• Level of crime in the area — check with local police if necessary.

Household Tips

Look for:

• Storage space and bedroom wardrobe (closet) space.

• Electrical points (outlets) for appliances, PC, TV & video, stereo, etc.

• Burglar and smoke alarms.

2

• Separate washing machine and dryer (they are often combined). If you do a lot of laundry and have a combination machine, you may want to ask your landlord to install a separate dryer if space permits.

• Refrigerator / freezer size (UK appliances are often smaller).

• Shower pressure (power showers).

• Access — are there too many stairs? Are the common areas of a good standard?

• Height and width of the corridors and stairwells (especially in conversions).

• Outside space — do you have access to the garden or will you have to share? Who is responsible for maintenance?

BUYING PROPERTY

For those not familiar with buying property in London, the experience can be daunting, distressing and expensive. It will pay dividends to acquaint yourself with basic procedures and terms and to obtain good professional advice.

Acquisition Costs

Finder's fee

The fee paid to a property search or purchase management company for representing you (the buyer) and finding your property. You do not have to pay this fee if you register with a normal estate agent and/or reply to an advertisement for a property. Remember that an estate agent represents the seller's interest — not yours.

2

Land Registry fees

The cost of registering the buyer as the new owner at the Land Registry will be about £220.

Legal fees

The solicitor's fee for acting on your behalf in the purchase. The fee can vary quite significantly so it is advisable to obtain a quotation from several solicitors before proceeding.

Lender's arrangement fee

Lenders may charge you for organising your house loan. This may be a flat fee or a percentage of the total advance. They may also require legal representation using a solicitor from their designated panel. Some lenders will make a contribution towards legal fees.

Local searches

These are searches undertaken by your solicitor with the local council to ensure there are no apparent reasons for not proceeding with the purchase. The searches take about two weeks and cost approximately £200.

Stamp duty

A government tax levied on the purchase price of a property. If the purchase price is £120,000 or less, you don't pay any stamp duty. If it is more than £120,000 you pay between 1% and 4% of the entire purchase price on a sliding scale. For details, visit www.direct.gov.uk.

Survey fees

The cost of the survey conducted to determine that the property has no significant structural faults. The lenders may insist on a particular type of survey, but they may make a contribution towards the cost of it.

2

Conveyancing (Legal) Process

Estate agent

The selling agents, who receive a fee from the seller to achieve a sale at the best possible price.

Formulating the offer

Your bid will be given to the estate agent, who will forward it to the seller for acceptance. Your ability to negotiate will depend on the current market. If you offer the asking price, you should ask for a period of exclusivity (when another contract cannot be issued) but this is not legally binding.

Legal exchange of contracts

At this stage, which takes place approximately one month after the initial offer, providing you have received your mortgage offer, you will enter into a legally binding contract with the seller, who can no longer accept other offers. You will normally pay a 10% deposit (although 5% is increasingly acceptable).

Legal completion

This usually occurs within one to four weeks after the exchange of contracts, at which time you become the legal owner of the property and obtain possession.

Insurance

If you are buying a house, you are responsible for buildings insurance from the exchange of contracts. With flats, you pay for this via the service charge. You will require contents insurance at completion to cover your belongings.

Mortgages

The term for a housing loan, normally up to 70% to 80% of the purchase price and for a period up to 30 years.

2

Capital repayment

In this type of mortgage, the instalment payment covers interest as well as repaying the capital borrowed.

Endowment

This mortgage uses the maturity value of an endowment policy to pay off the borrowing at the end of the term. Be aware that at maturity, the assurance policy may not cover the full loan sum.

Interest only

This type of mortgage payment only covers the interest that is accumulating on the loan. In this case it is advisable to have collateral security to pay off the capital at the end of the term.

Surveys

Homebuyer's report and valuation

Normally used by the homebuyer to obtain basic structural information.

Full structural survey

A more expensive but comprehensive report highlighting significant faults which may lead to further negotiation on the property purchase price.

Mortgage valuation

A visual inspection carried out by the bank to confirm the property valuation.

Types of Property Charges

Ground rent

The sum paid to the owner of the freehold for use of the land over which your property is built.

2

Service charge

Annual contribution to the running costs of a building (e.g., porter, lift, lighting, cleaning).

Sinking fund

Reserve fund collected annually to provide for major works (e.g., external redecoration).

Types of Tenure

Freehold

The outright purchase of a building, normally a house, and land "in perpetuity".

Leasehold

The purchase of a right to occupy a house or, more normally, a flat, for a specified number of years, up to 999 years. The land and main structure of the property is owned by the freeholder, who charges ground rent. Leases confer obligations on the lessee and the landlord. Property values diminish as leases shorten but owner-occupiers have a statutory right, subject to certain terms, to extend their lease for a further 90 years.

Share of freehold

In some cases, the building lessees combine together to buy the freehold. A management company is normally set up to purchase it and the lessees take a share. Among other benefits, it is then possible to extend the lease term without the payment of a premium.

BRITISH TERMINOLOGY

The following list of real estate terminology will hopefully eliminate any confusion in communication and help you interpret your property's particulars.

2

A Home By Any Other Name

There is a host of different descriptions for property, especially in London. Here are a few of the most common:

Bungalow	One-level ground floor house; very rare in Central London.
Conversion	A flat in a house that was originally built for single-family occupancy.
Cottage	Small rustic-style house, generally old, often with garden.
Detached house	A house that stands apart from any others, generally surrounded by its own garden.
Flat	An apartment, usually on one floor.
Maisonette	An apartment arranged over two or more floors.
Mansion block	Period apartment building often Victorian, Edwardian or Art Deco, built specifically to provide flats.
Mansion flat	Large, traditionally old-fashioned apartment, usually in a good area; often possessing large rooms, good storage space and lacking modern conveniences until refurbished.
Mews house	Converted "carriage" house with small rooms and a lot of character; often with garage.
New build	A new development of flats or houses.

Purpose-built block	A modern building of flats built specifically for this purpose.
Semi-detached house	A house that is joined to another house on one side only, often with its own garden.
Studio flat	A one-room flat with a separate bathroom and kitchen or kitchenette.
Terraced house	One of a row of similar houses joined together.
Townhouse	Typical Central London home, often located in a Georgian or Victorian terrace, usually two to five storeys high.

The ABCs of Property

Know your abbreviations. These are some of the most commonly used.

CH	Central heating.
CHW	Constant hot water.
F/F	Fully furnished: Equipped with furniture, soft furnishings and accessories for immediate occupation.
GFCH or GCH	Gas-fired central heating.
OSP	Off-street parking which is free and unrestricted.
Respark	Residents parking: Council-approved on-street parking. Usually unrestricted access in allocated areas for two vehicles per household for a small annual fee.

U/F   Unfurnished: No furniture but generally with carpets, light fixtures and appliances.

WC   Literally "water closet", but really a room with toilet and wash basin.

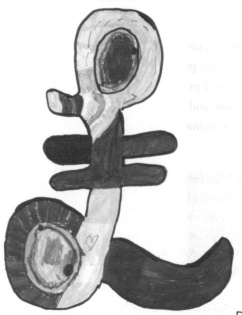

Drawn by Kate

Money, Banking and Taxation

BRITISH CURRENCY

British currency, normally referred to as "sterling", is comprised of two monetary units: the pence and the pound. One pound equals 100 pence. Coins include the 1 penny, 2 pence, 5 pence, 10 pence, 20 pence, 50 pence, the 1 pound coin, and the 2 pound coin. The bills are called "pound notes" and come in denominations of 5, 10, 20 and 50. There are no paper versions of the 1 and 2 pound coins. Pence are commonly abbreviated as "p" (e.g., 10p), and pounds are symbolised by "£" (e.g., £10). You may hear a pound called a "quid".

Did you know?...The term "quid" comes from the Latin expression "quid pro quo" meaning one thing in return for another, no doubt dating back to the Roman occupation of Britain.

THE EURO

The euro is the legal tender of 12 of the 25 countries that make up the European Union (EU). The symbol for the euro is "€".

As of this printing, euro notes and coins have replaced the national currencies of the following EU countries: Austria, Belgium, Finland, France, Germany, Greece, Ireland, Italy, Luxembourg, the Netherlands, Portugal and Spain. Three EU countries – Denmark, Sweden, and the UK – have chosen not to use the single currency. The 10 newest Member States that joined the EU in 2004 – Cypress, the Czech Republic, Estonia, Hungary, Latvia, Lithuania, Malta, Poland, Slovakia and Slovenia – are committed to adopting the euro, but they will not be ready to make the change until 2007.

The euro is divided into 100 cents, with coins and notes issued in a similar fashion to the British pound. In addition to the cent coins (issued in denominations of 1, 2, 5, 10, 20 and 50 cents), there is a 1 euro coin and a 2 euro coin. Bills are issued in denominations of 5, 10, 20, 50, 100, 200 and 500 euros. Euro notes are identical in all countries but each country issues its own coins with one common European side and one side displaying a distinctive national emblem. All of the notes and coins can be used anywhere in the euro area. Some retail outlets in countries outside the euro area will accept payment in euros as well as the national currency, but they are not legally obliged to do so.

> *Did you know?...Many services, particularly shops and taxis, don't like to or can't change large notes. Asking for smaller notes when banking will make life easier.*

There has been, and continues to be, fierce debate in the UK regarding participation in the euro. Although most of the British support strengthening ties between European states in a political sense, many question the merits of joining the monetary unit of the euro. The main cause for concern is the relative strength of the British pound today compared to the euro. To many, abandoning the pound and joining the euro is synonymous to propping up Europe's economy at the expense of the UK. However, it will likely become increasingly difficult for the UK to participate effectively in other issues facing the EU without adopting the unified currency.

THE EUROPEAN UNION

The European Union is an institutional system of 25 countries (called "Member States") which aim to represent its members on issues of interest to all. The idea was suggested by France and came to fruition in the 1950s because Europeans were determined to prevent the killing and destruction that occurred in World War II from happening again. In the beginning, the cooperation was between six countries, concerned primarily with trade and the economy. The current 25 Member States' objectives include: establishing European citizenship; ensuring freedom, security and justice; promoting economic and social progress; and asserting Europe's role in the world. The Member States are: Austria, Belgium, Cypress, the Czech Republic, Denmark, Estonia, Finland, France, Germany, Greece, Hungary, Ireland, Italy, Latvia, Lithuania, Luxembourg, Malta, the Netherlands, Poland, Portugal, Slovakia, Slovenia, Spain, Sweden and the UK. Life has become much easier for the traveler in the EU, with the removal of most passport formalities between countries and the sharing of a common currency (the euro), which makes price comparisons easy and eliminates the need to carry and convert different forms of money.

BANKS IN LONDON

Many of your banking needs will likely be determined by your main source of income. If you are moving to the UK as an expatriate, your company may choose to continue to pay your salary in your local currency, and provide an adjustment for the difference in the cost of living. If this is the case, note that although many of the major overseas banks have branches in London, many of them do not offer "retail" or personal banking services. Contact your London branch to see if they will provide chequing and savings account services.

It is generally a good idea to open a local currency account with a UK bank. The major banks offer essentially the same services (and can provide accounts that hold multiple currencies). Therefore, you will probably choose the bank with which your company has a business relationship, or the bank located nearest to your home or office. Some of the largest UK banks, with branches throughout London and the UK, are:

Barclays Bank (www.barclays.com, www.internationalbanking.barclays.com)

Lloyds TSB Bank (www.lloydstsb.com)

Royal Bank of Scotland (www.rbs.co.uk)

National Westminster Bank (www.natwest.co.uk)

HSBC (www.hsbc.co.uk)

Citibank (www.citibank.com)

Banks in the UK are acutely aware of the risk of fraud and money laundering and take several measures to prevent such crimes, which are particularly noticeable to persons opening accounts. It can take up to six weeks just to open an account.

The verification of the identity of new customers may be a rigorous process, including requiring original identity documents (e.g., passport, identity card and/or utility bills) or certified copies of the same. A letter of introduction from your firm helps and if you require immediate credit facilities, copies of your previous country's bank statements or a letter of introduction from your previous bank will also speed the process.

BANKING SERVICES

The UK banks offer two basic types of accounts: "current" (chequing) accounts and "deposit" (savings) accounts, although there are variations of each type of account. "Building societies" (similar to the US savings and loans associations) also offer current accounts. Most British banks now offer interest on current accounts. Most banks will provide "sweep" accounts. This means that the bank will automatically transfer excess funds from your current account to your deposit account. In reverse, the bank will move funds from your deposit account to your current account to maintain the agreed credit balance. You should obtain a "direct debit/cheque guarantee card" for your current account (see *Cheques and Debit Cards* below). At the request of the customer, statements are sent quarterly or monthly. Cancelled cheques are returned only if requested and a fee is frequently charged. Free banking is currently offered by most banks as long as you maintain a credit balance.

Monthly or quarterly bills (telephone, electricity, gas, water and council tax) may be paid at your bank by two methods. One method is to use the *"giro slips"* attached to most bills. The slips can be grouped together and all paid with a single cheque. The bank stamps your bill to provide a record of payment, proving beneficial as cheques are not normally returned by the bank. Other methods of payment, and perhaps the easiest, are the use of "standing orders" or *"direct debit"*. With a standing order, you instruct your bank to pay a fixed amount to a specified payee at regular intervals, usually on a certain day each month (e.g., £1,000 rent on the 15th of every month to the landlord or estate office). With a direct debit, you authorise your bank to pay on demand varying amounts as specified by a particular supplier (e.g., whatever the electricity company states is your monthly or quarterly bill). For additional information on paying utilities, see *Chapter 5: Utilities.*

Bank Hours

Regular banking hours are 09:00-17:00 or 09:30-16:30 Monday through Friday, with Wednesday hours often slightly

Did you know?...ATMs in the UK do not accept deposits.

shorter. Saturday hours (usually 09:30-12:00) are currently being offered by some UK clearing banks. This is mainly in, but not limited to, their suburban locations.

All banks are closed on holidays (hence the term "bank holiday"). Please see *Chapter 17: Annual Events* for a listing of bank holidays in the UK. Many banks close at 12:00 on Christmas Eve and do not reopen until after Boxing Day. All major banks have cash machines that operate 24 hours a day at most of their branches and, increasingly, elsewhere.

Cheques and Debit Cards

Writing a sterling cheque may differ slightly from writing cheques elsewhere. When drafting a cheque there are two important points to remember:

1. The date is written with the day, the month and then the year (e.g., 5

March 2007 or 5-3-07). Do remember either to put the day first or spell out the month.

2. To write the amount, you must write "pounds" and "p" or "pence". For example, £10.62 is written "Ten pounds and 62p" or "Ten pounds and sixty-two pence".

Sterling cheques are usually "crossed", meaning that they have two vertical lines running down the middle. A crossed cheque is for deposit only and cannot be cashed by a third party. Hence, cheques are not endorsed for cash in the UK.

All UK banks are now on a three to five day clearing cycle at the bank's discretion. Cash deposits, however, are credited immediately by most banks.

Importantly, you should obtain a direct debit/cheque guarantee card for your current account, in addition to any credit cards you may apply for. Well-known versions of the direct debit card are **Maestro®** and **Visa®**. This card will let you pay for goods and services wherever you see the Maestro® or Visa® logo and gives you access to your money from cash machines across the UK, as well as guaranteeing your cheque up to the amount shown on the card. Although you may cash a cheque for any amount at your own bank branch (where you opened the account), you will be required to show your cheque card when cashing a cheque at either another branch of your bank or at another chain of banks. If the cheque amount is over the limit stated on your card, you will often need to make prior arrangements to do so even within your own branch in order to cash it.

Whenever you use your direct debit/ cheque guarantee card, the transactions

> *Did you know?... In February 2006, the UK introduced what is called "Chip and PIN". Chip and PIN is the new, more secure way to pay with credit or debit cards in the UK. Instead of using your signature to verify payments, you will be asked to enter a four-digit Personal Identification Number (PIN) known only to you. If you don't know your PIN, you will be asked to use an alternative method of payment.*

will appear on your account statement, so you will have a clear audit trail of your transactions. Purchases are limited, however, to available funds (or an agreed overdraft).

Bank Credit Cards

Most major banks issue credit cards in the form of a **Visa®** or **MasterCard®**, which can be used throughout the UK and in Europe where the appropriate sign is displayed. Similar cards from other countries are also accepted. Attaining a UK credit card can be difficult initially if you don't already have a credit record in the UK. A letter or phone call from your company can speed the process.

Traveller's Cheques

Traveller's cheques and foreign currency can be purchased from all major UK banks; however, it is usually necessary to give a few days' notice and order ahead. Traveller's cheques can also be obtained from **Thomas Cook** and **American Express®** offices located throughout the UK. Importantly, foreign currency can also be ordered at most UK post office branches (but not often at the postal counters that can be found in retail stores like your local chemist or newsstand).

Transferring Money

If you want to transfer money from your previous home country to your UK current account you can have it sent by wire transfer with the help of your previous banker; a transfer by telex can be completed in 48 hours. Alternatively, you can purchase sterling from your UK bank with a foreign currency cheque (e.g., in dollars drawn on your US bank account). The time it takes for the foreign cheque to clear and be credited to your UK account will vary by type of currency and the size of the cheque. If timing is important, be sure to check with your bank before you proceed.

> *Did you know?... As an expatriate living in the UK, you pay UK taxes on any money you bring into the country.*

If you wish to remit money to another foreign country, you can ask your UK bank to draw a draft on your behalf against the sterling in your current account or to transfer the amount to a foreign bank account by mail, cable or telex.

Safety Deposit Boxes

Although local commercial banks often provide "strong rooms" for storing their customers' valuables, they do not have facilities for individual safety deposit boxes. These boxes are offered instead by privately run safety deposit centres. **Metropolitan Safe Deposits** (www.metrosafe.co.uk) is the UK's leading independent safe deposit company. There are three locations in London: Belgravia, Knightsbridge and St. John's Wood. Visit the website for more details.

Offshore Banking

Several banks provide an offshore banking option in addition to local services. The rationales for obtaining and utilising an offshore account vary according to your individual situation. They may include tax savings, shelter from monetary instability or an investment opportunity.

As a UK resident, offshore banking may provide a tax benefit because any income earned while you are physically located in another country is not subject to UK tax provided that the money is deposited into an offshore account and does not make it back to the UK. For example, if you spend two months working in Germany for your company, you would not be liable to pay UK income tax on those two months of wages provided that the wages were deposited in an offshore account and are not brought into the UK. For more details on this and other benefits of an offshore account, contact your financial adviser or Ben Snee at **UBS,** Private Wealth Management, 1 Curzon Street; W1; 0207 567 8855 (mobile 077 9540 2208).

TAXATION

When you come to reside in the UK, your tax status changes and the Inland Revenue – the UK's tax office – has primary jurisdiction over your income. Depending on where you have come from, you may have a tax obligation to your "home" country and may be required to report and pay income tax there as well. (Since this is true for American citizens, there is a section in this chapter on American taxes). In almost all cases, however, you will want to consult a tax accountant soon after you arrive regarding your tax status and filing requirements.

UNITED KINGDOM TAXES

The UK tax year runs from 6 April to the following 5 April. Returns should be filed by 30 September following the end of the tax year if you want Inland Revenue to work out your liability, and by 31 January following the end of the tax year if you calculate your own tax liability on income and capital gains (called "self-assessment"). Interest will be charged on tax not paid by the due date and penalties will be levied for tax returns filed late.

If you are employed by a firm in the UK, the tax on your earnings will be calculated and withheld at source via the PAYE (Pay As You Earn) system. If you are self-employed, your accountant can advise you on how to make estimated payments or you may consult with your nearest Inland Revenue office, which is listed in the telephone directory. In addition to wages, you will be taxed on any investment income that is sourced in the UK, along with any income from your investments outside the UK that is remitted to the UK. Publication IR20 *Residents and Non-Residents: Liability to Tax in the United Kingdom* is available from the Inland Revenue (and online); it addresses many of the issues of individual taxation in the UK. Their website is www.inlandrevenue.gov.uk.

National Insurance taxes (similar to the US social security tax) in the UK are payable through withholding if you are an employee and payable with your income tax or by direct debit if you are self-employed. If you are an American working in the UK, you will be required to pay either Social Security tax to the US or National Insurance tax to the UK, but not both. The length of your anticipated stay in the UK should determine into which plan you should pay.

Finally, VAT (Value Added Tax) is a tax that you pay as a consumer when you buy goods and services in the European Union. Each country in the EU has its own rate for VAT. In the UK the standard rate, which applies to most goods and services, is 17.5 per cent. Some items, like domestic power, are charged at a reduced rate of 5 per cent. You do not pay VAT on items such as newspapers, children's clothing and most groceries.

AMERICAN TAXES

American citizens are taxed by the US on their worldwide income but are given a tax credit, subject to limitations, for foreign income taxes paid. In general, American citizens, wherever they live in the world, must file a tax return if their income exceeds a certain amount. Filing dates are automatically extended for Americans abroad from 15 April to 15 June – and can be extended even further by application – but interest is applied from 15 April to any tax due.

Publication 54, *Tax Guide for US Citizens and Resident Aliens Abroad*, is available at the IRS office of the **US Embassy**, 24 Grosvenor Square, W1A 1AE (Marble Arch or Bond Street tube stops); 020 7408 8076, or you may write to **Forms Distribution Center**, P.O. Box 25866, Richmond, VA 23260, USA, or find it online at www.irs.gov.

Importantly, US taxpayers living in the UK are entitled to two potentially sizeable exclusions/deductions on their foreign earned income if they meet one of two conditions involving the length of their stay in the UK: the "bona fide residence test" or the "physical presence test" (spelled out in detail on 1040 Form 2555). The exclusions are as follows:

1. **Foreign Earned Income Exclusion**: If your tax home is a foreign country (e.g., the UK) and you qualify under either the bona fide residence test or the physical presence test, you can exclude the actual amount of foreign income earned during the year, up to a current maximum of $80,000. If husband and wife both work they are each entitled to the exclusion.

2. **Housing Cost Amount Exclusion:** A qualified taxpayer may also choose to exclude from gross income any qualified housing costs in excess

of a specified base amount.

After these deductions, any remaining earned income and all unearned income is taxed as if it were the only income and, therefore, will generally be taxed at a lower effective tax rate. If both husband and wife work, the foreign earned income exclusion is computed separately, even if they file jointly.

When it comes time to compute your US tax bill on Form 1040, you may be able to take a credit for some, if not all, of the foreign income taxes paid to the **UK Inland Revenue** (reported on Form 1116). Although you are generally subject to tax both in the UK and the US, this credit has the potential to limit your US liability.

In terms of state and local taxes, depending on the state from which you have moved, you may be liable for these income taxes while living abroad. Check with your tax accountant to be sure. However, you remain liable for any taxes on property (real estate or personal property) that generates income in the US.

Tax Assistance

For further information on your UK or US tax obligations, you may contact the Inland Revenue, your UK or US accountant or lawyer, or your company's personnel or expatriate employee departments. For UK tax enquiries, there are various local enquiry offices in London listed under "Inland Revenue" in the telephone directory. The IRS office in the US **Embassy** can assist you, at no cost, in filing your US returns and the Consular Office of the US Embassy has lists of American accountants and lawyers who can assist you for a fee.

There are a few small UK firms who specialise in US expatriates residing in the UK. These include:

Buzzacott & Livingstone, 12 New Fetter Lane, London EC4A 1AG; 020 7556 1200; www.ustax.co.uk.

Expatriate Tax Management, Unit 107, 16 Brune Street, London E1; 020 7721 7993.

MacIntyre Hudson, Greenwood House, 4/7 Salisbury Court, London EC4Y 8TB; 020 7583 7575; www.macintyrehudson.co.uk.

CANADIAN TAXES

In general, if you can establish that you are no longer a resident of Canada, you do not have to pay taxes in Canada on income earned outside Canada. Specific questions can be directed to the **International Tax Office**, 2540 Lancaster Road, Ottawa, Ontario K1A 1A8, Canada; +1 613 952 3741. Information may also be accessed on the **Canada Customs and Revenue Agency** website at www.ccra-adrc.gc.ca.

3

Drawn by Joao

Working

JOB SEARCH

Job hunting is a creative task that often requires considerable effort from the individual. Listed below are some resources that can help start your career search in London.

FOCUS Information Services

FOCUS is a not-for-profit, volunteer-run organisation that provides its members with programmes on working in the UK and operates a resource centre with information useful to a job seeker.

FOCUS publishes several books to aid the expatriate in establishing life in the UK, one of which is the FOCUS *Job Guide: Launching Your Career in the UK*, which is designed particularly for partners of expatriate employees. Topics include British curriculum vitae (CV; a résumé) preparation, job websites, resource lists, networking groups and tips, interviewing strategies and much more.

FOCUS Information Services, 13 Prince of Wales Terrace, W8; 020 7937 7799; www.focus-info.org.

Online Job Postings

A few of the larger UK job search websites include:

www.efinancialcareers.com

www.jobsite.co.uk

www.totallylegal.com

www.jobserve.com

www.reed.co.uk

www.topjobs.co.uk

www.newmonday.co.uk

www.monster.co.uk

www.workthing.com

Newspapers

Classified job advertisements can be found in most UK newspapers. Many national newspapers post job vacancies for particular sectors on a regular schedule. A selection of these follows:

Job advertisements can also be found on the websites of many newspapers:

Times / Sunday Times — www.timesonline.co.uk/jobs

Financial Times — http://news.ft.com/jobs

Evening Standard — www.londonjobs.co.uk

Guardian — www.guardian.co.uk/jobs

Independent — www.londoncareers.net

Daily Telegraph — www.jobs.telegraph.co.uk

RECRUITMENT CONSULTANTS

The Executive Grapevine: The UK Directory of Recruitment Consultants (Executive Grapevine Publishers) is an annual publication that will help you identify the top recruitment consultants in the UK by salary range,

Job Category	Monday	Tuesday	Wednesday	Thursday	Friday	Saturday	Sunday
Accountancy	Financial Times	Evening Standard					
Charities / Public Sector & Policy	Evening Standard	Times					
Creative / Media / Fashion	Guardian Independent	Evening Standard	Evening Standard	Evening Standard			
Education		Guardian		Evening Standard Independent			
Engineering					Evening Standard		
Executive / Management			Guardian	Times		Guardian	Times
Finance / Banking	Financial Times	Evening Standard	Guardian	Guardian		Guardian	
General			Guardian	Financial Times Daily Telegraph Daily Express			Sunday Telegraph Daily Express
Hotel / Catering				Evening Standard			
Human Resources				Evening Standard		Guardian	
Legal		Times	Guardian				
Medical / Health			Guardian	Daily Telegraph			
PA / Secretarial	Guardian		Times				
Sales / Marketing / Public Relations	Guardian		Evening Standard	Evening Standard Daily Telegraph		Guardian	
Science / Technology Information Technology			Evening Standard	Guardian Daily Telegraph			

67

function, industry and location. This book can often be found at major libraries in the careers section, or can be purchased directly from the publisher for £249.

Executive Grapevine International Limited, New Barnes Mill, Cottonmill Lane, St Albans, AL1 2HA; 01727 844 335; www.askgrapevine.com.

The distinctions between different types of recruitment firms may not always be clear to a job searcher. Recruitment consultants often work in at least one of the following ways:

Executive Search

Executive search firms (often referred to as "head hunters") are retained by a corporate client on a fee basis to find an appropriate candidate to fill a particular role. This type of search is typically for senior-level positions for which the pool of suitable candidates is relatively small. Executive search firms target the best candidates for a position, whether or not they are actively looking for a new job.

Advertised Selection

Recruitment firms are retained by a corporate client to advertise in the press to find candidates for a particular role. This approach relies on job candidates actively searching newspapers and trade publications to find job listings that may be of interest to them. Usually the recruitment firm will review all cover letters and CVs received, and then interview the most relevant candidates. A short list of interviewed candidates is then presented to the client for the next stage of the interview process. Advertised selection is most frequently used for hiring middle-management positions.

Contingent Recruitment

Fees charged to a corporate client by a contingent recruitment firm are conditional on a job placement being made. This type of recruitment relies on job seekers registering their CV with the recruitment firm or job seekers responding to an advertised position.

Typically, corporate clients will select more than one contingent recruitment firm for a particular search to find the best pool of candidates at a given time. This type of recruitment is most common with lower salary bands, as well as temporary and contract positions. Contingent recruitment is also used for more senior roles in markets where there is a large supply of suitable candidates.

It is important to understand how the firm will use any personal information that you provide. It is a good idea to make sure your personal details are not passed on to a potential employer without your approval.

Did you know?... In the UK, a CV will often contain personal information such as date of birth, marital status, nationality and whether or not the applicant has a UK driving licence. The CV should always include contact information, education, relevant experience, key skills (e.g., computer programmes or languages), and extracurricular activities where relevant, and be no more than 2-3 pages in length (one page is preferred, when possible).

LIBRARIES

A visit to a large reference library can be helpful in finding information on companies, industries and recruitment firms. Libraries can be a great source for trade journals, newspapers and other periodicals. Listed below are two of the best reference libraries in London for a job search:

City Business Library, 1 Brewers' Hall Garden (off Aldermanbury Square), EC2; 020 7332 1812; www.cityoflondon.gov.uk.
Opening hours: Monday to Friday 9:30-17:00.

Westminster Reference Library, 35 St. Martin's Street, WC2; 020 7641 1300; www.westminster.gov.uk/libraries.
Opening hours: Monday to Friday 10:00-20:00, Saturday 10:00-17:00.

Company Information Websites

The following websites provide career information, including profiles of companies and industry sectors: www.wetfeet.com, www.vault.com.

NETWORKING

Networking is often a key aspect of any job search. Most jobs are never advertised and are filled by word of mouth and personal recommendation. Friends, relatives, former employers, former colleagues, members of professional organisations and neighbours are all potential networking contacts. It may be helpful to have business or social cards printed with your name, phone number and e-mail address to pass out to contacts.

Alumni associations and clubs in London can often be good sources for networking. There are also numerous networking groups in the UK that welcome newcomers. The **FOCUS Resource Centre** (see the discussion at the beginning of this chapter) maintains an extensive list of networking organisations for its members.

Maintaining a good network is demanding work and needs constant development. Acquaintances that do not have employment information today may have some tomorrow.

Key networking tips:

- Keep good records of all networking contacts in one place.

- Keep in touch with networking contacts regularly, but not obtrusively.

Volunteering

Volunteering for an organisation can be a temporary or long-term alternative to full-time paid employment. Volunteering offers a great way to build your CV while you look for paid employment, as well as another source for networking contacts.

The following organisations can help you identify an appropriate volunteer position for your needs and interests:

TimeBank, 1 London Bridge, SE1; 0845 456 1668; www.timebank.org.uk.

Volunteering England, Regent's Wharf, 8 All Saints Street, N1; 0845 305 6979; www.volunteering.org.uk.

REACH, 89 Albert Embankment, SE1; 020 7582 6543; www.reach-online.org.uk. Enables voluntary organisations to benefit from the business, managerial, technical and professional expertise of people who want to offer their career skills working as volunteers.

Do-it, 3rd Floor, 2-3 Upper Street, N1; 020 7226 8008; www.do-it.org.uk. National database of volunteering opportunities in the UK; can advise you where to find your local volunteer bureau.

VISAS AND WORK PERMITS

Note: *This is not intended to be a complete guide to getting authorisation to work in the UK or to obtaining necessary visas. Advice specific to a situation should be sought when pursuing a visa to work in the UK.*

Most citizens living in the **European Economic Area (EEA)** are entitled to take employment in the UK without a visa or a work permit. Nationals of the Czech Republic, Estonia, Hungary, Latvia, Lithuania, Poland, Slovakia or Slovenia who are working in the UK may need to register under the Worker Registration Scheme. After one year of continuous work in the UK, these workers may apply for a residence permit to confirm their right to live and work in the UK. If the EEA citizen has non-EEA dependants or is intending to apply for permanent UK residency or a British passport, the EEA citizen should apply for a residence permit.

Non-EEA persons will need to obtain a visa that allows them to work in the UK. If a person does not qualify for a visa that permits them to seek work in the UK, then they will have to obtain a work permit through a UK employer. The employer will have to make an application to the Home Office, providing detailed information about the position and why the non-EEA person is the best person to fill it.

The following is a selection of the most common visas that allow a person to work in the UK.

Working Holiday Visas

Citizens of Commonwealth countries (e.g., Canada, Australia, New Zealand and South Africa) who are 17-30 years old with no dependents are eligible for a two-year working holiday visa. This visa must be applied for at a British High Commission outside the UK. The visa is issued with a restriction that the visa holder must not work for more than 52 weeks of their two-year stay. The main reason for visiting the UK must be for travel and any work must be incidental to the holiday. After 12 months, some working holiday visa holders may switch to work permit status (those who qualify on the skills shortage list) or the highly skilled migrant programme (see the discussion below), subject to fulfilling the appropriate criteria.

Ancestry Visas

Commonwealth citizens who can prove that a parent or grandparent was born in Britain are entitled to an ancestry visa for up to four years, which allows the visa holder to seek employment in the UK. A condition of this visa is that the applicant is able to work in the UK and intends to do so.

Highly Skilled Migrant Programme

The highly skilled migrant programme (HSMP) is a points-based scheme through which highly skilled persons may relocate to the UK to look for employment or self-employment opportunities. The application criteria are different for persons under age 28 and those over age 28. Applications are considered and points are assessed on the following criteria: education qualifications, work experience, past earnings, achievement in the chosen field and the applicant's partner's achievements.

If the application is granted, a one-year visa is granted to seek employment in the UK. The visa expires after that year unless the visa holder applies to stay longer, but "economic activity" (i.e., gainful employment) must be demonstrated.

Work Permits

If a person is not entitled to the above types of visas, then they can seek a work permit as a means of obtaining a visa that will allow them to work in the UK. A UK employer needs to apply for a work permit on the prospective employee's behalf. The work permit will apply to a specific role and is not transferable to other positions within the company. The employer has responsibility for proving it has gone to all reasonable lengths to find an EEA worker before looking elsewhere. Work permits typically are for a five-year period.

The application process for a work permit is fairly rigorous. The employer will need to provide information about the prospective employee, including work references, education, career history and professional qualifications, as well as the company's annual reports and accounts. The employer will also need to provide a job description and information about its recruitment advertising or other efforts made to fill the position. Work permits are rarely granted for manual, secretarial or domestic positions or for salaries of less than £20,000 per year.

After a work permit has been obtained, work permit holders who wish to come to the UK for more than six months must obtain "entry clearance" before travelling. Entry clearance is the formal term used to describe the application process for a visa that will allow a person to remain in the UK. The entry clearance certificate – the visa – is placed in the passport or travel document.

Additional Visas

This is not an exhaustive list of visas to work in the UK. For more information on this complex subject, refer to:

- **UK Visas, Foreign and Commonwealth Office**, SW1; 020 7008 8438; www.ukvisas.gov.uk. Jointly run by the Home Office and the Foreign and Commonwealth Office to handle UK visa services through diplomatic posts overseas. Opening hours: Monday-Friday: 9:30 – 13:30.

- **The UK Home Office Immigration and Nationality Directorate**, Lunar House, 40 Wellesley Road, Croydon, CR9 2BY;

0870 606 7766 (General information) or 0114 207 4074 (Work permit information); www.ind.homeoffice.gov.uk and www. workingintheuk.gov.uk.

INDEFINITE LEAVE TO REMAIN

Many UK immigration categories lead, after a period of time, to indefinite leave to remain. In addition to other categories, those living and working in the UK on a work permit (or the HSMP and later a work permit) for five continuous years are eligible to apply for indefinite leave to remain (permanent residence), which if granted will remove restrictions on the work or business you may do in the UK and eliminate any time limits on your stay in the UK.

For more advice regarding extending your stay once in the UK, contact the UK Home Office Immigration and Nationality Directorate (above).

EMPLOYMENT RIGHTS

All UK employers need to provide a statement of employment to the employee that clearly indicates the following information:

- The names of the employer and employee.

- The job title or a brief job description.

- Where the employee is expected to work.

- The date the employment started (or is to start).

- Details of salary and when payment will be made (e.g., weekly or monthly).

Hours of work, and any related issues such as overtime. An employee may be expected to work beyond the contractual hours for no additional pay if more work is required.

- Holiday entitlement (most UK workers receive 20-25 days

per year).

• Sick pay entitlement and procedures.

• Notice of termination period – standard notice is one month, but this can vary between industries and positions within a company.

• Pension scheme details.

• The length of the contract if the employee is working for a fixed time period.

• Details of the existence of any relevant collective agreements that directly affect the terms and conditions of employment.

More information on employment rights is available through the **Department of Trade and Industry: Employment Relations Directorate** (www.dti.gov.uk/er) or the **Department for Education and Skills** (www. dfes.gov.uk).

NATIONAL INSURANCE NUMBERS

National Insurance (NI) numbers are unique numbers assigned to individuals who reside in the UK for use when dealing with the **Inland Revenue and the Department of Work and Pensions**. The NI number ensures correct credit and a record of National Insurance benefits. Employers use the number for deducting taxes and National Insurance contributions from employees' pay.

If you are working in the UK, you will have to obtain an NI number promptly. You should contact a Department of Work and Pensions office (often a Jobcentre office) and ask for an appointment to be interviewed for an NI number. You will have to complete an application form and submit to an evidence of identity interview, and provide various documents to prove your identity and employment in the UK.

More information can be obtained from the **Department for Work and Pensions** (www.dwp.gov.uk). The website lists a variety of local offices, departments and phone numbers for information regarding specific types of enquiries.

FAST PATH APPLICATIONS

UK employers who have applied for a work permit under the Business and Commercial Scheme can complete a postal National Insurance number application form (signed by both the employer and employee); the employee will not have to attend the evidence of identity interview.

For more information on the fast path schemes, contact **Fast Path Internet Enquiries**, CCU Admin Team, 5th Floor, Portcullis House, 21 India Street, Glasgow, G2 4PH; 0845 641 5047.

4

Drawn by Mo

Utilities

THE POST OFFICE

The Post Office™ is a public corporation owned, but not managed, by the UK Government. **Royal Mail Group plc** is comprised of three separate businesses: **Post Office**, **Royal Mail** and **Parcelforce Worldwide**. Post Office manages the post office outlets; Royal Mail is the branch that handles the delivery of all mail within the UK; and Parcelforce Worldwide handles the movement of mail to and from overseas destinations.

Post Office™

The Post Office has a very helpful website at www.postoffice.co.uk. Here you can locate your local **post office** branch, track and trace mail posted in the UK, locate a UK address and learn about all of the services provided.

Post Office™ has a nationwide network of about 16,000 offices. Most are open Monday to Friday from 09:00 to 17:30 and on Saturday from 09:00 to 12:00. Neighbourhood Post Office hours vary.

The Post Office™ at 24/28 William IV Street, WC2, 020 7484 9307 (near Trafalgar Square), is open Monday to Friday from 08:00 to 20:00 and on Saturday from 09:00 to 20:00.

National Helpline, 0845 722 3344. This line is open on weekdays from 08:15 to 18:00, and on Saturdays from 08:30 to 19:00.

The UK postal service provides a wider range of functions than in most other countries, offering over 170 products and services that include the following (note that services may vary from branch to branch):

- **Paying household bills**. All payments such as phone, digital TV, utilities and council tax can be processed.

- **Banking.** Basic banking services are available to customers at most high street branches of the Post Office.

- **Travel services.** Foreign currency exchange and/or pre-order currency service, **American Express®** traveller's cheques, travel insurance and passport validation service.

- **Motor vehicle licences.**

- **TV licences.**

- **Lottery products.**

- **Mobile telephones and telephone calling cards.**

- **Postal orders.** Available at all branches of the Post Office. These can be used to pay household bills, pay someone who does not have access to a current (cheque) account, and to send money domestically or internationally. Postal orders are valid for up to six months. If sending a postal order internationally, you should verify that a British postal order can be cashed when presented in that country.

- **Transferring money overseas**. Available at over 1,500 post offices, Moneygram is a fast and safe way to send and receive money around the world in minutes.

- **Post shops.** Stationery and special stamps are available at some Post Office branches, as well as boxes in a variety of sizes.

- **Photo booths.**

- **Outdoor activity licences.** Gaming and fishing licences are available at certain branches that serve particular areas.

- **Flowers and chocolates.** Can be ordered for special events.

OTHER POST OFFICE™ SERVICES

Mail Redirection Service / Advice of Delivery

The **Post Office**™ enables you to have mail redirected for one, three, six, or 12 months for a variable fee. This service is renewable for up to two years. Mail can be redirected to a permanent or temporary address, either within the UK or abroad. Fill out a forwarding form at the Post Office (or download it from the website) at least a couple of weeks in advance of your move.

Keepsafe

The **Post Office**™ can hold your household's mail safely while you are away for up to two months, and then deliver it on a day that you specify. Requires at least one week's notice for this service, and charges a fee.

PO Box

As an alternative to receiving mail at home, you can set up a PO Box.

Apply and find out about the full terms and conditions of the service by contacting your local Sales Centre on 0845 795 0950.

Poste Restante (holding mail)

Mail can be received free of charge via the main **Post Office**™ of any town in Britain for a maximum of three months. However, the mail will be returned to the sender if you do not collect it within 14 days (one month if sent from abroad). Photo identification is necessary when you collect the mail. This service can be quite useful if you are going to be living at a certain address for a short amount of time. Letters should be addressed as follows:

> Your Name
>
> Post Restante
>
> Address of Post Office, including postcode

Several **American Express®** offices, including the branch at 30-31 Haymarket, SW1; 020 7484 9610, also provide poste restante services for its customers' letters for up to 30 days. The service is free to American Express ® cardholders and traveller's cheque holders; all others pay a small fee.

ROYAL MAIL

Royal Mail collects, sorts and delivers the mail. Royal Mail provides a wide range of services, including signature on delivery, guaranteed next working day delivery, and extra compensation cover for loss, damage or delay. The Royal Mail National Enquiry number is 0845 774 0740. The Royal Mail Postal Enquiry Line is 0845 711 1222. Their website is www.royalmail.com.

Parcelforce Worldwide

Parcelforce Worldwide provides a worldwide delivery service to over 200 countries. The Parcelforce Worldwide National Enquiry Centre can be contacted on 0870 850 1150 or try the website at www.parcelforce.com.

Sending Mail (all costs accurate at the time of publication)

Postage stamps can be bought at post offices, grocery stores, newsagents and even some petrol stations. A pre-paid envelope can be recognised by two thick vertical bars it has on the top right-hand side.

Sending Mail within the UK

Two rates apply for sending letters in the UK:

• First Class postage stamps cost 32 pence for up to 60 grams. First Class post will usually arrive the next business day within the UK.

• Second Class postage stamps cost 23 pence for up to 60 grams. Second Class is for sending less-urgent items and usually takes about three business days for delivery.

Recorded Mail provides additional reassurance by allowing for confirmation of delivery of important (but not valuable) items. You can check if an item has been delivered by visiting www.royalmail.com or calling 0845 927 2100. A "Proof of Delivery", which is a copy of the recipient's signature, is available by calling 0845 774 0740.

Special Delivery is recommended for valuable and time-critical items. This service provides the following benefits:

• Up-to-date delivery tracking

• A record of time and signature upon delivery (not necessarily the addressee's)

• Confirmation of delivery by visiting www.royalmail.com or calling 0845 700 1200

• "While you were out" cards for the recipient if no one was able to accept the package. The recipient can then collect it from the Royal Mail address on the card, or have the item delivered on another day or to another address.

Sending Mail Abroad

Letters and postcards. The maximum weight for an overseas letter or postcard is 2 kg and all post goes by air.

Small packets

A convenient and economical way to send goods and gifts is via the "small packet" service. When using this service, write SMALL PACKET in the top left corner on the front of the item. A customs declaration form must also be attached (most EU destinations are exempted). The maximum weight you can send is 2 kg (except for Saudi Arabia, which only accepts small packages of 1 kg or less).

Printed papers

A cost-effective way to send pamphlets, books, magazines and newspapers abroad is the printed papers service. When using this service, write PRINTED PAPERS in the top left corner on the front of the item. You can't include personal correspondence. The maximum weight for most places is 2 kg, or 5 kg for books and pamphlets.

Parcels

A variety of services is offered depending on how fast you want the package to be delivered. A customs declaration form must be attached to the parcel (EU destinations are exempt). Contact **Parcelforce** for more information.

Airmail

Items need an airmail sticker, or "By Airmail – Par Avion" written in the top left corner on the front of the item.

International Mail and Parcel Services

International Signed For

The international signed-for service allows you to send insured packages and ensure a signature is recorded upon delivery. This service is not available for all countries and the maximum compensation may be lower for some countries.

Airsure

This service is for express airmail. Mail is placed on the next available flight to the required destination. Airsure does not guarantee delivery times as postal standards vary in countries.

Shipment of Goods into the UK

Care should be taken regarding the shipment of goods into the UK. Customs services may stop incoming shipments and levy VAT charges and import duties on the value of the incoming shipment.

TELEPHONE

Public Phone Boxes

Phone boxes (public telephones) can be found in larger shops, in pubs and along the street. The minimum charge is 20 pence. Coin-operated telephones generally take 10p, 20p, 50p and £1 coins, and/or phone cards. Most new phones require you to insert the coin before dialling. When using older phones, dial the number and wait for the beeping sound before inserting coins. If an additional coin is required, ample warning is given by another beeping sound. Do not ask someone to ring you at the payphone unless you are certain that it will accept incoming calls.

Many new public telephones operate on phone cards available from most newsagents and post offices. These phone cards are composed of units of 10p and come in values of £3, £5, £10 and £20. If you plan on using the public telephones, it is useful to buy and carry a phone card with you, as coin-operated phones are being phased out.

Telephone Companies

You can choose from a large variety of fixed-line telephone service providers, including:

British Gas; 0845 600 6311; www.house.co.uk.
BT (British Telecommunications); 0800 800 150; www.BT.com.
NTL; 0800 183 1234; www.ntl.com.
Telewest; 0845 142 0200; www.telewest.co.uk.
Tesco; 0906 301 8000; www.tesco.com.

For help and advice on telephone companies and services, the UK's **Office of Telecommunications** has a useful website (www.oftel.gov.uk). Also, the **Industry Forum**, which consists of the main fixed-line phone companies, publishes a guide to quality of service, called the Comparative Performance Indicators (CPI). You can get a copy of CPI by e-mailing cpi@cpi.org.uk or visiting www.cpi.org.uk.

It is fairly easy to switch phone companies. In the UK, if you change your phone line and stay at the same address(or within the same telephone area), you can keep your phone number. However, phone companies may make a reasonable charge for this "number portability".

Before making any final decision, it is recommended that you check with the individual telephone companies for their latest prices, and other factors such as services offered and quality of service. Bundling telephone services with another utility service provider, such as broadband, pay TV services or gas, might enable you to take advantage of some special discounts.

Calculating the cost of various phone services can be complicated because you need to consider:

• Line rental

• Cost of calls

• Discount packages

• Number of calls you make and when

• The type of calls you mostly make (local, national, international or internet).

Currently, most calls, including local calls, are charged on a per minute and per unit basis. Telephone charges are based on metered units. The unit charge varies according to the time the call is made for local, national and international calls. Calls tend to be less expensive between 18:00 and 08:00.

Some free numbers include those with prefixes of 0800, 0808 or 0321. Numbers with the prefix 0345 or 0845 are charged at local rates. Numbers with the prefix 0900 or 0870 are charged at the national rate even if you make a local call.

New telephone equipment is available at a local **BT** shop, or any high street electronics retailer such as **Dixons**. New telephone equipment can also be rented from several of the telephone service suppliers, including BT. You can also purchase a phone adapter that will enable you to use a foreign telephone in the UK.

Telephone directories, including **Yellow Pages**™, are published for London and the other cities and towns in Great Britain. The dialling codes for all UK cities and towns are listed in the front of each directory.

Voice-over-Internet Protocol

A growing service for long distance and international calls is the voice-over-internet protocol (VoIP). Several companies provide this service and if you make frequent international or long distance calls this service may prove to be less expensive. The quality of the lines vary (usually depending on the time of day and the speed of your internet connection) but services are improving.

Some companies that provide this service include:

BT Anytime Call Plan; 0800 800 150; www.BT.com.

Just Dial VOIP Max; 07005 963 875; www.cheap-dial-international.com.

Skype; www.skype.com.

Tesco Internet Phone; 0906 301 8000; www.tesco.com.

VOIP Cheap; www.VOIPcheap.co.uk.

Vonage; 0800 008 6000; www.vonage.co.uk.

MOBILE TELEPHONES

Mobile phones are very popular in the UK. Common providers include **T-Mobile, Orange** and **Virgin**. Most of these companies offer services that will work throughout Continental Europe. To help decide on the right provider and plan, consider how often and where you will use your mobile (UK, Europe or the rest of the world), how long you want your service contract to last, and the ease of ending the contract.

Many mobile providers have stand-alone shops on most high streets and throughout London. If you change providers, it is usually possible to keep your mobile number. However, this is based on agreements between mobile phone companies. You do not have a legal right to keep the same number.

THE INTERNET

There are three different internet services you can subscribe to: ISPS, broadband or wireless.

ISPS is the oldest (and usually the slowest), for which internet service is provided via a dial-up connection over your landline telephone.

Broadband (ASDL) service is generally faster and requires that you purchase a modem. The monthly fee for ADSL broadband is typically between £15 to £40 depending on which services you require. Sometimes, additional equipment and set-up charges are added on top of the monthly fee.

Wireless (Wi-Fi) internet allows you to access the internet anywhere in your house. This is particularly useful if you have more than one home computer or prefer to use a notebook computer. Some of the common internet providers include:

AOL; www.aol.co.uk; 0800 376 5599.
BT; www.btopenworld.com; 0845 601 5190.
Telewest; www.telewest.co.uk; 0845 142 0200.
Tesco; www.tesco.com; 0906 301 8000.
Virgin; www.virgin.net; 0845 650 1000.
Wanadoo; www.wanadoo.co.uk; 0845 330 7124.

Internet Cafes

London also has many internet cafes. Two of the larger chains are:

Easy Internet; 020 7241 9000; www.easyeverything.com. Cafes are located throughout London, including Kensington High Street, Tottenham Court Road, Trafalgar Square, Oxford Street and the King's Road.

Internet Exchange; 020 7792 6200; www.internet-exchange.co.uk. Cafes are located on Baker Street, Bayswater, Covent Garden, Queensway and Shaftesbury Avenue (in the Trocodero).

UTILITIES

With the exception of water, consumers in the London area have a variety of utility suppliers. For electricity and gas, a wide range of services and price structures is available. Moreover, switching from one supplier to another is relatively easy.

To compare major utility prices and services in your area, visit the following websites:

www.buy.co.uk.

www.ofgem.gov.uk.

www.saveonyourbills.com.

www.unravelit.com.

www.uswitch.com.

ELECTRICITY & GAS

Electricity and gas meters are generally read quarterly and bills are sent following the reading. The bill will include electricity units used and their unit price, plus a quarterly standing charge.

If you intend to install gas appliances, you should choose a gas fitter who is registered with **The Council of Registered Gas Installers** (CORGI), 1 Elmwood, Chineham Business Park, Crockford Lane, Baskingstoke, Hants RG24 8WG; 012 5637 2300; www.corgi-gas.com. CORGI will provide the names of members in your area.

If you have individual gas and water heaters for bathrooms or the kitchen, you must have them serviced every year and make sure the rooms are well ventilated. A significant number of fatal accidents have occurred because of defective gas heaters.

The electrical supply in London is 240V AC. England has several types of electrical plugs; the most common is a square-shaped, three-pin plug. It requires a fuse and has a "ground" wire. The fuse is located inside the plug itself rather than at a central box; each electrical outlet has a switch to turn electricity on and off at the individual outlet.

The UK has several types of light bulbs, including a "screw in" and a "bayonet" variety. When purchasing replacement bulbs, you will need to know the size and type of bulb the lamp requires.

For more information on electricity, see *Chapter 1: Moving, under Electrical Differences*.

WATER

Thames Water supplies water for much of London (0845 9200 888; (www.thameswater.co.uk). Detailed information and telephone numbers can be found in the telephone directory. Many water bills are not based on a consumption rate, but on the value of the property plus a standing charge. Usually, you can improve on your water bill if your home is fitted with a water meter, which Thames Water will fit free of charge. You may not use a sprinkler to water your garden unless you have a water meter.

Water bills are sent semi-annually and include charges for water plus sewage services. If you rent your property, the landlord may pay this charge.

In most houses, the only drinkable tap water is from the tap in the kitchen. Water from other taps comes from storage tanks on the premises, rather than from the main line. Water in London is very hard so you will need to use a decalcification liquid to rid appliances such as kettles, irons and washers from the limescale that accumulates with use. For your washing machine, water softening tablets are available. For your dishwasher, salt is used to soften and prevent the deposit and stain of lime on kitchen utensils.

If your water looks cloudy, discoloured, tastes different or smells funny, contact the **Drinking Water Inspectorate** 020 7944 5956; www.dwi.gov.uk; or via email at dwi_enquiries@detr.gov.uk).

TELEVISION

All users of television sets must possess an annual TV licence, obtainable from any **Post Office**™. One licence covers all of the television sets in a household. The charge for a colour television licence is £126.50, and one for black and white televisions is £42.00. Each licence is valid for 12 months, and is automatically renewed. There is no charge for a television licence if you are over 75 years old. Fines for not having a TV licence can be as much as £1,000. Radios do not require a licence.

For more information about television licences, call 0870 241 6468 or visit www.tvlicensing.co.uk. If you leave the country before the expiry of the licence, you can obtain a refund by contacting **Customer Services, TV Licensing**, Freepost BS6689, Bristol BS98 ITL.

If you have a television with teletext it will enable you to read news, weather and future programming. **Ceefax** and **Oracle** are the two teletext information services available in the UK.

Digital and Satellite TV

In addition to the five terrestrial channels available with your television licence (**BBC 1**, **BBC 2**, **ITV**, **Channel 4** and **Channel 5**), cable, digital and satellite television may be available in your area.

Digital suppliers include **NTL, Telewest** and **Sky Digital**. Digital offers several advantages to the viewer, such as wide-screen pictures, CD-quality sound and video-on-demand. Interactive services such as home banking, home shopping and connection to the internet are also now available digitally through the TV in some areas. All TV in the UK will be digital by 2012. Visit www.dtg.org.uk/consumer and www.itc.org.uk/the_digital_age for more information about digital television.

In order to receive satellite communications, you may either purchase or rent an individual satellite dish to be installed at your residence. You must then subscribe to a plan, which will be payable on a monthly basis. Satellite dishes are available from many local high street electronic and appliance shops as well as from signal suppliers. Packages are available to rent from **Boxclever** (0870 333 4140; www.boxclever.co.uk). To subscribe to channels such as CNN, MTV and Sky, contact Sky at 0870 240 4040; www.sky.com or Telewest at 0845 142 0220; www.telewest.com.

Did you know?... Some residential estates offer satellite TV reception via a central dish. Other buildings do not allow satellite dishes at all. Be sure to check before purchasing this service.

Freeview

A less expensive alternative to pay-for digital TV services or satellite TV is called **Freeview**. This digital TV service requires that you purchase an electronic Freeview box (usually around £30 - £50), which you hook up to your TV and aerial. Freeview boxes are available at your local electrical retailer. There are no additional fees other than the cost of the Freeview box.

Freeview digital TV includes access to nearly 30 TV channels, including all-day children's programming and round-the-clock news as well as several digital radio stations.

For more information, contact Freeview at www.freeview.co.uk.

LOCAL COUNCILS

Each council works to meet the needs of residents and to provide various community services, including:

- Operating some of the best schools in London

- Maintaining roads and pavements

- Ensuring rubbish is promptly collected.

Council contact details for Central London are:

Corporation of London,
PO Box 270, Guildhall, EC2P 2EJ; www.cityoflondon.gov.uk.
General: 020 7606 3030

Recycling: 020 7236 9541

Refuse collection and street cleaning: 020 7236 9541

London Borough of Camden,

Camden Town Hall, Judd Street, WC1H 9JE; www.camden.gov.uk.

General: 020 7278 4444

Recycling: 020 7485 1553

Refuse collection and street cleaning: 020 7974 6914/5

London Borough of Hackney,

Hackney Town Hall, Mare Street, Hackney, E8 1EA; www.hackney.gov.uk.

General: 020 8356 5000

Emergencies: 020 8356 2300

Recycling and refuse collection: 020 8985 4681

London Borough of Hammersmith and Fulham,

Town Hall, King Street, Hammersmith, W6 9JU; www.lbhf.gov.uk.

General: 020 8748 3020

Emergencies (out of hours): 020 8753 1100

London Borough of Islington,

Islington Town Hall, 222 Upper Street, Islington, N1 1XR;

www.islington.gov.uk.

General: 020 7527 2000

Recycling: 020 7527 4679

Refuse collection: 020 7527 4692

Royal Borough of Kensington and Chelsea,

The Town Hall, Hornton Street, W8 7NX; www.rbkc.gov.uk.

General: 020 7937 5464

Emergencies (out of hours): 020 7361 3484

Recycling: 020 7341 5148

Refuse collection & street cleaning: 020 7341 5284

London Borough of Lambeth,
Lambeth Town Hall, Brixton Hill, SW2 1RW; www.lambeth.gov.uk.
General: 020 7926 1000
Refuse collection and street cleaning: 020 7926 9000

London Borough of Southwark,
Southwark Town Hall, Peckham Road, SE5 5UB; www.southwark.gov.uk.
General: 020 7525 5000
Recycling: 020 7703 8030
Refuse collection and street cleaning: 020 7525 2183 / 2188

Westminster City Council,
PO Box 240, Westminster City Hall, 64 Victoria Street, SW1E 6QP;
www.westminster.gov.uk.
General: 020 7641 6000
Recycling, refuse collection and street cleaning: 020 7641 2000

RECYCLING AND WASTE

Recycling centres for bottles, cans, clothes and paper products are widespread in London. Several methods of recycling are available to most London residents, including doorstep recycling collection, blue bins (larger recycling bins found throughout London neighbourhoods in designated areas), mini recycling centres and composting.

Most residents receive one or two domestic waste collections each week and one weekly recycling collection. Normal refuse should be put in strong plastic bags and securely tied. There are usually no domestic collections on New Year's Day, Easter, May Day, Christmas and bank holidays. Most councils also operate a "Too Big for the Bin" service for items that are too bulky to fit in with your normal refuse. Payment must be made in advance, and usually can be made by credit and debit card, cash, cheques or postal orders. This service tends to be fairly popular, with waiting times of up to four weeks. For specific details on all of the recycling and waste services available in your area, contact your local council.

Disposing of Bulky Items of Household Waste

At the following sites, residents can dispose of up to five black plastic bags of waste or five bulky items (furniture, carpets, etc). Residents who need to dispose of more than five bags must complete a C.A1 form and provide proof of residence.

Cremorne Wharf Recycling Centre, 27 Lots Road, SW10; 020 7376 4527. Open Monday to Friday from 07:30 to 16:30 and Saturday from 08:00 to 12:00.

This site also has collection facilities for books, clothes, oil and household electrical goods.

Western Riverside Waste Authority, Smugglers Way, Wandsworth, London SW18; 020 8871 2788. Open from 07:30 to 18:00, seven days a week.

Car batteries can be taken to this site, where the sulphuric acid is drained and the metal sent for recycling.

Cringle Dock, Cringle Street, Battersea, London, SW8; 020 7622 6233. Open from 08:00 to 20:00, seven days a week.

Motor oil

It is illegal to pour motor oil down the drain. For information on safe disposal, contact the Oil Bank Line (0800 663 366).

Old cars

If you want to dispose of your vehicle, or report apparently abandoned vehicles, contact your local council.

Recovery of lost items in gullies / storm drains. Lost items (such as jewellery or keys) can be recovered from gullies and storm drains for a fee. Contact your local council to get referred to the appropriate water refuse contractor for your area.

USEFUL TELEPHONE NUMBERS

Ambulance, Fire, Police (for immediate danger)   999 or 112
For non-urgent incidents – contact your local police station*.

Crimestoppers (anonymous)	0800 555 111
Electrical Emergency	0800 096 9000
Gas Emergency	0800 111 999
Directory Enquiries, UK	118 500/118 118
Directory Enquiries, International	118 505
Operator Assistance, UK	100
Operator Assistance, International	155
Telephone Repairs	151
Time (from area codes 0207 / 0208)	123
London Underground	020 7222 1234
National Rail Enquiries	0845 748 4950
National Bus Service (National Express)	0870 580 8080
Racial Harassment Reporting Hotline	0800 138 1661

* Contact your local council for other key numbers specific to your area.

5

Drawn by Zainab

Transportation

CONTENTS

- Public Transportation
- Driving in Britain
- London Airports

The best way to get to know London is on foot. Buy a good street guide (such as *London A to Z*, available in any bookshop or newsagent) and off you go! Just remember that cars travel on the left side of the road, so traffic will be coming from the right and pedestrians do not have the right of way, except at a "zebra crossing" (a pedestrian crosswalk), which is clearly marked with black and white stripes painted on the road surface or on poles and a flashing yellow light.

PUBLIC TRANSPORTATION

The most comprehensive resource for planning a trip by public transportation is the **Transport for London** (TfL) website found at www.tfl. gov.uk. The TfL phone number for general enquiries is 020 7222 1234.

The Underground, commonly called the Tube, and bus systems can take you almost anywhere you want to go. Free maps of the Tube and bus routes are available at all London Transport ticket offices. The routes of both systems are clearly colour coded.

Various types of tickets and passes can be purchased ranging from Travelcards for one to seven days to monthly passes for one to twelve months. You can also purchase a "bus saver" which is a booklet of six discounted bus tickets. Many of these tickets and passes can be purchased at newsagents displaying a red "Pass Agent" sign or at Underground ticket windows and machines. In addition, tickets purchased after 09:30 weekdays and all day Saturday and Sunday are considered off-peak and are therefore, less expensive than peak fares. All Travelcards can be used on the Tube and buses in the London area.

Did you know?...You can plan your journey online before you head out the door. If you want to plan a journey online, to include the Tube, buses, tramlink, DLR or river bus services, visit www.tfl.gov.uk. This very useful site includes both a journey planner and real-time travel updates.

"Oyster" is London's travel smartcard and is best suited to persons living in London rather than tourists. The Oystercard can store your Travelcard season ticket or Pre-Pay (pay-as-you-go travel), or a combination of both. Oyster is valid on the Tube, buses, Docklands Light Railway (DLR) and trams. It can be "topped up" when your season ticket expires or your pre-pay runs out. If you are making multiple journeys in one day, the Oyster card will cap the price you pay to the price of a one-day Travelcard or one-day bus ticket. Note that it's not yet valid for suburban trains.

The Underground (Tube)

In order to purchase an Underground ticket, go to the ticket window in Underground stations and ask for a ticket to your destination or use the self-service ticket machines that exist in most stations. Signs are posted over the machines listing fares. Newer machines accept both cash, debit and credit cards; older machines require coins rather than notes, and occasionally exact change is required. Tickets must be put through the scanner at the barrier at both the beginning and end of your journey, so remember to keep your ticket in order to exit at your destination. If you are travelling with children, be sure to hang on to their tickets as well.

Fares are based on the distance traveled. London is divided into six bands called "travel zones" for Tube fares. The more zones you cross, the higher the fare. Children under five ride free and children under 16 and adults over 60 are entitled to reduced fares.

The Underground operates from 05:30 until approximately midnight daily with reduced schedules on Sunday and holidays. Rush hours (for "peak" fares) are 08:00 to 09:30 and 16:30 to 19:00. Smoking is not permitted on the Underground trains or in the stations. Dogs are allowed to travel on the Underground. Often stations close due to construction so it is wise to check before you begin your journey. If you forget to check for closings before you depart, look for the white boards at the station's entrance. These boards often list current service disruptions.

Buses

Buses are less expensive than the Underground but can be slower in heavy traffic. Most buses run until 23:00 with different timetables on Sunday and holidays. However, several "night bus" routes operate after 23:00. Most bus stops have placards indicating which bus routes stop there. Some stops are "request" stops, which are marked with red signs. At a request stop, you must signal the driver to stop the bus by holding out your hand. Most buses are now "one man buses" where you pay the driver as you enter. Fare collectors may not have change for large bills so carry small change whenever possible.

If boarding a bus at a Central London bus stop, a bus ticket must be purchased before boarding. The red ticket machines are located at most Central London bus stops and require exact change.

Children under 16 ride free of charge on buses and trams and adults over 60 are entitled to ride or free or at reduced fares. From September 2006, free bus and tram travel will be extended to those under 18 in full-time education.

If you are outside of Central London, pay the fare to the driver and he or she will hand you a ticket. If you are using an Oyster card, press one side of the card to the electronic scanner next to the driver. Keep your ticket during your ride, as inspectors occasionally conduct checks. You cannot transfer from one bus to another without paying an additional full fare unless you have an all-day ticket.

Red Arrow buses offer a limited stop or express service between Victoria, Waterloo, London Bridge and Liverpool Street stations and major shopping and business areas. Red Arrow buses require exact fare.

Green Line coaches serve communities within a 40-mile radius of Central London. The company also runs coaches to Luton Airport. There are stops within London, indicated by green bus stop signs. For information, call 0870 608 7261 or visit www.greenline.co.uk.

National Express Coaches and **Euroline link London** with other cities in the United Kingdom, Ireland and Continental Europe; for bookings and enquiries, call 0870 580 8080 or visit www.gobycoach.com.

Trains

The major cities in Britain are linked by modern, high-speed trains. There are also commuter lines between towns and outlying areas. Tickets can be purchased at any train station, online or by phone and at most travel agencies. There are various ticket schemes, such as "cheap day" return (round trip), excursion, seasonal and family rail cards. You should ask about the most economical way to get to your destination before purchasing a ticket. Hold on to your ticket throughout your journey. If you have a Travelcard, it may be valid for train journeys that are within the zones covered by your Travelcard — ask a ticket agent.

The 24-hour telephone number for all national train times and fares is 0845 748 4950.

Trains for various destinations depart from different London stations:

The North & Central Britain:
Euston
King's Cross
St. Pancras

The South:
Charing Cross
London Bridge
Victoria
Waterloo

The West Country, Wales
& South Midlands:
Paddington
Waterloo
Marylebone

The East, East Anglia & Essex:
Liverpool Street
Victoria
Fenchurch Street

Express Trains to London Airports

Gatwick Express
Victoria, Blackfriars,
Moorgate, Farringdon
and London Bridge stations

Heathrow Express
Paddington station

Stansted Express
Liverpool Street station

For more detailed information regarding transportation to London airports, please read the segment on airports at the end of this chapter.

Taxis

The familiar black London taxi (now often painted in other colours yet still commonly referred to as the "black cab"), is the most expensive but often the most convenient and reliable form of transportation. Taxis are controlled strictly by law and all areas within London are regulated by meters.

During periods of fare increases and before meters are adjusted, your fare may be higher than the meter indicates but the new fares will be explained and posted inside the cab. It is customary to tip by rounding up the charge (e.g., pay £6 for a £5.50 fare) or by giving approximately 10%.

Taxis are limited by law to carrying five adults. You can hail a taxi that has a lit "for hire" sign on its roof, "queue" (line up) at an appointed taxi stand or ring one of the taxi companies directly.

London also has "minicabs" (also listed under "Taxis") that are both licensed and unlicensed. Minicabs cannot be hailed in the street and must be booked ahead of time. It is important to verify or even negotiate a minicab price when you book and it is helpful to have a good idea of where you are going, as minicab drivers are not required to know London streets and directions.

Even though unlicensed minicab drivers exist, they are not recommended. If a minicab stops you in the street and offers you a ride, you should always refuse the offer.

> Did you know?...Even London taxi drivers and natives keep good maps of London in their automobiles. Some of the most useful are London A to Z, Nicholson's London Street Guide, Geographer's and One Way London. You can also plan your route in advance on line at www.mapquest.co.uk or www.streetmap.co.uk.

If you use a reputable taxi company, and become comfortable with them, not only will they offer a courier service (pick-up and delivery of goods, packages and food), but they will also take your children to and from school and home or wherever necessary. Personal and corporate accounts can be set up.

For a few minicab recommendations, see *Chapter 11: Services.*

DRIVING IN BRITAIN

Owning a car is not essential in Central London because of the comprehensive public transportation. If you prefer the convenience of a car, you can buy, lease or rent a vehicle easily. It is strongly recommended that you purchase and read *The Highway Code* (available in most bookshops), which outlines the British driving regulations before beginning to drive in Britain. The differences do not end with driving on the left-hand side of the road!

Traffic and congestion are problems, as in any other major city, and petrol (gasoline) is expensive. There is a "congestion zone" in London whereby you must pay a fee to drive within Central London during specified hours. Parking is limited to car parks (parking lots) or meters for non-residents in certain areas, and street parking in these restricted areas is only possible for residents with permits. Parking violations may result in fines, towing or "clamping", all of which involve considerable expense and inconvenience. On the other hand, having a car makes picking up groceries and other bulky items easier and getting out of the city for a weekend much more convenient.

For national traffic information call the **Royal Automobile Club** traffic line on 0906 470 1740. For car problems, call the **Automobile Association** (AA) 24-hour Breakdown line on 0800 887 766, or the Royal Automobile Club (RAC) 24-hour Rescue Service linkline on 0800 828 282. For European breakdown service, contact the AA on 0800 085 2840. You need to be a member of these organisations to enjoy their service, so before you head out on the roads please refer to the section following on Automobile Associations.

Congestion Charge

In an effort to reduce congestion and encourage the use of other modes of transport in London, all drivers must pay a congestion charge when entering the congestion zone from Monday – Friday between 07:00 and 18:30. The zone is clearly marked with traffic signs in London.

You can pay the congestion charge either in advance or on the day of travel before, during or after the journey. The charge is £8 if you pay by 22:00 on the day of travel. An additional £2 surcharge will apply if you pay from 22:00 until midnight on the day of travel. If you forget to pay, a penalty notice will be issued to the vehicle registrant. You can pay the charge online, via email or text, by phone, by post and at various shops throughout London. For detailed information regarding the congestion charge, visit: www.cclondon.com.

Driving Licences

It is important to obtain a proper driver's licence, because driving without one is illegal and will affect your insurance. **The Department of Transport's Driver and Vehicle Licensing Centre**, 0870 240 0009, is open for calls Monday to Friday 08:15 to 16:30.

Generally, if you hold a valid driving licence or International Driving Permit (and are not barred from driving in Great Britain) you may drive vehicles covered by your licence here for 12 months. If you are in the UK as a visitor, the 12 months begins on the date that you last entered Great Britain. If you are a new resident, the 12 months begins on the date you took up residence in the UK.

At the end of your first 12 months, you must hold a valid British driving licence if you wish to continue driving in the UK. You should allow at least three weeks for the licence to be issued. If you are entitled to apply for a full Great Britain licence you should send proof of your entitlement with the application form. If you wish to exchange an EC licence, you must also apply within one year of coming to live here.

You may take a driving test before or after the 12-month time limit has expired providing you hold a driving licence that entitles you to drive in the UK. There are often delays in scheduling a test appointment. If you wish to expedite the application process, you might state that you are willing to take the test at any time and at any location.

There are many firms offering driving lessons. The best known is the **British School of Motoring** (BSM), which can be reached on 0845 727 6276 or at www.bsm.co.uk. Motoring schools can advise you on the requirements, handle applications and instruct you in techniques required to pass the British driving test. Consult the phone book for additional schools of motoring in your area or try the following services:

International Drivers Service, Suite No 10, Noel Court, Bath Road, Hounslow, Middlesex, TW4 7DD; 020 8570 9190; www.internationaldriversservice.com.

Provides overseas licence holders driver training courses and preparation for obtaining a UK driver's licence.

The Driving Test published by the **Department of Transport** is also a useful tool. It lists available driving instructors and test centres, and breaks down the driving test components. The driving test begins with a written theory test on *The Highway Code* and *The Complete Theory Test for Cars and Motorcycles*. Both of these publications are available at most bookstores. The written theory test is followed by an eye test and a 20-30 minute driving test. There is no limit to the number of times that these tests can be taken.

If you wish, the driving school instructor will accompany you to the test and acquaint you with the test route. It is important to remember that if you take the test driving a car with an automatic transmission, your licence will be restricted to automatic transmissions. However, if you take the test on a vehicle with a manual transmission, your licence will be valid for vehicles with automatic and manual transmissions.

Insurance

Third-party insurance is compulsory and it is advisable to have comprehensive insurance as well. "No claim" reductions and other options are available. You might bring a letter from your previous insurance agency stating that you are entitled to "no claim" insurance for the past five years. It is recommended that you contact several insurance companies regarding types of coverage and cost. You should also have a clear understanding with your insurance company regarding claims and the kind of licence you possess.

Purchasing a Car

Purchasing a car in Britain is expensive but there is a good market for second-hand cars. The London evening papers, Sunday papers, specialised car magazines (*The Auto Trader, Loot* and *The American*) are all good sources. There is also a monthly magazine called the *Motorist's Guide to New and Used Car Prices*. Both the **AA** and the **RAC** will thoroughly inspect and value second-hand cars for their members for a fee.

Road Tax

A compulsory Road Tax must be paid each year for each car. Upon paying your Road Tax, you will receive a round sticker ("tax disc") to display inside your windscreen. If you are buying a car through a dealer, they will generally take care of this detail as part of the sales procedure but it is up to you to renew it for subsequent years. If you have brought a car with you to the UK, forms are available at your local post office. Annual renewal forms will be sent to you automatically.

M.O.T.

If your car is more than three years old, you must have a **Ministry of Transport** (M.O.T.) test each year to prove its roadworthiness. Garages licensed by the Ministry of Transport to conduct this test can perform the test within 24 hours, or while you wait. There is a fee for this service. You must present your M.O.T. certificate along with proof of insurance when paying your Road Tax.

Leasing and Renting Cars

Leasing cars by companies is a common practice in Britain and dealers can supply details of the various lengths of time and conditions. Car rental firms provide the usual services. Cars with manual transmission are most common and less expensive than automatics. Car rental companies are listed in the **Yellow Pages**™ of the phone directory under "Car Hire—Self Drive". **Hertz, Avis, Budget, Enterprise, Europcar, Kenning** and **Thrifty** are well-known rental agencies.

Automobile Associations

You may consider joining the **AA** or the **RAC** for emergency services (see the "Driving in Britain" section for their emergency phone numbers), as there is no other way of ensuring service in an emergency. These organisations also offer breakdown insurance for trips to the Continent and can even provide legal service in court.

The Automobile Association, Fanum House, Basing View, Basingstoke, Hants, RG21 2EA; 0870 600 0371; www.theaa.com.

The Royal Automobile Club Motoring Services, P.O. Box 700, Bristol, BS9 91RB; 0800 029 029; www.rac.co.uk.

Garages

While all garages are different, it is not unusual to have to book weeks in advance in order to get your car serviced or repaired.

Resident's Parking

In many areas of London, you are entitled to purchase a Resident's Parking Permit (check with your council at your town hall for eligibility). Residents' areas are patrolled regularly by traffic wardens and fines are given if you are in a restricted area without the proper parking permit. Resident parking regulations vary from area to area so it is imperative to read signs thoroughly.

If you are not fortunate enough to locate a parking meter on the street, you may opt for a car park. Blue signs with a white 'P' direct you to public parking in unfamiliar surroundings. Three central public parking garages are:

Drury Lane Car Park, Parker Street, WC2; 020 7242 8611

Selfridges Ltd., Edwards Mews, off Duke Street, W1; 020 7629 1234

Barbican Centre Garage, Silk Street, EC2; 020 7638 4141.

Clamping

In the unfortunate case of "getting clamped", you can call your local council to get it removed. If you would like someone to perform the service for you, **Clampbusters** (020 7735 7235) are happy to help. For an annual fee and a service charge, they will unclamp your car, deliver it to your home and handle the paperwork.

Petrol Stations

Petrol stations in Britain accept **Visa®**, **Mastercard®** and sometimes **Diners Club®** and **American Express®**. Some stations offer personal accounts that are payable monthly. BP/Mobil and Shell both offer a charge card.

LONDON AIRPORTS

There are five airports conveniently located to London: City, Gatwick, Heathrow, Luton and Stansted. **The British Airport Authority** (BAA) operates the largest three (Heathrow, Gatwick and Stansted) and has a very informative website (www.baa.co.uk) for real-time arrivals and departures information, directions, methods of public transport available and more.

HEATHROW

Hounslow, Middlesex TW6 1JH; 087 0000 0123; www.heathrowairport.com

Heathrow, located 15 miles to the west

Did you know?...You can check your baggage for some airlines at Paddington Station.

of London, is the busiest international airport in the world. It is also very large with four terminals and a fifth one under construction. Terminal 4, the newest, is a considerable distance by road from the others, and extra time should be allowed to reach it, or to transfer between terminals. Check your departure terminal (can be found on the website above) before you begin your journey to Heathrow.

Traveling to Heathrow

You can travel to Heathrow by train, tube, bus, taxi or car. Most services run between 05:00 and 23:30.

Train

The Heathrow Express (0845 600 1515; www.heathrowexpress.com) is the fastest way to reach the airport from Central London. The journey takes 15 minutes from Paddington Station to Terminals 1, 2 or 3 and 20 minutes to Terminal 4. Trains run every 15 minutes. A one-way ticket costs £14 (£26 return) if bought at the station, or £13 (£25 return) if purchased online. Tickets are available on board the train at a premium. If you have heavy luggage, be warned that there may be a long walk after arriving at the airport to reach the terminal.

Tube

The Piccadilly Line connects central London and Heathrow's two tube stations (one station for Terminals 1, 2 and 3, and one for Terminal 4). Trains run every five minutes at peak times and every nine minutes off-peak and on weekends. Journey time is roughly one hour from Central London. The Heathrow stations are located in zone 6 for Tube ticket buying purposes.

Due to work on extending the Piccadilly line, there is no underground service to Terminal 4 until September 2006. Passengers travelling to and from Terminal 4 can use the replacement bus service between Hatton Cross underground station and Terminal 4.

Bus

National Express Coaches offer service to Heathrow from various pick-up points throughout London. Visit www.nationalexpress.com or telephone: 0870 580 8080 for details.

Licensed Black Cabs

In central London, a black cab will always take passengers to Heathrow. The fare will vary on traffic and time of day but is generally £40-£50 from Central London. Only some black cabs will accept pre-booked trips for a set fare whereas most mini-cab companies offer fares to Heathrow for a set price. See *Chapter 11: Services – Taxis and Minicab Services* for recommendations.

Fly Away Meet & Greet Valet

This is a service for travellers who wish to drive themselves to the airport. A representative will collect your vehicle from you at the terminal, and have it waiting for you upon your return. For an additional fee they will wash, wax and service your car while you are away. Telephone: 020 8759 1567 / 020 8759 2020 with your terminal, travel dates and time. For more details and other parking options visit: www.airport-parking-shop.co.uk/heathrow.

GATWICK

Gatwick, West Sussex RH6 ONP; 087 0000 2468; www.gatwickairport.com

Gatwick, 28 miles to the south of London, is the second largest airport in the UK. Although it is farther from central London than Heathrow, many consider travelling from Gatwick to be a more pleasant experience.

There are two terminals at Gatwick: the north terminal, mainly dedicated to British Airways scheduled flights, and the south terminal, from which most other scheduled services and all holiday charter flights depart. The main train station is in the South terminal, but there is a free, shuttle train service that will take you to the North terminal; the ride between terminals lasts a few minutes.

Train

The fastest and best value way to reach Gatwick is via the **Gatwick Express**, a non-stop service to/from Victoria Station. Trains leave every 15 minutes between 05:00 and midnight. Trains run less frequently outside of this time frame – check the website for details. Journey time is 30-35 minutes and a one-way fare is £13 (£24 return). Booking is not necessary; you can purchase your ticket on the train at no extra cost. Go to www.gatwickexpress.co.uk or call 08705 30 15 30 for the latest schedules and further information.

Bus

National Express Coaches offer service to Gatwick from various pick-up points throughout London. Visit www.nationalexpress.com or telephone: 0870 580 8080 for details.

Local bus services also run direct to and from both Gatwick terminals into Crawley, Horley and Redhill, as well as other local destinations. See www.gatwickairport.com for details.

Taxi

The train is a faster and more reliable route to Gatwick than via car/taxi from central London. The black cab fare is roughly £80 from central London, and takes about 90 minutes. A chauffeured car will be slightly less expensive and more luxurious. Try Checker Cars which charges approximately £75 one-way. (Departing the South Terminal: 012 9350 2808; departing the North Terminal: 012 9350 1377). Most mini-cab companies also offer fares to Gatwick for a set fare that should run you less than the prices above. See *Chapter 11: Services – Taxis and Minicab Services* for further recommendations.

Car

Gatwick is directly linked to the M23 at Junction 9 and to the A23 London-Brighton Road. Just a ten minute drive away, the M25 further connects with the UK's extensive road and motorway network. Pre-book your airport parking directly on the Gatwick Airport website (see above).

STANSTED

Essex, CM24 1QW; 012 7968 0500; www.stanstedairport.com.

Stansted is a very modern airport, 37 miles northeast of London and is the fourth busiest airport in the UK. Several low-cost airlines, including Ryanair, have made Stansted their base.

Train

The Stansted Express is a fast and convenient way to and from Stansted Airport, with trains departing every 15 or 30 minutes, with an average journey time of approximately 45 minutes. The one-way fare is £14.50 (£26.00 return). For the latest information and timetables, please visit www.stanstedexpress.com or telephone 0845 607 245.

Bus

National Express Coaches offer service to Stansted from various pick-up points throughout London. Visit www.nationalexpress.com or telephone: 0870 580 8080 for details.

LONDON CITY

Royal Docks, E16 2PX; 020 7646 0000; www.londoncityairport.com.

London City Airport is situated just 10 miles (16km) from the West End.

Tube and DLR Combined

The recommended route for the London City airport is to take the Tube and connect with the Docklands Light Railway (DLR). Journey time is just a few minutes to the airport on the DLR and the train runs every few minutes (Timing varies based on location. Visit the website for complete details).

Bus and Taxi Service

Local buses will also take you to the airport as well as cabs. If you choose to drive, there is a choice of short term and long term car parks, which are conveniently located adjacent to the Terminal.

LUTON

Luton, Bedfordshire, LU2 9LY; 015 8240 5100; www.london-luton.co.uk.

London Luton Airport is about 32 miles northwest of Central London and is one of the UK's fastest growing airports.

Train

Thameslink operates a fast, frequent rail service direct between central London and Luton Airport Parkway train station. Luton Airport Parkway is around 35 minutes away from King's Cross Thameslink station. Catch the free Luton Airport Express shuttle bus from outside the train station and it will take you directly to the airport in 5-10 minutes.

Coach and Bus

National Express Coaches offer service to Luton from various pick-up points throughout London. Visit www.nationalexpress.com or telephone: 0870 580 8080 for details. Local bus service is also available. Check the Luton Airport website for details.

6

Healthcare

CONTENTS

BRITISH HEALTH SYSTEM

Healthcare in the UK is exceptionally good and in most cases is free of charge for UK citizens and residents.

Healthcare providers in the UK fall into two categories: **National Health Service (NHS)** providers, most of whose services are free of charge, and private medical practitioners, who charge a fee. Some doctors see patients both privately and under the NHS.

This chapter explains the services provided by NHS and private healthcare centres and lists contact details and information for both.

THE NATIONAL HEALTH SERVICE

Great Britain has a government-subsidised national health service. If you pay National Insurance as a resident of the UK, you are entitled to medical coverage at little or no additional cost. This service includes:

Doctor care

Dentistry

Specialist and hospital care

Eye examinations and glasses

Child-care clinics for under-fives

Well-man and well-woman clinics

Marriage counselling

Family planning services

This service is also available to foreign visitors on an emergency basis. British taxes paid by you or your employer go towards these services, so eligibility should be verified. Advice on eligibility is available from the **Department of Health and Social Security (DHSS)**. The head office is located in Richmond House, 79 Whitehall, London, SW1A 2NL; 020 7210 3000.

Some other useful health service contact telephone numbers include:

Health enquiries: 020 7210 4850

Social security enquiries: 020 7712 2171.

The Department of Health website is www.dh.gov.uk. Please consult the website for various help-lines and information. DHSS offices are located throughout London.

Telephone numbers and locations are listed on the website and in the telephone directory under "Health and Social Security, Department of".

The Citizens' Advice Bureau provides free information and advice about the NHS. Check the telephone directory for the nearest office location, ask at a local library or visit the National Association of Citizens' Advice Bureaus' website at www.nacab.org.uk, and www.adviceguide.org.uk.

The NHS produces several leaflets explaining its different services. They are usually available at your doctor's office and through the **Department of Health Publications**, PO Box 777, London, SE1 6XH; email doh@prolog. uk.com; 0870 155 5455. For additional information on your local NHS services visit www.nhs.uk.

Healthcare While Travelling Abroad

Please read "Health and Safety" in *Chapter 15: Travel.*

NHS Registration

All permanent UK residents are eligible to register with the NHS. Eligibility for temporary residents depends on whether you or your spouse is paying British income tax and National Insurance (NI). For an expatriate and his or her family, the individual's company will often obtain an NI number, which is needed in order to apply for NHS registration. If this is not the case, you may obtain an NI number by applying in person at one of the DHSS offices. Bring your passport to the office, proof of residence and marriage certificate (if the name on the passport differs).

To obtain an NHS number, you must register with a local doctor (known as a "GP", or general practitioner) who has vacancies for NHS patients. (Note: not all GPs handle NHS patients; some handle only private patients). It is up to the discretion of the GP to register temporary residents with the NHS. If the GP decides to accept you as a patient, he or she will take your personal details (including your NI number and length of stay in the UK) and then apply to the local **Family Health Service Authority (FHSA)** for your NHS number.

For a complete listing of GP surgeries (offices) in your area, visit www.nhsdirect. nhs.uk/localisation. The website will provide an address, phone number and map, and may identify whether or not the GP is accepting new NHS patients. As an alternative, contact your local council's FHSA for the names, addresses and telephone numbers of GPs in your area. Lists of doctors can also be found at local

> *Did you know?...In the UK, specialists and general practitioners are addressed as "doctor". Surgeons, including dental surgeons, obstetricians and gynaecologists, are referred to as "Mr", "Mrs" or "Miss". The "surgery" or "operating room" in a hospital is called a "theatre", and the office of a medical professional is called a "surgery". In some instances the surgery is located in a home instead of a clinic or office building. Patients go "to hospital" rather than "to the hospital".*

libraries, main post offices, Community Health Councils and the Citizens' Advice Bureau. Local chemists (pharmacists) may have a list, but they are not officially permitted to make specific recommendations.

There are often waiting lists for many NHS doctors. Sometimes it is easiest to sign up with a local GP practice as a private patient and ask to be placed on their NHS waiting list. This may be the best way to get into the local practice of your choice.

For medical attention other than general family care, you must be referred by your GP. Known in the UK as a "consultant", the specialist is anyone other than a GP. Most consultants practise under the NHS and privately.

A drawback of the NHS is that if your complaint is not an emergency, you may be required to wait before receiving attention (this includes non-emergency operations). In these instances, consulting a private doctor may be an advantage as there would be no waiting list. Under certain circumstances, both NHS and private doctors are willing to make house calls.

NHS Direct

For information on NHS services, doctors, dentists, hospitals or self-help groups contact NHS Direct on 0845 4647, available 24 hours a day, seven days a week (www.nhsdirect.nhs.uk).

NHS Direct also provides a service whereby a nurse will advise on particular symptoms or medical treatment for adults and children confidentially over the telephone allowing you to get early advice without leaving home.

PRIVATE MEDICAL CARE

An alternative to NHS medical care is private treatment. Although much more costly, it allows you to have control over when treatment should take place and who should perform it. The Consular Section at the **US Embassy** has a list of doctors available at www.usembassy.org.uk.

Additionally, there are several privately staffed and run hospitals in the London area. These facilities are available to private-care patients only. These hospitals are usually modern, offer private rooms and overall good facilities. They may not offer the emergency care of the NHS hospitals and are not subject to the same regulation as NHS hospitals.

Employer-sponsored group health plans issued in other countries may be extended to the UK with employer consent. Any questions regarding the extent of coverage should be directed to your employer's personnel department. You may wish to consider subscribing to a British form of medical insurance. **BUPA, PPP** and **Standard Life** are three of the most popular plans. *The Which Report,* a consumer magazine published by the *Consumers Association,* gives a factual comparison of each plan. This report can be obtained by contacting the **Consumers Association** on 0845 307 4000 or via the website at www.which.net.

COUNSELLING

To find information about where to receive counselling locally, approach your GP, local library, the **Citizens' Advice Bureau**, the **Council for Voluntary Service** or the local **Marriage Guidance Council** (RELATE).

Nationally, the **British Association for Counselling and Psychotherapy** can supply some information about counselling services and specialist organisations, including counsellors in your local area. The association also publishes a nationwide directory of counselling and psychotherapy resources.

Some useful addresses and telephone numbers:

Al Anon/Al ateen,
020 7403 0888 for a 24-hour telephone service to help relatives and friends of problem drinkers.

Alcoholics Anonymous,
PO Box 1, Stonebow House, Stonebow, York YO1; London Helpline: 0845 769 7555; www.alcoholics-anonymous.org.uk.

American Church in London (ACL),
79 Tottenham Court Road, W1; 020 7580 2791; www.americanchurchinlondon.org.

American Psychotherapy Associates, Ltd.,
39A Welbeck Street, W1; 020 7486 9255; www.apapsychotherapy.com.
US-trained psychotherapists who serve the international expatriate
community. They provide services for adults, children, couples and families.

British Association for Counselling and Psychotherapy,
1 Regent Place, Rugby, Warwickshire CV21 2PJ; 087 0443 5252;
www.bac.co.uk.

CRUSE (Bereavement),
126 Sheen Road, Richmond, Surrey, TW9; 0870 167 1677;
www.crusebereavementcare.org.uk. Anyone can contact CRUSE if they
want to talk about themselves or someone they know who has been
affected by a death.

London Marriage Guidance Council,
020 7580 1087; www.dfes.gov.uk/marriageandrelationshipsupport/
marsdir/index.shtml. A nonprofit organisation that is very compassionate
and highly trained. They frequently deal with expatriate issues.

Narcotics Anonymous, helpline,
020 7730 0009 or 0845 373 3366; www.ukna.org.

RELATE (National Marriage Guidance),
Herbert Gray College, Little Church Street, Rugby, Warwickshire CV21
3AP; 01788 573 241 or locally on 020 7336 0144; www.relate.org.uk.

Samaritans, Central London helpline,
0845 7909 090, www.samaritans.org.uk

Westminster Pastoral Foundation,
23 Kensington Square, W8; 020 73614800; www.wpf.org.uk.

DENTAL SERVICES

Dental care is available through the NHS (much the same as medical care) at a reduced cost. As an NHS dental patient you are expected to pay a percentage of the cost of the work done. There is an upper limit set on the contribution you will be asked to make for one course of treatment. Expect to be asked to pay all or part of the charge in advance. Before each and every visit you must ascertain that the dentist will treat you as an NHS patient, otherwise you could be treated as a private patient. The difficulty however, is that the majority of dentists in London are private; meaning that you will be asked to pay the full cost of your dental treatment (and will only be reimbursed if you have alternative private dental insurance coverage).

Did you know?...Tap water in London is not fluorinated.

If you are interested in trying to locate a dentist using the NHS, lists of NHS dentists are posted in the same fashion as NHS doctors at www.nhsdirect.nhs.uk.

You are automatically entitled to free dental healthcare through the NHS if:

1. You are under 16 years of age, or a student under 19 years of age and still in full-time education.

2. You are expecting a baby and were pregnant when the dentist accepted you for treatment.

3. You have had a baby during the 12 months before your treatment began.

For further information, consult the **Department of Health** on 0870 155 5455; www.dh.gov.uk; email dh@prolog.uk.com.

A couple of recommended dentists are:
Carnaby Street Dental Practice,
Dr Peter Mendelsohn, BDS (Syd) and Dr John Stolz, BDS (Adel), 31 Carnaby Street, W1; 020 7734 6421; www.carnabystreetdentist.co.uk.

Dental practice offering very high-quality dentistry using the latest technology.

The Q Clinic,
Dr Elisabeth Hersey, 139 Harley Street, W1G 6BG; 020 7317 1111; www.qclinic.com. American-trained dentist at this full-service, state-of-the-art dental practice which offers a broad range of procedures and services.

OPHTHALMICS

Your sight can be tested only by a registered ophthalmic optician (optometrist) or an ophthalmic medical practitioner. If you want to find an optician, go to your local library for a list of registered opticians in your area, ask at your local **Citizens' Advice Bureau** or look in the **Yellow Pages**™ under "Opticians".

Free eye tests are available to people under 16 years of age (or under 19 years of age if still in full-time education), and to those over 60 years of age.

The optician MUST give you a prescription (or a certificate that you do not need glasses), even if your sight has not changed. You cannot be asked to pay for your eye test until you have been given your prescription. You are under no obligation to buy your eyeglasses from the same optician who gave you the test. Your prescription is valid for two years.

All charges for sight tests can be found in NHS leaflet HC.12, Benefits enquiry line 0800 882 200 or at the **Department of Health** (0870 155 5455; www.dh.gov.uk).

For further information, consult NHS leaflet HC.12.

FAMILY PLANNING

A full range of family planning services is available through your GP or local clinic as well as specific family planning clinics run by the NHS. The larger clinics will offer all types of birth control for both men and women, well-women clinics, psycho-sexual counselling, termination referrals and follow-up, and post-natal examinations. All services are available free of charge, on a walk-in basis. For further information contact:

The Family Planning Association,
2-12 Pentonville Road, N19; 020 7837 5432; www.fpa.org.uk.

Maternity Services

If you are expecting a baby, it is necessary to become a patient of an obstetrician promptly. Your GP can recommend an obstetrician and you must decide on whether to have your baby with the NHS or privately.

If you decide to use the NHS, you will have free care throughout your pregnancy and delivery. In the case of a normal delivery, the NHS provides a midwife to attend your birth along with an obstetrician and full medical support staff on call at the hospital in case of complications. You will have a

> *Did you know?...Black cabs may refuse to transport you to hospital once in labour. If you are planning to deliver at a private hospital and need transportation, contact the hospital to arrange for a private ambulance. If you call 999 for an ambulance, they must take you to the nearest hospital.*

private birthing room, but during recovery you will be on an NHS ward, which usually has four to eight beds. Private or semi-private rooms may be available but only if you make prior arrangements with the hospital.

A midwife is a specialist in normal pregnancy, birth and the post-natal period. As well as performing ante-natal checks, she can deliver your baby, perform ultrasound scans and care for you once you have had your baby. She may work in the hospital or be based in the community. In some areas, you can book directly with a midwife instead of your GP. Telephone the Director of Midwifery at your local hospital and ask if there is a midwives clinic or a GP/midwives clinic in the community.

Traditionally, you are booked under a consultant at the hospital and receive your ante-natal care from members of his or her team, including midwives. You visit the clinic for all of your ante-natal care, and your baby is delivered by labour-ward midwives or the obstetrician on duty at the time you arrive to deliver your baby. Although the consultant leads the team, you may never actually see him or her unless your pregnancy is complicated.

There are many options for delivery within the NHS. Call your local hospital or speak to your GP to see whether these options are available in your area:

Shared Care

You visit the hospital two or three times during your pregnancy and for any special ultrasounds and tests. The rest of the time, you are cared for by your GP and/or your community midwife. When you go into the hospital to have your baby, your baby will be delivered by hospital midwives.

Midwives Clinic

Most of your ante-natal care is done by a team of midwives at the hospital who may work in teams under a consultant. Your baby is then delivered by the same team of midwives, who take care of you on the post-natal ward, too.

GP/Midwife Care

Your ante-natal care is done by your GP or community midwife at the surgery or local health centre. When you go into labour, you are cared for by community midwives and your GP is informed. If complications arise, you will be transferred to consultant care.

Domino Scheme/Midwife Care

Your ante-natal care may be shared between the community midwife and your GP, or done by the community midwife at the surgery or local health centre. The midwife may visit you at home for ante-natal checks, and you may go into hospital for any special tests. When you go into hospital to deliver your baby, your midwife or another on her team will attend the birth and provide your post-natal care once you have returned home.

HOME BIRTH

Home births are becoming more common in the UK as they are gaining support from the medical community. Your ante-natal care may be under taken entirely by your community or independent midwife with your own GP or another doctor acting as back-up. The midwife will deliver your baby at home and also provide your post-natal care.

If you choose private care, you are assured that your obstetrician and a midwife will assist your delivery. In the case of an unexpected emergency situation, there is always an obstetrician on call in both private and NHS hospitals. Private doctors may use both NHS and private hospital facilities.

However, if your pregnancy is considered "high risk", you may not be allowed to delivery your baby at a private hospital; instead, you may have to deliver your baby at an NHS hospital that has more appropriate facilities to care for you and the baby in the case of an emergency.

Whether you choose the NHS or private care, your choice of hospitals for your delivery will be limited to the hospital or hospitals at which your obstetrician is registered. In the case of a private hospital, accommodation must be reserved well in advance of your baby's due date. Hospitals may also request a deposit at the time of reservation.

In London, most large hospitals offer good maternity facilities. Some hospitals with exceptional maternity facilities are listed below. Note that not all hospitals have neonatal intensive care units.

Chelsea & Westminster Hospital,
369 Fulham Road, SW10; 020 8746 8000; www.chelwest.nhs.uk. Has excellent childbirth facilities including birthing pools and a new private maternity wing. (NHS/Private).

Guys and St. Thomas' Hospital,
Lambeth Palace Road, SE1; 020 7188 7188;
www.guysandstthomas.nhs.uk. (NHS/Private).

Hammersmith Hospital,
150 Du Cane Road, W12; 020 8743 2030; www.hhnt.org. (NHS/Private).

Portland Hospital for Women and Children,
209 Great Portland Street, W1; 020 7580 4400;
www.theportlandhospital.com. (Private).

Queen Charlotte's Maternity Hospital,
150 Du Cane Road, W12; 020 8383 1111; www.hhnt.org. (NHS/Private).

St. Mary's Hospital,
Praed Street, W2; 020 7886 6666; www.st-marys.nhs.uk. (NHS/Private–
Lindo wing).

The Hospital of St. John & St. Elizabeth,
60 Grove End Road, NW8; 020 7806 4000; www.hje.org.uk. (NHS/Private).

The Wellington Hospital,
8a Wellington Place, NW8; 020 7586 5959;
www.thewellingtonhospital.com. (Private).

The NHS and most private hospitals offer preparatory "parent classes" at local hospitals and clinics. A listing of independent ante-natal courses and refresher courses for repeat mums is available through your GP.

An additional organisation involved in natural birth preparation classes nationwide is **The National Childbirth Trust (NCT)**, Alexandra House, Oldham Terrace, Acton, W3; 0870 770 3236; www.nctpregnancyandbaby care.com.

The NCT is a non-profit organisation formed expressly for the purpose of education for pregnancy, birth and parenthood. Contact them for information on what courses are offered in your area. You must contact them early in your pregnancy if you are interested in ante-natal classes in London.

UK BIRTH REGISTRATION

All births taking place in the UK must be registered. The hospital where the birth occurs will notify the local Registrar of Births with details of the birth. The parents (mother or father, if the parents are legally married) must register the child at the local office within 42 days of the birth. Either a short or long form of birth certificate is available for a fee. The long form is more detailed and in some countries, it is considered to be the only "official" birth certificate. Therefore, it is often helpful to obtain several official long form birth certificates at the time of registration so that they are readily available when required.

Foreign Nationals Born in the UK

It is recommended that babies born in the UK to resident foreign nationals register at the appropriate foreign embassy or high commission to receive proper citizenship papers and passports. Each country's laws differ, so it is best to check with your embassy's website (see *Chapter 17: Organisations* for a list of foreign embassies in London). There is usually a fee for this service.

Obtaining British Nationality for a Child Born to Foreign Nationals

In certain circumstances, it will also be possible to register a child born in the UK as a UK national, and to obtain a British passport for the child. (This may or may not affect the child's primary citizenship.) Parents interested in this possibility should contact the **Immigration and Nationality Division**, 0870 606 7766.

Obtaining Child Benefit

If your child is born in the UK, you are eligible to claim for a weekly Child Benefit Allowance until your child leaves school. Child Benefit is a tax-free benefit that does not depend on how much money you earn or on how much savings you have. For information regarding the *Child Benefit Allowance* call your local Social Security office. The phone number and address are in the telephone book under "Social Security" or "Benefits Agency". Your local baby clinic usually has information as well.

PAEDIATRICS

Your local health clinic or GP offers a full service of paediatrics, as well as Child Health Clinics, which specialise in children only. Check with your local FHSA for one close to you. The following services are available:

1. Immunisations and boosters.

2. Developmental checks (i.e., hearing, vision, weight, height) at six weeks, eight months, 18 months, three years and four years (pre-school). The service then continues via the school system.

3. Child health care including: psychotherapy; educational psychology for learning and behaviour problems; speech therapy; and orthopaedics.

4. Health Visitors who make house calls to answer any questions you may have, discuss problems, remind you of injection dates and help orient you to local play groups, and registered childminders in the area.

> *Did you know?...There are several "Medicentres" throughout London, including locations at Victoria Station and Euston Station. These are privately run walk-in clinics, many of which are open seven days a week. They are an excellent resource for conditions that are not quite 'emergency room' emergencies. They are also useful to visitors who might need a doctor's aid. For a list of locations and services, telephone 0870 600 0870 (www.medicentre.co.uk).*

All clinics have emergency numbers to be used after hours. GPs or their deputies will make house calls in emergency situations.

IMMUNISATIONS AND VACCINATIONS

Many countries require you to have certain immunisations and vaccinations. Please read *Chapter 15: Travel and Culture* for details.

For information regarding immunisations for babies, please read *Chapter 7: Healthcare* (under "Paediatrics") or *Chapter 8: Children*.

EMERGENCY FACILITIES AND CASUALTY UNITS

If an emergency does arise, proceed immediately to a hospital with an Accident and Emergency (A&E) department. It is most important to know the nearest A&E department in your area. IN A SERIOUS EMERGENCY, DIAL 999 and ask for the ambulance service. Emergency service to a resident is provided free of charge by the NHS and is available to anyone, including tourists.

NHS Walk-in Centres provide treatment for minor injuries and illnesses seven days a week. You do not need an appointment and will be seen by an experienced NHS nurse. To locate the Walk-in Centre nearest you (located in Soho, Fulham, Whitechapel, Parsons Green, Tooting and Charing Cross), visit www.nhs.uk/england/search.aspx.

Each police station keeps a list of emergency doctors and chemists who are available on a 24-hour basis.

Nearly all London NHS hospitals have a 24-hour A&E department. Listed below are some of the larger ones throughout London.

LONDON HOSPITALS WITH 24-HOUR ACCIDENT AND EMERGENCY DEPARTMENTS (Partial List)

SE1

Guy's Hospital,
St. Thomas Street, SE1; 020 7188 7188.

St. Thomas' Hospital,
Lambeth Palace Road, SE1; 020 7188 7188.

W2, W9 and W10

St. Mary's Hospital,
Praed Street, W2; 020 7886 6666.

SW1, SW3, SW7, SW10

Chelsea & Westminster Hospital,
369 Fulham Road, SW10; 020 8746 8000.

SW6, W14, W6, W12
Charing Cross Hospital,
Fulham Palace Road, W6; 020 8846 1234.

Hammersmith Hospital,
1234 Hammersmith Hospital, Du Cane Road, W12; 020 8743 2030.

NW3, NW4, NW6, NW8, NW11
Royal Free Hospital,
Pond Street, NW3; 020 7794 0500.

University College Hospital,
235 Euston St, NW1; 0845 155 5000.

Eye Emergencies Only
Moorfields Eye Hospital,
162 City Road, EC1; 020 7253 3411.

Children's Emergencies Only
Chelsea & Westminster Children's Hospital,
369 Fulham Road, SW10; 020 8746 8000.

Dental Emergencies Only
NHS Direct on 0845 4647 is a 24-hour information line that can refer you to a surgery open for treatment (private or NHS). In addition, the NHS website search function includes an option to search by opening hours. Visit www.nhs.uk for more details.

Animal Emergencies
The Blue Cross Animal Hospital,
1-5 Hugh Street, SW1; 020 7834 4224 for 24-hour emergency veterinary service. (Read *Chapter 11: Services* under "Veterinarians" for veterinarians with 24-hour emergency service.)

AMBULANCE SERVICES

London Ambulance Service (NHS); 999

St. John's Ambulance Service,
NW1, non-emergency (private); 020 7258 3456.

LATE NIGHT CHEMISTS

Bliss Chemists,
50-56 Willesden Lane, Kilburn, NW6; 020 7624 8000. Open 09:00 to
23:00, 365 days a year.

Bliss Chemists,
5 Marble Arch, W1; 020 7723 6116. Open 09:00 to midnight, 365 days a year.

Boots The Chemist,
West Concourse, Victoria Station; 020 7834 0676. Open 07:30 to 21:00
(Monday to Friday), 09:00 to 19:00 (Saturday).

Dajani,
92 Old Brompton Road, SW7; 020 7589 8600; www.dajanipharmancy.
com. Open 09:00-22:00 Monday- Friday, 9:00 to 20:00 Saturday & 10:00-
20:00 Sunday. Also open 10:00-20:00 on Bank Holidays.

Warman Freed,
45 Golders Green, NW11; 020 8455 4351. Open 08:30-24:00 every day
(Including Bank Holidays).

Zafash,
233-235 Old Brompton Road, SW5; 020 7373 2798. Only 24 hour
chemist in London.

ALTERNATIVE MEDICINE

Your local health food store or chemist can be a good resource for alternative medicine services and products in your area.

Bioenergetic Medical Centre,

Drs. Tatyana and Damir Shakamber; 23 Manchester St, W1; 020 7935 6866. Alternative health specialists, combining Shiatsu, acupuncture, aromatherapy, psychoanalysis; overall philosophy that mind and body must be in tune.

Eden Medical Centre,

For excellent chiropractor and holistic health practitioners in the city.

Hale Clinic,

7 Park Crescent, W1; 020 7631 0156; www.haleclinic.com. Integrates conventional and complementary medicine under one roof.

Homeopathic Clinic serving North London, St Albans and Southwest London; Katherine Allison, 07913 401 107 and Catherine Wilkerson, 07913 401 109; email ckhomeopathy@aol.com for more information.

Neal's Yard Therapy Rooms,

2 Neal's Yard, WC2; 020 7379 7662; www.nealsyardremedies.com.

HOMEOPATHIC PRODUCTS

Culpeper,

8 The Market, Covent Garden, WC2; 020 7379 6698 and 236D Fulham, SW10; 020 7352 5603; www.culpeper.co.uk. 17th century apothecary and herbalist; the oldest chain of herbal shops in England. Natural and herbal products for bath, body and home. Aromatherapy and essential oils, natural and organic foods, medical herbs and tinctures.

Sloane Health Shop,

27 King's Road, SW3 4RT; 020 7730 7046. Vitamins, nutritional

supplements, homeopathic remedies, aromatherapy products and natural cosmetics.

Sloane Health Clinic,
27 King's Road, SW3; 020 7730 1328.

AIR QUALITY

To check the air quality in your area ring the Air Pollution Bulletin Service operated by the **Department of the Environment, Food and Rural Affairs** on 0845 933 5577 (www.defra.gov.uk), or try www.airquality.co.uk. Information is updated hourly.

National Asthma Campaign,
Providence House, Providence Place, N1; 0845 701 0203; www.asthma.org.uk.

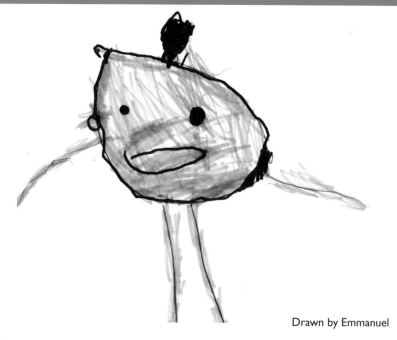

Drawn by Emmanuel

Children

CONTENTS

Moving overseas with children can be a complicated task. Fortunately, London has plenty of offerings for the younger set — it's just a matter of becoming familiar with all of the options! The following information has been shared by London mums who have successfully survived the experience.

BABY CARE PRODUCTS

Many popular foreign brands are widely available in the UK; however, you will find that the selection can vary depending on the store or chemist, which often means you'll have to visit a few different places in order to find everything you're looking for.

Johnson & Johnson®, Pampers® and *Huggies®* products are carried by most supermarket and chemist chains in the UK. Large supermarkets and chemists such as **Sainsbury's, Tesco** and **Boots** also carry their own lines of wipes and nappies.

Vaseline® and A&D® ointment are sold in the UK. There are also several British-made nappy rash ointments such as *Sudocrem®* and *Kamillosan®* that work very well.

Formula / Breastfeeding

Ready-to-feed or powdered infant formulas are commonly offered in the following brands: *SMA®*, *Cow and Gate®*, *Wysoy®* (a soya milk formula) and *Hipp Organic®*. It is also possible to find brands such as *Aptamil®* and *Enfamil®* as well as specialised (such as hypoallergenic) formulas, but you may need to search a bit more, as these items are generally not carried in most chemists or supermarkets.

The most popular and widely distributed brand of feeding accessories is *Avent®*, offering everything from bottles and nipples to breast pumps, shields and storage bags. *Medela®* breast pumps, a well-regarded brand, can be ordered through selected chemists, via the website (www.breastpumps. co.uk) or through **Central Medical Supplies** (015 3839 9541; www. centralmedical.co.uk).

In addition, the *Mamm®*, *Maws®* and *Nuk®* brands all have breastfeeding accessories, bottles and pacifiers.

Baby Food / Feeding Items

Popular UK brands include *Heinz®*, *BabyNat®* and *Hipp Organic®*, which is made with fresh, organic ingredients, free from all pesticides and chemical fertilisers. Hipp Organic® has a full line of cereals, vegetables, desserts, juices, snacks and toddler meals.

> *Did you know?...UK bed and linen sizes (including those for baby cots) may vary from your home country. If moving to the UK with your bed and linens, remember to bring everything you will need.*

Beechnut® baby food (fruits, vegetables and juices only) is available at selected outlets. Sippy cups, bibs, feeding bowls and accessories made by *Avent®*, *Tommee Tippee®* and *Maws®* are readily available.

Detergents

A good detergent for young babies and people with sensitive skin is *Filetti®*. There is also a handy product called *Napisan®*, which safely removes germs and stains from children's clothes.

Quick Glossary of Terms

English	American
Cot	Crib
Dummy	Pacifier
Nappies	Diapers
Pushchair/Buggy	Stroller
Teet	Nipple

MEDICAL NEEDS

Baby First Aid / Safety

Below are some helpful contacts for baby first aid and safety.

Child Alert; www.childalert.co.uk.

A comprehensive reference/guidance website that focuses on addressing a variety of child safety topics and parenting concerns. There is a section on child-proofing, plus the opportunity to arrange for complimentary baby-proofing advice.

The Parent Company; 6 Jacob's Well Mews, W1; 020 7935 9635; www.theparentcompany.co.uk.

Offers classes in first aid and basic life support and can arrange private sessions in your home.

Did you know?...Electrical outlets may differ from your home country and some baby monitors may not work without an adapter and transformer (Tomy® and Safe'n'Sound® are good UK brands).

The Portland Hospital, Physiotherapy Department; 205-209 Great Portland Street, W1; 020 7580 4400; www.theportlandhospital.com.

Offers a 2½-hour baby / toddler first aid class taught by a midwife. Topics include how to make your house safer, what to do in emergencies and how to administer CPR, with practice on a dummy. Classes are held approximately every six weeks.

Healthcare / Illness

You can see a **National Health Service (NHS)** doctor or a private GP for emergency or routine medical care. (See *Chapter 7: Healthcare*.) Pædiatricians are considered specialists and generally are seen annually or when referred by a GP. You can make an appointment directly if you wish, although there may be a fee for doing so if you do not have comprehensive private health insurance.

Immunisations for babies and regular health checks are available free of charge through your local NHS well-baby clinic. The current immunisation schedule for babies in the UK is very similar to the schedule in other countries. The UK strongly encourages, but does not require by law, that children be immunised.

See *Chapter 7: Healthcare* for more information on the NHS and pædiatrics. See *Chapter 11: Services* for late-night chemists.

Medicines

Over-the-counter medicines for children's health are readily available although they may carry different brand names than you are used to. Most chemist shops have a pharmacist on duty that can help you find the medicine you need for your child's illness.

Pain relievers for children usually contain either paracetemol such as *Calpol®* or ibuprofen, such as *Nurofen®*. These usually come in a liquid form for younger children.

Some children's medicines and products are:

Calpol® – pain reliever containing paracetamol

Nurofen® – pain reliever containing ibuprofen

Gripe water – colic and hiccups

Infacol® – colic

Piriton Syrup® – antihistamine

Sudacrem® – nappy rash

Zinc and castor oil lotion – nappy rash

E45 Cream® – dry skin

Aqueous Cream® – dry skin

Dentinox® – teething pain

Oilatum® – cradle cap, eczema

Dioralyte® – rehydration powder (to be mixed with water).

PREGNANCY

One of the first decisions you will have to make when you become pregnant is whether or not you plan to use the NHS or private healthcare. Most British policies, such as BUPA, do not consider pregnancy a medical condition and will not cover private healthcare costs unless you have a scheduled C-section or other high-risk condition. Some private health insurance policies that specialise in coverage for expatriates living in the UK will cover maternity care — check with your policy provider for details.

Whether using the NHS or private healthcare, a Health Visitor will come to your home after you have given birth to check that you and your baby are healthy and are adjusting to life at home. They will schedule the visits with you for up to 10 days after the birth.

See *Chapter 7: Healthcare* for more information on Maternity Services and Birth Registrations.

The National Childbirth Trust

For recent arrivals to the UK or anyone with young children, **The National Childbirth Trust (NCT)** is a tremendous resource.

The NCT is a non-profit organisation and a registered charity full of excellent information on all matters relating to childbirth and early parenting. Many of the neighbourhood branches of the NCT have produced wonderful information packs on having a baby in London that can be a great help to a pregnant expatriate.

The National Childbirth Trust; Alexandra House, Oldham Terrace, Acton, W3; 0870 444 8707; www.nctpregnancyandbabycare.com.

For information on branches all over London, contact this, the main branch.

Working Families; 1-3 Berry Street, EC1; 020 7253 7243; www.workingfamilies.org.uk.

Under the NCT umbrella, this group's goal is to help working parents find a better balance between home and work responsibilities. They have a free help line and fact sheets on issues such as maternity rights, legal and practical advice for returning to work, establishing a flexible work schedule and helping working parents with a disabled child.

The NCT branches have published many helpful books about children in London such as: *Clapham for Kids, Chiswick for Kids* and *Under Fives: Welcome in and around Westminster.* These can be obtained from your local Social Services Department.

The NCT also publishes the *Working Mothers' Handbook,* an excellent book on the various types of care one can expect to get for children in London. It also discusses interviewing techniques, training standards, costs associated with childcare and authoritative bodies which oversee these employees.

Ante-Natal Classes

Ante-natal (pre-natal) classes are available at some hospitals. Independent of any hospital, the following offer ante-natal preparatory classes and post-natal exercise classes:

The Life Centre; 15 Edge Street, W8; 020 7221 4602; www.thelifecentre.com.

Offers yoga for pregnancy and post-natal. Also offers baby massage classes.

The National Childbirth Trust (NCT); listed above. For general information and also to organise pregnancy support groups.

Triyoga; Neal's Yard Therapy Rooms, Neal's Yard, WC1 and 6 Erskine Road, NW1; 020 7483 3344; www.triyoga.co.uk.
Offers ante-natal Pilates, yoga classes and treatments.

Maternity Wear
Some major department stores offer a small selection of maternity clothes and a large and varied selection of baby equipment.

Blooming Marvellous; 725 Fulham Road, SW6; 0845 458 7429 (mail order 0870 7518944); www.bloomingmarvellous.co.uk.
Sells children's wear and toys.

Formes; 28 Henrietta Street, WC2; 020 7240 4777; www.formes.fr.
French company that offers a stylish line of maternity clothes. Multiple locations.

H&M; 481-483 Oxford Street, W1; 020 7493 8557; www.hm.com.
This well-known Swedish chain carries a line of trendy, fun maternity clothes under the "Mama" label. Multiple locations.

Great Expectations and Night Owls; 78 Fulham Road, SW3; 020 7584 2451.
Designer maternity clothes and underwear.

Mothercare; 174-176 Oxford Street, W1; 020 7629 6621; www.mothercare.com.
Complete range of items for mothers-to-be and children up to size 10, including baby beds, linens and toiletries. Multiple locations.

9 London; 8 Hollywood Road, SW10; 020 7352 7600; www.9london.com.
Offers a range of designer maternity wear from names such as Juicy Couture,

Diane von Furstenberg, Earl Jean, Expecting, Chaiken, Liz Lange and more.

Rigby & Peller; 22 Conduit Street, W1; 020 7491 2200, and 2 Hans Road, SW3; 020 7589 9293.
Good source for nursing bras and maternity underwear.

Top Shop; 272-286 Regent Street, W1; 020 7636 7700; www.topshop.co.uk.
Offers hip, inexpensive maternity wear. Multiple locations.

Websites

There are many websites for expectant and new mums. They cover many topics including how to conceive a baby, breastfeeding, furniture and equipment, buying guides, and finding good childcare. Some of the most useful sites that we have found are listed below.

Babyworld; www.babyworld.co.uk. Information and tips on many aspects of pregnancy and child rearing, a monthly panel test of baby products and a section for you to pose questions to doctors and midwives. Online shopping and a discussion group for dads.

Babycentre; www.babycentre.co.uk. Articles and interactive tools developed by British experts in women's and children's health and development. Online shopping, plus buying guides for baby products.

Ivillage; www.ivillage.co.uk. Informative articles on pregnancy and parenting. Also, a handy pregnancy calendar, due date calculator, baby name finder and more.

CHILDCARE

Once you arrive in the UK, you may wish to take advantage of the wonderful childcare that seems to be readily available. Before deciding on help with the children and/or housekeeping, it is helpful to be aware of the distinctions between the following:

Au Pair — A young girl who comes to live with a family in order to learn the English language. She will help with childcare and light housework for up to 30 hours per week in exchange for her room and board and pocket money. She is usually a student and may not speak fluent English.

Mother's helper — A non-professional who will do housework and care for children either full- or part-time.

Nanny — A certified nursery nurse who holds a Nursery Nursing Examination Board Certificate (NNEB). She does not do housework or meal preparation for the family but does take care of all needs of the children, including their laundry and meal preparation. She can live in or out.

Agencies

When working with an agency, make sure that you have a complete understanding of the fees charged. There are membership fees, engagement fees and booking fees depending on the situation and agency. These fees vary widely.

The Good Nanny Guide is an indispensable resource book outlining the traditional duties and pay scales for all types of help; it can be found at most bookstores. It is advisable to contact more than one agency. Finding a good match for your specific needs will depend on the sort of people a given agency has on its books at the time you call. Help can be found to suit most permanent and part-time requirements.

Below is a short list of agencies.

Annie's Nannies; 83 Victoria Street, SW1; 0870 0132944.

Live-out nannies, mother's helpers, nannyshares and babysitters; both long term and temporary.

Childminders; 6 Nottingham Street, W1; 020 7935 3000; www.babysitter.co.uk.

Babysitting service. Also provides light domestic help such as cleaners, ironers and party staff.

Elite Nannies; 22 Rowena Crescent, SW11; 020 7801 0061;
www.elitenannies.co.uk.

Permanent and temporary nannies, mother's helpers and maternity nurses.

Kensington Nannies; 3 Hornton Place, W8; 020 7937 3299 / 2333;
www.kensington-nannies.com.

Nannies and mother's helpers, both full- and part-time.

Maternally Yours; 17 Radley Mews, W8; 020 7795 6299;
www.imperialnannies.com.

Specialises in maternity nurses.

Night Nannies; 0207 731 6168; www.night-nannies.com.

Experienced night nannies.

Quick Help Agency; 307A Finchley Road, NW3; 020 7794 8666;
www.quickhelp.co.uk.

Nannies, mother's helpers, au pairs, cleaners and care for the elderly.

The Nanny Service; 6 Nottingham Street, W1; 020 7935 3515 or
020 7935 6976; www.nannyservice.co.uk.

Specialises in Australian, New Zealand and British nannies on a temporary
or permanent basis — both daily and live-in.

Tinies; Unit 14, Elysium Gate, 126-128 New Kings Road, SW6;
020 3166 5050; www.tinieschildcare.co.uk.

The UK's leading nanny agency with six branches across London. They
also own www.emergencychildcare.co.uk, which is a great site for getting
last-minute nannies or nursery places.

Sharingcare; www.sharingcare.co.uk.

This is a website that puts you in touch with other local parents so that
you can share the cost of a nanny.

Universal Aunts; Clapham, SW4; 020 7738 8937; www.universalaunts.co.uk.
Nannies, mother's helpers, cleaners, butlers and cooks.

Three additional excellent sources for childminders, full- or part-time are:

The Lady; 39-40 Bedford Street, WC2; 020 7379 4717; www.lady.co.uk.
A weekly (Tuesday) magazine publication available at newsagents listing situations vacant for all domestic help. Good responses can be had by placing ads listing personal requirements.

Best Bear; 0870 7201 277; www.bestbear.co.uk.
This agency rates and recommends nanny services. They pose as interested childcare workers and conduct interviews with services to see what type of childminders they hire.

Gumtree; www.gumtree.com.
A website where you can post advertisements for childcare and potential nannies will contact you.

Nanny Tax

If you employ a nanny on a part- or full-time basis, you are required by law to pay regular tax and National Insurance contributions to the Inland Revenue on the nanny's behalf, as well as provide the nanny with regular pay slips. There are two payroll service companies that can take care of all the details for a fee: **Nannytax** (0845 226 2203; www.nannytax.co.uk) and **Taxing Nannies** (020 8882 6847; www.taxingnannies.co.uk).

Gym Crèches

For mums who like to get a bit of exercise, there are several London sports clubs that have crèche (nursery) facilities for children, including **Holmes Place, David Lloyd, Esporta** and **The Harbour Club**. The amenities vary between locations and companies, so telephone or visit before making your decision. See *Chapter 14: Sports and Leisure* for contact information.

SHOPPING

Books

The large bookstores such as **Waterstone's** have extensive children's book areas. **Daisy & Tom, Daunt Books** and **Mothercare** also have a good selection of children's books. **Amazon** (www.amazon.co.uk) is a convenient way to purchase books for children as well.

Barefoot Books; 0800 328 2640; www.barefoot-books.com.
Books that focus on our cultural differences; themes that encourage independence of spirit, enthusiasm for learning, and sharing of the world's diversity.

The Children's Book Centre; 237 Kensington High Street, W8; 020 79377497.
Also sells toys and gifts.

Children's Wear

Most department stores such as **John Lewis, Peter Jones** and **Debenhams** have children's departments with a large selection. Stores such as **Marks & Spencer** and **BHS** are also excellent for competitively priced, unfussy clothes for boys and girls from 0-14 years of age.

Benetton; 255/259 Regent Street; 020 7647 4220; www.benetton.com.
Colour co-ordinated trousers, shirts and sweaters for boys and girls. Multiple locations.

Bonpoint; 15 Sloane Street, SW1; 020 7235 1441, and 17 Victoria Grove, W8; 020 7584 5131.
Exclusive French children's wear.

Daisy & Tom; 181 King's Road, SW3; 020 7349 5800; www.daisyandtom.com.
Large store with clothes, toys, books and nursery furniture and equipment.

They also have a carousel, a small puppet theatre, a children's café and children's haircutters.

Gap Kids; 315-321 Oxford Street, W1; 020 7493 3316.
American chain with contemporary children's wear, great designs and frequent sales. Multiple locations.

Green Baby; 345 Upper Street, N1; 0870 240 6894; www.greenbaby.co.uk.
Specialises in environmentally friendly clothing and nappies. Mail order business and multiple retail locations throughout London.

H&M; 261-271 Regent Street (at Oxford Circus), W1; 020 7493 4004; www.hm.com.
Swedish chain with well-priced contemporary children's wear. Multiple locations.

Mini Boden; 0845 677 5000; www.boden.co.uk.
Mail order catalogue or order online at their website. Fun, playful clothes, shoes and accessories for babies through to teens.

Mothercare; 461 Oxford Street, W1; 020 7629 6621; www.mothercare.com.
Absolutely everything can be bought here, including children's clothing from 0-8 years, maternity clothes, pushchairs, nursery furniture, home and car safety equipment. Multiple locations.

Next; 508 Oxford Street, W1; 0207 659 9730.
Reliable children's wear. Multiple locations.

Did you know?...When shopping for baby clothes, it's helpful to remember that generally, British sizes are spot on, European sizes are a tighter fit and American sizes tend to be cut generously. For example, an average-sized 3-month-old baby will usually fit British and American clothes marked as 3 months, but will fit European clothes marked as 6 months. It is therefore best to buy European baby clothes at least one size up.

Petit Bateau; 62 South Molton Street, W1; 020 7491 4498.

Excellent-quality French children's clothing brand. Multiple locations.

Rachel Riley; 82 Marylebone High Street, W1; 020 7935 7007, and 14 Pont Street, SW1; 020 7259 5969.

Traditional English clothes with a French influence. Also has a mail order catalogue (020 7935 7007).

Trotters; 34 King's Road, SW3; 020 7259 9620, and 127 Kensington High Street, W8; 020 7937 9373; www.trotters.co.uk.

Wide range of clothing and shoes. Also children's haircuts.

Costumes / Fancy Dress

Mystical Fairies; 12 Flask Walk, NW3; 020 7431 1888; www.mysticalfairies.co.uk.

Will fulfil the dreams of any little princess. Carries every magical and mystifying fairy item imaginable.

Charliecrow; 01782 417 133; www.charliecrow.com.

Online company offering a large collection of costumes for imaginative play.

Equipment Hire / Nappy and Household Goods Delivery

See *Chapter 11: Services* for a more complete list of food and nappy delivery services.

Chelsea Baby Hire; 31 Osborne House, 414 Wimbledon Park Road, SW1; 020 8789 9673; www.chelseababyhire.com.

Little Green Earthlets; Unit 17, Silveroaks Farm, Waldron, East Sussex, TN21 0RS; 0845 072 4462; www.earthlets.co.uk.

A full range of natural baby essentials, pregnancy products and other quality baby products. We are also "cloth nappy specialists" and stock the award winning Mother-ease fitted cloth nappies.

Little Stars; 020 8621 4378; www.littlestars.co.uk.

Started by two mums who come to your house and help you to locate anything or everything! They will order directly from the manufacturer in many case, so you don't pay the steep retail prices. Also have a wide range of equipment and toys for hire.

Olimia Ltd.; 1b Church Street, Reigate, Surrey, RH2 0AA; 017 3722 3355; www.olimia.com.

A one-stop shop for natural everyday essentials for you and your family, including our fantastic range of frozen babyfood and toddler meals, washable and eco-friendlier disposable nappies. Products are additive free and predominantly organic.

If you are looking to acquire gently used baby items, such as pushchairs, highchairs, furniture and clothing, the NCT runs a series of "Nearly New" sales throughout the country. For dates and schedules, contact the NCT through the main number listed above.

The Hampstead Women's Club and **Kensington Chelsea Women's Club** hold "Nearly New" sales in the spring and autumn respectively. They specialise in gently used children's clothes, equipment and toys. Contact details for these clubs can be found in *Chapter 18: Organisations*.

Nursery Equipment and Furniture

John Lewis, Mothercare, Harrods and **Marks & Spencer** have good baby and children departments. Mothercare and **The Early Learning Centre** (see "Toys") specialise in baby's and children's items. Other stores that specialise in nursery items include:

Aspace; 01985 301 222; www.aspaceuk.com. Visit the website for furniture selection and to order a catalogue.

Baby List; 50 Sulivan Road, SW6; 020 7371 5145; www.babylist.co.uk.

Large variety of brand name items. For a fee, they will help put together a list of complete nursery needs.

The Children's Furniture Company; 020 7737 7303; www.thechildrensfurniturecompany.com.

Beautiful and sturdy handmade children's furniture to be ordered direct.

Daisy & Tom (see "Children's Wear").

Dragon's of Walton Street; 23 Walton Street, SW3; 020 7589 3795; www.dragonsofwaltonstreet.com. Specialising in hand-painted furniture.

Kiddicare; www.kiddicare.co.uk.

The leading online retailer for nursery equipment and furniture within the UK. Offer free delivery.

The Nursery Window; 83 Walton Street, SW3; 020 7581 3358; www.thenurserywindow.co.uk.

Specialising in layettes and items for newborns made from the shop's own fabric.

Urchin; 0870 112 6006; www.urchin.co.uk.

Visit the website or call for the mail order catalogue. Kitchen, bath, and travel accessories, furniture, toys and games.

Wigwam; 0870 902 7500; www.wigwamkids.co.uk.

Visit the website or call for the mail order catalogue. Contemporary children's furniture and accessories.

TOYS

Most major department stores such as **John Lewis** and **Harrod's** have large toy departments, and **Hamley's** has everything!

Cheeky Monkeys; 202 Kensington Park Road, W11; 020 7792 9022; www.cheekymonkeys.com.
   Unusual and traditional children's toys and gifts, furniture, china, dressing-up, etc. Multiple locations.

Daisy & Tom (see "Children's Wear").

Early Learning Centre; 36 King's Road, SW3; 020 7581 5764; www.elc.co.uk.
   Specialising in educational toys for young children. Multiple locations.

Great Little Trading Company; 0870 850 6000; www.gltc.co.uk.
   Practical, innovative products for children and parents. By mail order only.

Hamley's; 188-196 Regent Street, W1; 0870 333 2455; www.hamleys.co.uk. World's largest toy shop!

J.J. Toys; 138 St. John's Wood High Street, NW8; 020 7722 4855.

Mulberry Bush; 014 0375 4400; www.mulberrybush.co.uk.
   An established specialist mail order company, selling traditional and innovative toys and gifts for babies and young children up to age 12.

Myriad Natural Toys, Ringwood, Hampshire; 017 2551 7085; www.myriadonline.co.uk. Fantastic wooden toys, arts, crafts, and books.

The Disney Store; 360-366 Oxford Street W1; 0207 491 9136; www.disneystore.co.uk. Multiple locations.

Toys 'R' Us; Tilling Road, Brent Cross Shopping Centre, NW2; 020 8209 0019; www.toysrus.co.uk. Multiple locations.

Traditional Toys; 53 Godfrey Street, SW3; 020 7352 1718.

ENTERTAINING YOUR CHILDREN

One of the greatest things about living in London is that there is no shortage of things to do. It is often a difficult task to narrow down the choices. Despite all of the various venues, activities and special events, you will not find one source that lists everything that's on and when. Some key websites, magazines and guidebooks are listed at the end of this chapter. You should also contact your local council, and visit your local library, town hall (if applicable), local parks/playgrounds and schools. You will be amazed at what isn't advertised in the local newspaper or magazine!

When planning any sort of outing in London, it is always a good idea to call ahead to verify operating hours and the schedule of events. Things have a tendency to change in London on short notice and there is nothing worse than an unhappy child after a long journey.

Adventure (Multi-Activity Play Areas)

Bramley's Big Adventure; 136 Bramley Road, W10; 020 8960 1515; www.bramleysbig.co.uk.

Three-level indoor playground for children 0-11 years' old. Will also host children's parties.

Chessington World of Adventures; Letterhead Road, Chessington, Kent; 0870 999 0045; www.chessington.com. Theme park and zoo.

Diggerland; Roman Way, Medway Valley Leisure Park, Stroud, Kent; 0870 034 4437; www.diggerland.com.

A must for Bob the Builder fans. Allows children to "dig" in real mini-diggers.

Legoland Windsor; Winkfield Road, Berkshire; 0870 504 0404; www.legoland.co.uk.

Open late March through November. Over 50 rides and attractions, plus seasonal special events.

Snakes and Ladders; Syon Park, Brentford, Middlesex TW8; 020 8847 0946;

www.snakes-and-ladders.co.uk.

Vast building housing three separate play areas for toddlers, intermediate and older children under 12. Also has a café and garden, and can host children's parties.

Talacre Community Sports Centre; Dalby Street, NW5; 020 7974 8765; www.camden.gov.uk/sport.

An indoor soft play area for young children. A separate play area for the under-5s. Also a gymnastics training centre and classes (with a very long wait list).

Topsy Turvy; Brent Cross Shopping Centre, NW2; 0800 587 5225; www.topsyturvyworld.com.

A popular and conveniently located indoor play centre. Hosts birthday parties.

Art

Art Start; 59a Portobello Road, W1; 078 1128 3679.

Classes and parties for ages 18 months and older.

Creative Wiz Kids; 020 7794 6797; www.creativewizkids.com.

Playgroups, after-school programmes and parties; creative play through art (music, painting, crafts). Ages 1-12.

The Art Workshop; 020 7794 0800; www.art4fun.com.

Three London branches in Chiswick, Muswell Hill and West Hampstead. Themed art activity centre focusing on painted ceramics. Birthday parties, holiday courses and classes.

London Brass Rubbing Centre; The Crypt, St. Martin in the Fields, WC2; 020 7930 9306. Brass rubbing.

Aquariums

The London Aquarium; County Hall, Westminster Bridge Road, SE1; 020 7967 8000; www.londonaquarium.co.uk.

Home to over 350 species including sharks, sting rays, crabs and more. Admission charge.

The Tropical Forest (formerly known as The Aquatic Experience); Syon Park, Brentford, Middlesex TW8; 020 8847 4730; www.thetropicalforest.co.uk.

A small centre with crocodiles, snakes, frogs and various fish (some which can be fed). The highlight is the animal talk — children can learn and touch some of the creatures. Admission charge.

Boat Trips

Canal Cruises; 250 Camden High Street, NW1; 020 7485 4433.

Canal trips on Regent's Canal and Camden Lock on the Jenny Wren (operates March to October) and the My Fair Lady (year round).

Guildford Boat House; Millbrook, Guildford, Surrey; 01483 504 494; www.guildfordboats.co.uk.

One-and-a-half-hour boat trip from Town Wharf to St. Catherine's Lock, rowing boats for daily hire, and canal boats for holiday hire (four days minimum). Open Easter to October.

Jason's Trips; Jason's Wharf, opposite 60 Blomfield Road, W9; 020 7286 3428; www.jasons.co.uk.

Boat trips (one way 45 minutes, return 1½ hours) from Little Venice to Camden Lock. March to September.

London Water Bus Company; Camden Place, NW1 and Little Venice, NW1; 020 7482 2550 (Office); 020 7482 2660 (Information); www.londonwaterbus.com.

Boat trips (one way 45 minutes, return 1½ hours) leaving from either

Camden Lock or Little Venice via the zoo. Open daily April to October and weekends in winter.

Westminster Passenger Services Association Up River; Westminster Pier, Victoria Embankment, SW1; 020 7930 2062; www.wpsa.co.uk.

Boat trips on the Thames to Richmond, the Tower of London, Greenwich, Kew Gardens and Hampton Court. Round-trip or one-way, returning by public transportation.

Also look at www.royalparks.gov.uk for paddle boat rides in Regent's Park and Hyde Park.

Cookery

Books for Cooks; 4 Blenheim Crescent, W11; 020 7221 1992; www.booksforcooks.com.

Special workshops for children ages 5-14.

Cookie Crumbles; 34 Marylebone High Street, W1; 0845 601 4173; www.cookiecrumbles.net.

Cooking parties for ages 5-16. Workshops held at the Divertimenti Cooking School.

Divertimenti Cookery School; 34 Marylebone High Street, W1; 020 7935 0689, and 227-229 Brompton Road, SW3; 0207 581 8065; www.divertimenti.co.uk.

Offers Saturday classes for little ones, covering themes such as "Italian Day" and "Party Food".

Kids Cookery School; 107 Gunnersbury Lane, W3; 020 8992 8882; www.kidscookeryschool.co.uk.

Offers holiday and half-term classes and workshops for ages 3 and up.

Dance

Cherry Childe School of Dancing; Trinity Hall, Hodford Road, NW11; 020 8458 6962.

Ballet, modern and tap classes for both boys and girls.

English National Ballet School; Carlyle Building, Hortensia Road, SW10; 020 7376 7076; www.enbschool.org.uk.

Two-year full-time classical ballet training for the serious student beginning at age 16. Caters to both boys and girls.

Rona Hart School of Dance; Rosslyn Hall, Willoughby Road, NW3; 020 7435 7073.

Offers ballet from age 2 ½ at several locations in Hampstead.

Royal Academy of Dance; 36 Battersea Square, SW11; 020 7326 8043; www.rad.org.uk.

Ballet, jazz and contemporary dance for all ages and abilities, for both boys and girls.

Royal Ballet School; White Lodge, Richmond Park; 020 8392 8000 (Lower School), and 46 Floral Street, WC2; 020 77836 8899 (Upper School); www.royal-ballet-school.org.uk.

Classical ballet classes for the serious student beginning at age 11. Upper School by audition only. Boys and girls.

Vacani School of Dancing; The Marylebone Ballet School, St Mary's Church Precinct, Wyndam Place, W1, and Moscow Road, W2; 07887 574 390; www.maryleboneballet.co.uk.

Classical ballet for boys and girls aged 2 and up.

Drama / Theatre

Many of the following listings offer excellent children's workshops and/ or performances.

Albert and Friends; Riverside Studios, Crisp Road, W6; 020 8237 1111/ 1170; www.albertandfriendsinstantcircus.co.uk or www.riversidestudios.co.uk.

Workshops for circus skills, dance, drama and music. Runs the largest children's circus in London.

Allsorts Drama; 020 8969 3249 / 020 8871 4987; www.allsortsdrama.com.

Drama courses for ages 3-16. Includes music and movement, improvisation, mime, characterisation, costume and stage makeup. Multiple locations.

Battersea Arts Centre; Lavender Hill, SW11; 020 7223 2223; www.bac.org.uk.

Drama, mask and model-making, puppetry, photography and music. Classes for age groups from 6 months to 15 years old. Films and mime shows on Saturdays.

Chicken Shed Theatre; Chase Side, Southgate, N14; 020 8351 6161; 020 8292 9222 (box office); www.chickenshed.org.uk.

Regular performances, special interactive theatrical productions for pre-schoolers and theatre education workshops for those aged 5-24.

The Colour House Theatre; Merton Abbey Mills, SW19; 020 8542 6644; www.wheelhouse.org.uk.

Children's shows for ages 3 and up.

The Little Angel Theatre; 14 Dagmar Passage, N1; 020 7226 1787; www.littleangeltheatre.com.

Puppet shows for ages 3 and up.

> *Did you know?...A Pantomime is a traditional British Christmas play performed at various theatres throughout the country over the holiday season. Pantomimes are great family entertainment; a mix of fairy stories, folk tales and much loved cartoons, which encourage audience participation. The male roles are often played by women and female roles by men.*

Polka Theatre; 240 The Broadway, Wimbledon, SW19; 020 8543 4888; www.polkatheatre.com.

Theatre for children aged 3 and up.

Puppet Theatre Barge; opposite 37 Blomfield Road, W9; 020 7249 6876; www.puppetbarge.com.

A floating theatre on a Thames barge. Marionette and puppet shows for children aged 4 and up. November to June at this location. In the summer months it stops at various locations along the Thames; call or visit the website for details.

Stagecoach; 0193 225 4333; www.stagecoach.co.uk.

Over 60 venues across London with no more than 15 per group. Drama, dance and singing classes for ages 4-16.

Tricycle Cinema and Theatre; 269 Kilburn High Road, NW6; 020 7328 1000; www.tricycle.co.uk.

Theatre productions and cinema screenings on Saturdays for children under 5, plus half-term workshops.

Unicorn Theatre for Children; 0870 053 4534; www.unicorntheatre.com.

Theatre for children ages 4 -12 years. Family show at Christmas. Theatre location varies, call for details.

Warehouse Theatre; 62 Dingwall Road, Croydon; 020 8681 1257; www.warehousetheatre.co.uk.

Plays and shows on Saturday morning for children aged 4-9.

Westminster School of Performing Arts; The Flat Street, Andrews Club, 12 Old Pye Street, SW1; 020 7222 8873.

Drama, music, gymnastics, singing and dance for ages 2-18.

Yvonne Arnaud Theatre; Millbrook, Guildford, Surrey; 0148 344 0000 (performances) and 0148 356 5191 (Youth Theatre, for summer workshops); www.yvonne-arnaud.co.uk.

Offers special children's activities on some weekends and holidays.

Entertainers / Party Venues

Magicians, clowns and mimes will organise children's parties (complete with prizes and favours) or just entertain at your direction. Be sure to book these popular entertainers well in advance (three to four months prior to the event) to avoid disappointment.

There are several terrific websites to help with birthday planning, offering tips on everything from party venues to themes, food, entertainment and party bags. Visit www.familiesonline.co.uk/topics/parties for helpful hints and links to other party websites; www.nonstopparty.co.uk for tableware, balloons and party products; and www.birthdayexpress.com for party themes, cakes, games and costumes.

Albert and Friends —see above.

Arda Halls; 020 8969 0154; puppet shows for the 5-and-under set.

Blueberry Playsongs; 020 8677 6871; www.blueberry.clara.co.uk.

Guitar, songs and puppets for children's parties.

Creative Wiz Kids; 020 7794 6797; www.creativewizkids.com.

Entertains children through art media: painting, music, games and creative crafts.

Crechendo; 020 8772 8120; www.crechendo.co.uk.

Themed parties and entertainers.

Gymboree; 020 7258 1415; www.gymboreeplayuk.com.

Parties with climbers, slides, balls and hoops, plus games, activities and music with a Gymboree teacher. Multiple locations.

Mr. Squash; 020 8808 1415; www.mr-squash.co.uk.
Puppets, magic and fun, from 2 years and up.

Oscar's Den; 127-129 Abbey Road, NW6; 020 7328 6683;
www.oscarsden.com.
Party and balloon shop, bouncy castles and other play equipment for hire;
tables, chairs and highchairs for hire; and entertainers.

Mystical Fairies; 12 Flask Walk, NW3; 020 7431 1888;
www.mysticalfairies.co.uk.
Will fulfil the dreams of any little princess. Carries every magical and
mystifying fairy item imaginable. Also caters children's parties (for fairies
and pirates) on the premises.

Rhubarb the Clown; 72 Hillside Road, N15; 020 8800 5009;
www.rhubarbtheclown.com.
Includes mime, magic, juggling and unicycles.

Smartie Artie; 01582 600 529; www.smartieartie.com.
Does one-hour party that includes puppets, games, comedy magic and
balloon making. For ages 3 and up.

Splodge Education; Box 31368, SW11; 020 7350 1477;
www.planetsplodge.com.
Helps plan interactive, themed parties that incorporate art, drama
and music for ages 2-12. Also offers half-term clubs and special school
workshops.

Twizzle Entertainment; Chantry House, 4 Umbria Street, SW15; 0208 789
3232; www.twizzle.co.uk.
Party entertainment that includes a clown, games, competitions and
magic. Also does themed parties, mini-discos, puppet shows and sing-alongs
with musical instruments for all ages.

Halloween

One popular and fun-filled Halloween event is a party hosted each year by the Kensington Chelsea Women's Club. Registration is usually at least a month in advance; contact them on 020 7863 7562 or visit www.kcwc.org.uk for more information.

Libraries

Your local library in London is well worth an investigative trip. In addition to excellent collections of children's books, many have video/DVD and cassette lending programmes and organised activities for children. Many libraries have story reading for younger children during term time or school holidays. The library is also a prime source of information on other local happenings for children, especially during the school holidays. Children receive their own lending cards by providing proof of local residence. The Information Service based at the **Library Association** (7 Ridgmount Street, WC1; 020 7636 7543) has a directory of all branches in the London area and will gladly assist you in finding the branch nearest your home.

Museums

There are countless museums in and around London of interest to children of all ages. The major museums in London have special activities, exhibits and quizzes during school holidays. Ring for information or consult weekly events magazines. The **Science Museum** on Exhibition Road and **The Royal Air Force Museum** in North London are excellent choices for entertaining young children on rainy days. See *Chapter 16: Culture* for a listing of museums and galleries. The listing indicates which ones are recommended for children.

Music and Movement

Bea's Baby Music School; 020 8670 9378; www.babymusic.co.uk.

Music classes held in Chelsea, Battersea, Barnes and Putney for children from 6 months to 6 years old.

Blueberry Playsongs; 020 8677 6871; www.blueberry.clara.co.uk.
Locations in Chelsea, Clapham, Notting Hill, Putney, Hammersmith and Richmond. Music classes for children from 9 months to 6 years old.

Budokwai; 4 Gilston Road, SW10; 020 7370 1000; www.budokwai.co.uk.
A popular judo and martial arts club.

Crêchendo; 020 8772 8120; www.crechendo.co.uk.
Active learning classes for children age 4 months to 7 years. Classes offer movement, music, sight and sound experiences. Multiple locations.

Culture Kids; 020 8540 4203; www.culture-kids.com.
Pre-school music classes in Chelsea, Hampstead and Kensington.

Gymboree Play & Music; 0800 092 0911; www.GymboreePlayUK.com.
Activity and music classes from birth to 5 years old. Multiple locations.

Monkey Music; 01582 766 464; www.monkeymusic.co.uk.
Music and movement classes for children from 6 months to 5 years old. Multiple locations.

Muzsika; 020 7794 4848.
Lively music workshops for children aged 6 months to 5 years old. Classes are held in Notting Hill and St. John's Wood.

Philharmonia Orchestra; First Floor, 125 High Holborn, WC1; 020 7242 5001; www.philharmonia.co.uk.
Resident at the Royal Festival Hall. Workshops, concerts and family music days are held throughout the season.

The Royal College of Music; Junior Department, Prince Consort Road, SW7; 020 7591 4334; www.rcm.ac.uk.
Instruction and recommended teachers.

Parks / Playgrounds

There are over 80 parks within a seven-mile radius of Hyde Park Corner. Most parks are open dawn until dusk. See *Chapter 14: Sports and Leisure* for a full listing of parks and details. Also look at www.royalparks.gov.uk for up-to-date activities and events being held in some of London's most popular parks.

Many parks and/or playgrounds around London have a One O'Clock Club, which usually consists of a separate indoor/outdoor play area specifically designed for children under 5 and their parents or caregivers to play together and make new friends. Toys, books, games and craft time are typically available. The clubs are generally open from 10:00 – 11:30 and 13:00–16:00, but times may vary based on location.

Some parks that are especially good for children are:

Battersea Park; Sun Gate entrance, Albert Bridge Road, SW11; 020 8871 7539; www.batterseapark.org.

Has a children's One O'clock Club, children's zoo and an adventure playground.

Coram's Fields; 93 Guildford Street, WC1.

This inner-city playground has an under-5s' sand and water themed play area (bring children a change of clothes), small animal enclosure, paddling pool and adventure play area for children aged 5 and up.

Golders Hill Park; North End Road, NW11.

Within Hampstead Heath. Playground and small zoo.

Hampstead Heath; Parliament Hill, NW3; www.cityoflondon.gov.uk/ Corporation/living_environment/open_spaces/hampstead_heath.htm.

Swimming pool (the Lido), One O'Clock Club, Adventure playground (Ages 8+), wading pool and children's playground (near Parliament Hill). Visit the website for special events and a map.

Holland Park; Ilchester Place, W8; 020 7471 9813; www.rbkc.gov.uk.

Lovely children's play area on the southwestern side of the park. Has sand, swings and other equipment for the under-5s. There is also a new adventure play park under construction for older children.

Primrose Hill; Prince Albert Road, NW8; www.royalparks.gov.uk.

Part of Regent's Park. Has a gated children's play area at the southern end of the park, bordering Prince Albert Road.

Diana Princess of Wales Memorial Playground; Orme Gate, Kensington Gardens, W8; 020 7298 2141; www.royalparks.gov.uk.

Large gated play area on the north side of Hyde Park with sand, swings, slides and lots of wooden play pieces, including a pirate ship for children to climb on.

Regent's Park; NW1; 020 7486 4216; www.royalparks.gov.uk.

Has three gated children's play areas, paddling and row boats, and at the northern end of the park, you will find London Zoo (which also contains a playground).

St. Luke's Gardens; Sydney Street, SW3; 020 7361 3003; www.rbkc.gov.uk.

Popular children's play area convenient for Chelsea and South Kensington.

Playgroups

The **NCT**, **Kensington and Chelsea Women's Club** (KCWC), **Hampstead Women's Club** (HWC), **One O'Clock Clubs** (see above under "Parks / Playgrounds"), your local library and your local health centre or clinic are all excellent sources for playgroups in your neighbourhood. See *Chapter 18: Organisations* for contact information.

Restaurants

There are a surprising number of London restaurants that positively welcome children. Sunday lunch is a popular family meal, so children are usually expected anywhere. Here is a small selection of child-friendly restaurants; you may also want to look in *Harden's*, the *Time Out Eating guide* or *Zagat's* for more options.

Big Easy; 332-334 Kings Road, SW3; 020 7352 4071; www.bigeasy.uk.com. Cajun-style food.

Blue Elephant; 3-6 Fulham Broadway, SW6; 020 7385 6595; www. blueelephant.com. Thai food with wild tropical plants and wood bridges.

Carluccio's Café; 8 Market Place, W1; 020 7636 2228; www.carluccios.com. Casual Italian restaurant with children's menu. Many branches have a takeaway Italian deli. Multiple locations.

Giraffe; 6-8 Blandford Street, W1; 020 7935 2333. Family friendly for breakfast, lunch and dinner; eclectic menu. Multiple locations.

La Famiglia; 7 Langton St, SW10; 020 7351 0761. Great local Italian.

Lemonia; 89 Regent's Park Road, NW1; 020 7586 7454. Greek food.

Rainforest Café; 20-24 Shaftesbury Avenue, W1; 020 7434 3111; www.therainforestcafe.co.uk. Full of screeching monkeys, jungle plants and baboons, for the young, or young at heart.

Tate Modern; Bankside, SE1; 020 7401 5020. Both restaurant and café are non-smoking and have high chairs.

TGI Fridays; 6 Bedford Street, WC2; 020 7379 0585. Multiple locations. Crayons, face painting and balloons available at some locations.

Tootsies; 35 James Street, W1; 020 7486 1611.
Basic American diner grub. Multiple locations.

Wagamama; 1 Tavistock Street, WC2; 020 7836 3330; www.wagamama.com.
Asian noodle restaurant where diners eat at communal tables. Multiple
locations.

GIRL GUIDES AND BOY SCOUTS
Girl Guides/Girl Scouts Association, World Bureau, Olave Centre,
12c Lyndhurst Road, NW3; 020 7794 1181; www.wagggsworld.org.

The Scout Association; Baden-Powell House, 65 Queens Gate, SW7;
0845 300 1818; www.scouts.org.uk.

For **American Boy Scouts and Girl Scouts**, contact the American School
in London (020 7449 1200).

SPORTS
In addition to the sports choices below, several health clubs offer excellent
children's programmes. See *Chapter 14: Sports and Leisure* for more
information.

Baseball
The Baseball Association (www.londonsports.com) has seven different
leagues (T-ball, Coach-pitch, Minor League, Major League, Juniors Baseball,
and junior and senior girls' softball). Practice sessions and games take place
at Wormwood Scrubs, Hammersmith during the spring.

Basketball
The Basketball Association (www.londonsports.com) has a winter
basketball programme for girls and boys aged 8-14. Many of the games are
played at the American School in St. John's Wood.

Cricket

At **Lord's Cricket Grounds** (St. John's Wood Road, NW8; 020 7616 8611; www.lords.org),
Children can learn cricket at the renowned "home of cricket".

Football (Soccer)

The London Football Association; www.londonsports.com.
Football practice for boys and girls at Wormwood Scrubs, Hammersmith during the school year.

The Chelsea Estates Youth Club; 020 7351 9478.
Runs a football club for 12-18 year olds.

Little Kickers; 01235 833 854; www.littlekickers.co.uk.
Pre-school classes for ages 2-4, year round in blocks of 12 weeks. Classes in Battersea, Fulham, Highgate, Chiswick and Hammersmith. For classes in Hampstead and Swiss Cottage, ring 020 8201 1084.

Riding

London has several equestrian schools. Most of the schools will expect their students to be properly attired and equipped; check with the school. Both lessons and hacking are offered. See *Chapter 14: Sports and Leisure* for details.

Skating

Alexandra Palace Ice Rink; Alexandra Palace Way, N22; 020 8365 4386; www.alexandrapalace.com.
Year-round ice rink, skating lessons and a café.

Queen's Ice and Bowl; 17 Queensway, W2; 020 7229 0172; www.queens iceandbowl.co.uk.
Two-to-three-hour skating sessions, seven days a week.

Swimming

Swimming pools offer lessons and regular activities for children as well as special programmes during school holidays. Many facilities have a separate shallow teaching pool for very small children, separate diving areas and wave machines. See *Chapter 14: Sports and Leisure* under "Swimming" for more information.

Aquababies; 017 0876 8400; www.aquababies-uk.com.

Swimming pools located throughout London. Swimming classes for ages 3 months to 4 years.

Little Dippers; 0870 758 0302; www.littledippers.co.uk.

Locations in London, Sussex and Kent. Infant water safety training classes for ages 0-1 year.

Mighty Ducks; 39-51 Highgate Road, Linton House, NW5; 020 7428 7715; www.mightyducks.co.uk.

Swimming classes for children of all ages and levels. Classes held at various North London locations.

Swimming Nature; 087 0094 9597; www.swimmingnature.co.uk.

Classes in Pimlico/Victoria, Chelsea, Notting Hill and Regent's Park for babies 6 months and older.

Tennis

To locate a tennis club that offers children's tennis lessons near you, visit www.totaltennis.net.

Zoos

Visit the Good Zoo Online (www.goodzoos.com), which has a complete listing of all of the zoos and wildlife parks in the UK.

Battersea Park Children's Zoo; Battersea Park; 020 7924 5826; www.batterseapark.org.

London Zoo; Outer Circle, Regent's Park, NW1; 020 7722 3333; www.zsl.org.

The London Butterfly House; Syon Park, Brentford, Middlesex; 020 8560 7272; www.londonbutterflyhouse.com.
A live butterfly zoo.

Whipsnade Wild Animal Park; Dunstable, Bedfordshire; 01582 872 171; www.zsl.org.
Walk or drive over 600 acres. Animals are enclosed in very large spaces.

GUIDEBOOKS AND MAGAZINES FOR PARENTS
Adore; 020 8440 1848.
A magazine for parents of very young children or parents-to-be. Distributed through selected nurseries, doctors' surgeries, maternity units, libraries and more. Also available through paid subscription.

Angels & Urchins; 020 7603 1366; www.angelsandurchins.co.uk.
An indispensable magazine for families living in London. Available in many children's stores, schools or by paid subscription.

Children's London, Evening Standard; www.thisislondon.com.
Comprehensive listings of all sorts of children's activities. Check out the "6 of the Best" section, listing everything from ice cream parlours to pottery cafes to bowling lanes and adventure playgrounds.

Families; 020 8696 9680; www.familiesonline.co.uk.
Useful magazine for families with young children in six London areas: SW, SE, W, N, NW and E. Available free in many children's stores, schools or by paid subscription. The website is a great resource, covering issues such as health, childcare, schools and birthday parties. The monthly "Out and About" section lists events, activities and entertainment.

Harden's London Baby Guide, by Kate Calvert; www.hardens.com.

Detailed reference book, with information on birthing options, shops and mail order suppliers, support groups, books, websites and a directory of practitioners who specialise in treating pregnant women and children.

The London Baby Directory: An A-Z of everything for pregnant women, babies and under 5s, edited by Karen Liebreid; www.babydirectory.com. Useful resource book available in various children's stores or by writing to Cuneix Interactive, 10 Grove Park Terrace, London W4 3QG. Updated annually.

Parents' Directory; Needwood, West Lavant, Chichester, West Sussex PO18 9AH; 01243 527 605.

Directories available for South West London, South East London and North West London. Summer and winter editions by subscription.

Time Out London. Weekly magazine found at newsagents; look for the section on children. Also publishes a *London for Kids guide* (available at newsagents and bookshops).

FURTHER REFERENCE INFORMATION

Camden Children Information Services; 020 7974 1679; cindex.camden.gov.uk.

Lists TONS of activities, schools, clubs, classes, farms, playgrounds, one o'clock clubs, parks and more for children, sorted by post code. There is both an "under 5s" listing and an "under 2s" listing. Copies available at your local library or ring to receive one by post. Listings are updated regularly.

London Tourist Board; www.visitlondon.com.

A good starting point for any information. There is a special kids section on their website at www.kidslovelondon.com.

Londonkidz; www.londonkidz.com.

Updated information on the latest children's events in and around London.

Drawn by Leon

Schools

CONTENTS

The London area is full of excellent schools. Finding the school that best meets the needs of one's child and family can take considerable time due to the choice available. The decision should involve a number of considerations, including: your estimated length of time in England, your children's ages, adaptability of the children, and the overall impact that a change to the English system might have on the children and family.

Before making a decision, families should talk to friends and colleagues with children of similar ages. Additionally, families should visit and speak to as many different schools as possible. Education consultants may also be a valuable resource in selecting the right school.

THE ENGLISH SCHOOL SYSTEM

Every child in the UK must be in full time education by the age of 5 (that means 5 on the 1st September in the year in which they are 5 years of age.) The date "1st September" is non-negotiable.

The system can be confusing to a newcomer and may differ from location to location. Within the English school system, schools are generally grouped into two categories: State Schools, run by the Government, and Independent Schools, privately run and fee-paying. Confusingly, Independent Schools are also referred to as Public Schools in many areas. State schools may also include religious foundations schools (ie., the Church of England and Roman Catholic schools).

State Schools

As in any country, some State Schools outperform Independent Schools in the same area. Therefore, choosing a State School may be a very viable option. However, places in the top State Schools are very competitive to obtain, as families move to the respective areas to register their children at a very early age. In many instances, matters are even more complicated for incoming families, as many State Schools restrict registration until a family can prove residence in the relevant catchment area. This makes it very difficult to simultaneously co-ordinate housing and schooling.

State Schools follow the National Curriculum and are subjected to periodic standardised testing called SATs (Standardized Assessment Tasks) up through the age of 13/14. At the age of 14, students commence their GCSE (General Certificate of Secondary Education), a two-year program ending in a standardised exam also known as the GCSE. Following GCSE, students will either move on to study a vocational trade or pursue "A levels", which are required for entrance to University. A student may take several "A level" courses, typically concentrating on the subjects he or she hopes to study at University (e.g., sciences or languages). Each "A level" course also concludes with a standardised test, and "A level" results are crucial to the British University Admissions Process. While Independent Schools are not obliged to comply with the "A level" curriculum, many do.

Each school (whether State or Independent) has its GCSE and "A Level" exam results published annually as part of the National "League Tables" which are released in the major British newspapers. They can be useful but, as their critics point out, they represent only one measure of each school's success. The Good Schools Guide (see more information below) has a good discussion on their limitations. Additionally, all State Schools are inspected by **Ofsted**, an independent organisation which objectively reports the standards and quality of each school, making recommendations where necessary. You can read each school's Ofsted report on the Ofsted website: www.ofsted.gov.uk.

To enrol your child in a State School, you should contact the school directly as well as the **Local Education Authority** (LEA) of the borough in which you plan to live.

In addition, the following organisations may also provide helpful advice:

The British Council; 10 Spring Gardens, SW1 2BN; 020 7930 8466; www.britishcouncil.org. An education information service.

The Department for Education; Sanctuary Buildings, Great Smith Street, SW1P 3BT; 0870 0002 288; www.dfee.gov.uk or www.edubase.co.uk.

Overall policy setting government department; they supply the telephone number for your Local Education Authority.

Ofsted, Alexandra House, 33 Kingsway, WC2B 6SE; 0845 6404 045; www.ofsted.gov.uk.

INDEPENDENT SCHOOLS

Independent Schools vary in size, facilities and most importantly, in philosophy towards education. For example, some schools adhere to sections of the National Curriculum, where others have abolished "A levels" and now offer the International Baccalaureate (covered in more detail below).

Entrance into most schools is determined by examination and/or personal interview. Due to the limited number of spaces, and high demand, many schools require long advance notice for admission. As a result, many parents register their children at birth. However, incoming parents should not be put off, nor should news that there is no place for your child at a particular school discourage you. Gracious determination sometimes pays dividends.

Although only about 7% of students in England attend Independent Schools, there are over 2,000 to choose from, including local day schools and boarding schools. The boarding school tradition is strong in the UK, and it is not uncommon for boys to be sent away at age eight, and girls at age eleven. Many good schools, both primary and secondary, are single-sex. A number of publications and consulting services are around to help you select a day or boarding school.

Examinations and interviews for entry into Independent Secondary Schools should be expected. Boys and girls take entrance exams at different ages. Boys take an exam for Preparatory School at age 7 or 8 years and the Common Entrance Exam at age 13 while girls take the "11+" or Common Entrance Exam at age 11, 12 or 13. Many schools have organised 'open days' when groups of prospective parents (and their children) are shown around the school, with opportunities to meet the staff.

All Independent Schools, including American / International Schools are inspected regularly by ISI (the Independent Schools Inspectorate), an independent body which reports on the standards and quality of Independent Schools. You can read a copy of each school's report on the ISI website: www.isinspect.org.uk/.

Did you know?... Independent Schools in England are often referred to as "Public" schools. Until 1902, there were no publicly-supported secondary schools in England. Public schools were supported by an endowment, with a governing body, available to all members of the public, provided they could pay for tuition costs. Private schools were run for private profit. In recent years, all schools formerly called Public Schools now refer to themselves as Independent Schools, but the national press (and many individuals) still use the term "Public School" when referring to Independent Schools. In particular, the older, more prestigious, fee-paying schools mentioned in the Public Schools Act of 1868 (Charterhouse, Eton, Harrow, Rugby, Shrewsbury, Westminster, Winchester, Merchant Taylors' and St. Paul's) are typically still referred to as Public Schools.

9

SCHOOLS

PUBLICATIONS

Gabbitas Guide to Independent Schools; Gabbitas Educational Consultants, Carrington House, 126-130 Regent Street, W1B 5EE; 020 7734 0161, www.gabbitas.net.

A comprehensive directory of independent schools (Pre-prep to senior) with a geographical directory and advertisements.

The Good Schools Guide; 3 Craven Mews, SW11 5PW; 020 7801 0191; www.goodschoolsguide.co.uk.

Information on over 350 top private and state schools in the UK (junior and senior, day and boarding).

Good Nursery Guide; written by Sue Woodford and Anne de Zoysa, Ebury Press. Advice on tailoring a child's nursery education to individual needs, how to locate the schools in any particular area of Britain and Northern Ireland, how to arrange a visit, what to look for, as well as the questions to ask and how to assess costs.

The ISCis Guide to Accredited Independent Schools; St Vincent's House, 30 Orange Street, WC2; 020 7766 7070; www.isc.co.uk.

An annual publication available from Independent Schools Council Information Service (ISCis) which offers a guide to the independent sector and the 1300 ISC schools, with their examination results, an interactive CDROM and a range of leaflets and other publications to help parents.

Which London School? Guide; published annually by John Catt. This guide lists details of independent day, boarding, nursery and international schools in London area. Can be purchased from the John Catt's website: www.schoolsearch.co.uk/.

EDUCATION CONSULTANTS

Educational Consultants can prove extremely valuable and helpful as one looks for schools in the London area. As mentioned above, Educational

Consultants are not only extremely knowledgeable about schools in the London area, but also often have good contacts at schools that may be helpful in obtaining a place. A good Educational Consultant will usually start by "interviewing" you to better understand what schools might be a good match. The Educational Consultant will usually arrange for you to receive school prospectuses. Additionally, he or she will typically arrange for visits to the school, possibly accompanying you on the visits, and then assisting you through the admissions process. However, a good Educational Consultant will not tell you which school to choose – that is a very personal choice.

Below are some Educational Consultants that Junior League of London members have utilised.

Humphrys Education Limited; Suite 203, 258 Belsize Road, NW6 4BT; 020 7625 4883, www.humphrys-education.com.

Martin Humphrys, the Managing Director, has been a teacher, housemaster, athletics coach, and the general manager for the University of Westminster Union in the UK. Additionally, he has advised the U.S. State Dept and various other Associations and Agencies on the position of schools within the UK.

Bowker Consulting Ltd; Gill Bowker, Suite 38, 500 Avebury Boulevard, Milton Keynes, MK9 2BE; 019 0854 7950; www.bowker.org.uk.

Gill Bowker has over 22 years of teaching experience, dealing with children ranging from five to sixteen. She also has experience teaching children with specific learning difficulties and was the Head of Middle School in a large International School.

Childtrack UK; Suite 61, 22 Nottinghill Gate, W11 3JE; 077 1158 1919; www.childtrackuk.com.

Most of Childtrack's referrals come from HR Departments of companies that transfer employees into London on a routine basis. Childtrack staff are trained and experienced teachers.

School Choice International, Inc.; 1600 Harrison Avenue, Suite 208, Mamaroneck, NY 10543, USA; 001 914 381 1788; www.schoolchoiceintl. com or email info@schoolchoiceintl.com.

Liz Perlstein, the President, has been a teacher, a primary school administrator, a university administrator and a board of education trustee. She lived in England for three years, during which time she visited numerous British schools and guided many families through the school selection process.

The Good Schools Guide Advisory Service; 3 Craven Mews, SW11 5PW; 020 7801 0191; www.goodschoolsguide.co.uk or email on editor@goodschools guide.co.uk.

A consultancy run by **The Good Schools Guide®** to advise parents, on a one-to-one basis, on choosing the best schools for their children.

DECIPHERING THE BRITISH SCHOOL SYSTEM

The school system in the U.K. can be confusing. The independent (or privately run) school system in particular, has no standard age at which nursery, junior or senior schools begin and end.

In general, nursery schools take children between the ages of 2 ½ and 5 years; junior schools will take children from age 5 - 11 or 13 and senior school begins at age 11 for girls and age 13 for boys.

State schools are a bit more straight forward. There is pre-school (for the under 5's), primary school (aged 5 – 11 or 13) and secondary school (until graduation at age 18).

ENGLISH SCHOOLS

Junior League of London members know a number of private or independent English schools. The schools have been divided into the following groups: nursery, junior / pre-prep schools and senior / preparatory schools.

Our list is by no means exhaustive; there are many more good schools than are listed here. These are simply schools recommended by at least one of our members.

Age and Grade Equivalents

The following chart may be helpful as you enquire about British Schools.

Age (in years) - Beginning of School Year	English Year	English Independent School System Level	English State School Level	American Grade	American School Level
4	Reception	Pre-Prep	Pre-School	Pre-Kindergarten	Pre-School
5	Year 1	Pre-Prep	Primary or Infant's School	Kindergarten	Elementary
6	Year 2	Pre-Prep	Primary or Infant's School	First Grade	Elementary
7	Year 3	Pre-Prep or Prep Depending on School	Primary or Junior's School	Second Grade	Elementary
8	Year 4	Pre-Prep or Prep Depending on School	Primary or Junior's School	Third Grade	Elementary
9	Year 5	Prep	Primary or Junior's School	Fourth Grade	Elementary or Middle Depending on School
10	Year 6	Prep	Primary or Junior's School	Fifth Grade	Elementary or Middle Depending on School
11	Year 7	Prep for boys, Senior for girls	Secondary School	Sixth Grade	Elementary or Middle Depending on School
12	Year 8	Prep for boys, Senior for girls	Secondary School	Seventh Grade	Elementary or Middle Depending on School
13	Year 9	Senior	Secondary School	Eighth Grade	Elementary or Middle Depending on School
14	Year 10, First year of GCSE	Senior	Secondary School	Ninth Grade	High School
15	Year 11, Second year of GCSE	Senior	Secondary School	Tenth Grade	High School
16	Year 12, First year of A Levels	Senior	Sixth Form College	Eleventh Grade	High School
17	Year 13, Second Year of A Levels	Senior	Sixth Form College	Twelfth Grade	High School

Nursery Schools in London (Boys and Girls)

Note that in many cases, it is wise to register a child for nursery school as soon as possible, even at birth. Unless otherwise noted, each school accepts children from the ages of 2 ½ to 5 years.

The following schools are for boys and girls under the age of five.

Acorn Nursery School; 2 Lansdowne Crescent, London W11 2NH; 020 7727 2122.

Asquith Nurseries; West Hampstead, 11 Woodchurch Rd, NW6; 020 7328 4787. (Ages 3 mos to 5 years).

The Boltons Nursery School; 262b, Fulham Rd, SW10; 020 7351 6993.
Broadhurst School; 19 Greencroft Gardens, NW6; 020 7328 4280.

The Chelsea Kindergarten; St. Andrew's Church Hall, Park Walk, SW10; 020 7352 4856.

Chelsea Open Air Nursery School; 51Glebe Place, SW3, 020 7352 8374. (Ages 3 to 5).

Eaton Square Nursery and Preparatory School; 79 Eccleston Square, SW1V, 020 7931 9469; www.eatonsquareschool.com. (Ages 2½ to 13)

Falkner House; 19 Brechin Place, SW7; 020 7373 4501; www.falknerhouse.co.uk. (Girls, ages 3 to 5).

 Garden House School; Turks Row, SW3; 020 7730 1652; www.gardenhouseschool.co.uk. (Ages 3 to 11).

Great Beginnings Montessori Nursery School; 37-39 Brendon Street, W1; 020 7258 1066. (Ages 2 to 6).

The Hampshire Schools; 63 Ennismore Gardens, SW7; 020 7584 3297. (Ages 3 to 5).

Hampstead Hill School; 53 Courthope Rd, NW3; 020 7482 0721.

 Holland Park Nursery School; The Undercroft, St. John's Church, Landsdown Crescent, W11; 020 7221 2194.

The Knightsbridge Kindergarten; St. Peter's Church, 119 Eaton Square, SW1; 020 7371 2306. (Ages 2 to 5).

Ladbroke Square Montessori School; 43 Ladbroke Square, W11; 020 7229 0125. (Ages 2½ to 5½).

The Maria Montessori School Hampstead; 26 Lyndhurst Gardens, NW3; 020 7435 3646. (Ages 2½ to 12). There are branches in Nottinghill, Bayswater and West Hampstead.

Minor's Nursery; 10 Pembridge Square, W2; 020 7727 7253. (Ages 2½ to 4½).

Miss Morley's Nursery School; Fountain Court Club Room, Ebury Square, SW1; 020 7730 5797. (Ages 2 to 5).

 Miss Willcocks Nursery School; Holy Trinity Church Hall, Prince Consort Road, SW7; 020 7937 2027.

North Bridge House; 33 Fitzjohn's Avenue, NW3; 020 7435 9641.

Oaktree Nursery; 6 Arkwright Rd, NW3; 020 7435 1916. (Starts at 2½. At pre-reception children join the Devonshire House School).

Paint Pots Montessori School; Chelsea Christian Centre, Edith Grove, SW10; 020 7376 5780. (Ages 18 mos to 8 years).

The Phoenix School; 36 College Crescent, NW3; 020 7722 4433. (Ages 3 to 7).

Rainbow Montessori School; 13 Woodchurch Road, NW6; 020 7328 8986.

Ravenstonehouse; 22 Queensbury Place, SW7, 020 7584 7955; www.ravenstonehouse.co.uk. (Ages 1 to 3).

Ravenstonehouse; Hyde Park, Albion Street, St Georges Fields; 020 7262 1190; www.ravenstonehouse.co.uk. (Ages 2 mos to 7 years).

Ringrose Kindergarten; 32a Lupus St, SW1; 020 7976 6511.

Ringrose Kindergarten (Chelsea); St. Lukes Church Hall, St. Lukes St, SW3; 020 7352 8784.

Rolfe's Montessori Nursery School; 206-208 Kensington Park Road, W11; 020 7727 8300.

St. Christina's School; 25 St. Edmund's Terrace, NW8; 020 7722 8784. (Boys, ages 3 to 7; girls, ages 3 to 11).

St. John's Wood Pre-Preparatory School; St. John's Hall, St. John's Wood High St, NW8; 020 7722 7149. (Ages 3 to 7).

Thomas's Kindergarten; 14 Ranelagh Grove, SW1; 020 7730 3596 and The Crypt, St. Mary's Church, Battersea Church Road, SW11; 020 7738 0400; www.thomas-s.co.uk.

Strawberry Fields Nursery School; 5, Pembridge Villas, W11;
020 7727 8363.

Toddlers Inn; Cicely Davis Hall; Cochrane St., NW8; 020 7586 0520.
(Ages 2 to 5).

Young England Kindergarten; St. Saviour's Hall, St. George's Square,
SW1; 020 7834 3171.

Boys' Junior and Preparatory Schools
Arnold House; 1-3 Loudoun Road, NW8; 020 7266 4840;
www.arnoldhouse.co.uk. (Ages 5 to 13).

Colet Court (St. Paul's Preparatory School); Lonsdale Road, SW13,
020 8748 3461; www.stpaulsschool.org.uk. (Ages 7 / 8 to 13).

Dulwich College Junior School; Dulwich Common, SE21;
www.dulwich.org.uk.

Eaton House Belgravia; 3-5 Eaton Gate, Eaton Square, SW1,
020 7730 9343; www.eatonhouseschools.com. (Ages 4 to 8).

Eaton Housel; The Manor; 58 Clapham Common Northside, SW4,
020 7924 6000; www.eatonhouseschools.com. (Boys, ages 8 to 13; also
pre-prep for boys and girls, ages 4 to 8).

The Falcons Pre-Preparatory School; 2 Burnaby Gardens, Chiswick, W4;
020 8747 8393. (Ages 3 to 8).

The Hall; 23 Crossfield Road, NW3; 020 7722 1700. (Boys, ages 5 to 13).

Hawkesdown House School; 27 Edge St, W8; 020 7727 9090;
www.hawkesdown.co.uk. (Ages 3 to 8).

Lyndhurst House School; 24, Lyndhurst Gardens, NW3; 020 7435 493; www.lyndhursthouse.co.uk. (Ages 6 to 13).

St Anthony's Preparatory School; 90 Fitzjohns Ave, NW3; 020 7431 1066. (Ages 5 to 13).

St. Philip's School; 6 Wetherby Place, SW7; 020 7373 3944. (Ages 7 to 13).

University College School Junior School; 11 Holly Hill, NW3; 020 7435 3068; www.ucs.squareeye.com. (Ages 7 to 11).

Sussex House; 68 Cadogan Square, SW1; 020 7584 1741. (Ages 8 to 13).

Wimbledon College Prep; Edge Hill, SW19; 020 8946 2533. (Ages 11 to 18).

Westminster Under School; Adrian House, 27 Vincent Square, SW1; 020 7821 5788; www.westimister.org.uk. (Ages 8 to 13).

Wetherby School; 11 Pembridge Square, W2; 020 7727 9581; www.wetherbyschool.org.uk. (Ages 4 to 8).

Boys' Senior Schools

The following schools are for boys aged 13 to 18 unless noted otherwise.

City of London School; Queen Victoria Street, EC4; 020 7489 0291; www.clsb.org. (Ages 10 to 18).

Dulwich College; Dulwich Common, SE21; 020 8693 3601; www.dulwich.org.uk. (Ages 7-18).

King's College School (Wimbledon); Wimbledon Common, SW19; 020 8255 5300; www.kcs.org.uk.

St. Paul's School; Lonsdale Road, SW13; 020 8748 9162;
www.stpaulsschool.org.uk.

University College School (UCS); Frognal, Hampstead, NW3;
020 7435 2215; www.ucs.squareeye.com. (Ages 11 to 18).

Westminster School; Little Dean's Yard, SW1; 020 7963 1003;
www.westminster.org.uk.

Wimbledon College; Edge Hill, SW19; 020 8946 2533;
www.wimbledoncollege.org.uk. (Ages 11 to 18).

BOARDING SCHOOLS FOR BOYS

The following boarding schools are affiliated with the Church of England:
Charterhouse; Godalming, Surrey, GU7; 014 8329 1501;
www.charterhouse.org.uk.

Eton College; Windsor, Berkshire, SL4; 017 5367 1249;
www.etoncollege.com.

Harrow School; 1 High Street, Harrow on the Hill, Middlesex, HA1;
020 8872 8007; www.harrowschoolorg.net.

Marlborough College; Wilshire, SN8; 016 7289 2300;
www.marlboroughcollege.org.

Millfield; Edgarley Hall, Glastonbury, Somerset, BA6; 014 5883 2446;
www.millfieldprep.com.

Radley; Abingdon, Oxford, OX14; 012 3554 3000; www.radley.org.uk.

Winchester College; College Street, Winchester, Hampshire, SO23;
019 6262 1247; www.winchestercollege.org.

For information on boys boarding schools administered by the Roman Catholic Church, contact: **Catholic Education Service for England and Wales**; 39 Eccleston Square, SW1; 020 7828 7604; www.cesew.org.uk.

Girls' Junior and Preparatory Schools

Bute House Preparatory School for Girls; Bute House, Luxemburg Gardens, W6; 020 7603 7381. (Ages 4 to 11).

Cavendish School; 179 Arlington Road, NW1; 020 7485 1958. (Ages 3 to 11).

Channing School; Fairseat, the Junior School, Highgate, N6; 020 8340 2328; www.channing.co.uk. (Ages 4 to 11).

City of London School for Girls; Barbican, EC2Y; 020 7628 0841; www.clsg.org.uk. (Ages 7 to 18).

Falkner House; 19 Brechin Place, SW7; 020 7373 4501. (Ages 4 to 11).

Francis Holland (Sloane Square); 39 Graham Terrace, SW1; 020 7730 2971. (Ages 4 to 18).

Glendower Preparatory School; 87 Queen's Gate, SW7; 020 7370 1927. (Ages 4 to 11).

James Allen's Girls' School (JAGS); East Dulwich Grove, SE22; 020 8693 1181. (Ages 4 to 19).

Kensington Preparatory School; 596 Fulham Road, SW6; 020 7731 9300. (Ages 4 to 11).

Notting Hill and Ealing High School; 2 Cleveland Road, W13; 020 8799 8400. (Ages 5 to 18).

Pembridge Hall School; 18 Pembridge Square, W2; 020 7229 0121.
(Ages 4½ to 11).

Putney High School; 35 Putney Hill, SW15; 020 8788 4886. (Ages 4 to 18).

Queen's College Preparatory School; 61 Portland Place, W1; 020 7291 0660. (Ages 3 ½-11).

Queen's Gate School; 131-133 Queen's Gate, SW7; 020 7589 3587. (Ages 4 to 18).

Royal School Hampstead; 65 Rosslyn Hill, NW3; 020 7794 7708. (Ages 3 to 18).

South Hampstead High School; 3 Maresfield Gardens, NW3; 020 7435 2899. (Ages 4 to 18).

Sarum Hall; 15 Eton Avenue, NW3; 020 7794 2261. (Ages 3 to 11).

St. Christopher's School; 32 Belsize Lane, NW3; 020 7435 1521. (Ages 4 to 11).

St. Margaret's School; 18 Kidderpore Gardens, NW3; 020 7435 2439. (Ages 4 to 16).

The Study Preparatory School; Wilberforce House, Camp Road, Wimbledon Common, SW19; 020 8947 6969; www.thestudyprep.co.uk. (Ages 4 to 11).

Tower House Preparatory School; 188 Sheen Lane, SW14; 020 8876 3323; www.towerhouse.richmond.sch.uk. (Ages 4 to 13).

Ursuline Convent Preparatory School; 18 The Downs, SW20;
020 8947 0859. (Ages 3 to 12).

Wimbledon High School; Mansel Road, SW19; 020 8971 0900.
(Ages 4 to 19).

Girls' Senior Schools

All schools accept girls from age 11 unless otherwise noted.
Channing School; Highgate, N6; 020 8340 2328; www.channing.co.uk.

City of London School for Girls; Barbican, EC2Y; 020 7628 0841;
www.clsg.org.uk.

Francis Holland; (Regents Park), Clarence Gate, NW1; 020 7723 0176;
www.francisholland.org.

The Godolphin and Latymer School; Iffley Road, W6; 020 8741 1936;
www.godolphinandlatymer.com.

James Allen's Girls' School (JAGS); East Dulwich Grove, SE22;
020 8693 1181. (Ages 4 to 19).

More House School; 22--24 Pont Street, SW1X; 020 7235 2855.

North London Collegiate School; Canons, Edgware, Middlesex, HA8;
020 8952 0912; www.nlcs.org.uk. (Ages 4 to 18).

Putney High School; 35 Putney Hill, SW15; 020 8788 4886.

Royal School Hampstead; 65 Rosslyn Hill, NW3; 020 7794 7708.
(Ages 3 to 18).

Queen's Gate School; 131-133 Queen's Gate, SW7; 020 7589 3587.

South Hampstead High School; 3 Maresfield Gardens, NW3;
020 7435 2899.

St. Paul's Girls' School; Brook Green, W6; 020 7603 2288; www.spgs.org.

Westminster School; Little Dean's Yard, SW1; 020 7963 1003.
(Girls accepted in Sixth Form).

Wimbledon High School; Mansel Road, SW19; 020 8971 0900.
(Ages 4 to 19).

Boarding Schools for Girls

The following boarding schools are affiliated with the Church of England:
Benenden School; Cranbrook, Kent, TN17 4AA; 015 8024 0592.

Heathfield School; London Road, Ascot, Berkshire, SL5; 013 4489 8342;
www.heathfieldschool.net.

St. Mary's School (Calne); Calne, Wiltshire, SN11; 012 4985 7200;
www.stmarycalne.org.

Cheltenham Ladies College; Bayshill Road, Cheltenham,
Glouchestershire, GL50; www.cheltladies.org.

Roedean School; Roedean Way, Brighton, BN2; 012 7366 7500;
www.roedean.co.uk.

St. Mary's School (Wantage); Newbury Street, Wantage, Oxfordshire,
OX12; 012 3577 3800.

Wycombe Abbey; Highwycombe, Buckinghamshire, HP11,
014 9452 0381; www.wycombeabbey.com.

Boarding Schools for Girls

The following boarding schools are affiliated with the Roman Catholic church:

Marymount International School; George Road, Kingston-upon-Thames, KT2; 020 8949 0571; www.marymount.kingston.sch.uk.

St. Mary's School (Ascot); Ascot, Berkshire, SL5; 013 4462 3721; www.st-marys-ascot.co.uk.

Woldingham School; Marden Park, Woldingham, Surrey, CR3; 018 8334 9431; www.woldinghamdschool.co.uk.

For additional information on girls' boarding schools administered by the Roman Catholic Church, contact: Catholic Education Service for England and Wales; 39 Eccleston Square, SW1; 020 7828 7604; www.cesew.org.uk.

Co-Educational Schools

Abercorn School; 28 Abercorn Place, NW8; 020 7286 4785. (Ages 2 to 13).

Belmont School; The Ridgeway, Mill Hill Village, NW7; 020 8959 1431. (Ages 7 to 13).

Cameron House; 4 The Vale, SW3; 020 7352 4040. (Ages 4½ to 11, 100 pupils).

Devonshire House Preparatory School; 69 Fitzjohn's Avenue, NW3; 020 7435 1916; www.devonshirehouseschool.co.uk. (Ages 2-13).

Finton House School; 171 Trinity Road, SW17; 020 8682 0921. (Ages 4 to 11).

Eaton Square School; 79 Eccleston Square, SW1; 020 7931 9469; www.eatonsquareschool.com. (Ages 2 to 13).

Eridge House School; 1 Fulham Park Road, SW6; 020 7371 9009. (Ages 2 to 11).

Emanuel School; Battersea Rise, SW11; 020 8870 4171. (Ages 10 to 18).

Garden House School; Turks Row, SW1; 020 7589 7708; www.gardenhouseschool.co.uk. (Ages 3 to 11).

The Hampshire Schools; Knightsbridge Upper School, 63 Ennismore Gardens, SW7; 020 7584 3297. (Ages 4 to 13).

Hampstead Hill School; St. Stephen's Hall, Pond Street, NW3; 020 7435 6262. (Ages 2 to 9).

The Hall School Wimbledon; 17 The Downs, SW20; 020 8879 9200; www.hsw.co.uk. (Ages 11 to 16).

The Harrodian School; Lonsdale Road, SW13; 020 8748 6117. (Ages 4 to 18).

Highgate School; 3 Bishopswood Road, N6; 020 8340 9193; www.highgateschoo.org.uk. (Ages 3 to18).

Hill House International Junior School; 17 Hans Place, SW1; 020 7584 1331. (Ages 3 to 13).

Hurlingham School; 122 Putney Bridge Road, SW15; 020 8874 7186; www.hurlinghamschool.co.uk. (Ages 4 to 11).

Ibstock Place School; Clarence Lane, SW15; 020 8876 9991. (Ages 3 to 18).

Lion House School; Old Methodist Hall, Gwendolen Avenue, SW15; 020 8780 9446. (Ages 2 to 18).

Newton Preparatory School; 149 Battersea Park Road, SW8; 020 7720 4091. (Ages 3 to 13).

Norland Place School; 162-166 Holland Park Avenue, W11; 020 7603 9103. (Ages 4 to 11).

North Bridge House School; 1 Gloucester Avenue, NW1; 020 7267 2542; www.northbridgehouse.com. (Ages 4 to 18).

Notting Hill Preparatory School; 95 Lancaster Road, W11; 020 7221 0727; www.nottinghillprep.com. (Ages 5 to 13).

Portland Place School; 56-58 Portland Place, W1; 020 7307 8700; www.portland-place.co.uk. (Ages 11 to 18).

Prospect House School; 75 Putney Hill, SW15; 020 8780 0456. (Ages 3 to 11).

Ravenscourt Park Preparatory School; 16 Ravenscourt Avenue, Ravenscourt Park, W6; 020 8846 9153. (Ages 4 to 11).

Redcliffe School; 47 Redcliffe Gardens, SW10; 020 7352 9247. (Ages 3 to 11).

The Roche School; 11 Frogmore, SW18; 020 8877 0823; www.therocheschool.co.uk. (Ages 2 to 11).

St. Christina's School; 25 St. Edmund's Terrace, NW8, 020 7722 8784. (Boys 3 to 7, girls 3 to 11).

St. Joseph's Roman Catholic Primary School; Highgate Hill, N19; 020 7272 2320.

Thomas's Preparatory School; 28-40 Battersea High Street, SW11, 020 7978 4224; www.thomas-s.co.uk. (Ages 4½ to 13). Also locations in Kensington; 020 7938 1931 and in Clapham; 020 7924 5006. (Ages 4½ to 11).

The Vale School; 2 Elvaston Place, SW7; 020 7584 9515. (Ages 4 to 11).

More and more boys' schools are taking in girls at sixth form and lower. Please consult the publications listed earlier in this chapter for up-to-date information.

INTERNATIONAL, NATIONAL AND AMERICAN SCHOOLS

There are a number of international schools in the London area that cater specifically to expatriate children. These schools are experienced in working with students and families making an international transition. While they all class themselves as international schools, some do specialise in a national curriculum, while others offer a much more international curriculum; many increasingly adopting the International Baccalaureate (IB) standards. Some of the schools provide education for students of specific nationalities with classes taught in their native tongue.

For information on all schools part of the **London International Schools Association**, LISA, visit the LISA website, www.lisa.org.uk.

THE INTERNATIONAL BACCALAUREATE, IB

The IB is commonly known for its Diploma Programme for 16 to 18 yrs (or the last two years of American High School). The IB Diploma is the only such certification recognised by universities internationally; in fact, it is not only accepted, but highly regarded as a rigorous programme by universities in over 120 countries, including the U.S., Canada and the UK. Often universities will offer university credit for competent completion of specific IB courses. The IB Diploma is increasingly offered in many top-performing High Schools in the U.S. and Canada, with students taking IB courses to fulfil requirements for their High School Diploma. A number of International and American Schools in London offer the IB Diploma alongside the American High School Diploma.

The IB Programme also includes the less well-known Middle Years Programme (MYP), for students in grades six through ten, and Primary Years Programme (PYP), for students in grades pre-kindergarten through five. Like the Diploma Programme, the MYP and PYP are increasingly offered in American, Canadian and International Schools around the world, making it very easy for children to transition from one IB school to another.

For more information on the IB, visit their website at www.ibo.org.

International Schools (Boarding and Day)

The following schools offer an international environment for students from all over the world.

The American School in London (ASL); 2-8 Loudoun Road, NW8; 020 74491200; www.asl.org. Co-educational day school, ages 4 to 18, 1200 pupils.

The oldest American School in London with a large modern campus. High percentage of American students.

ACS International Schools; www.acs-england.co.uk.

Three campuses in London (below). The schools are approximately 50 per cent American. The other 50 per cent represent more than 60 different nationalities.

ACS Cobham; "Heywood", Portsmouth Road, Cobham, Surrey, KT11; 019 3286 7251.

Co-educational boarding and day school, ages 3 to 19, 1,350 pupils. A 120-acre campus offering state of the art sports facilities. The IB Diploma is offered in 11th and 12th grade. Limited EAL support is offered in 8th grade through 12th grade.

ACS Egham; "Woodlee", London Road (A30), Egham, Surrey, TW20 0HS; 017 8443 0611. Offers the IB Diploma, MYP and PYP.

ACS Hillingdon; "Hillingdon Court", 108 Vine Lane, Hillingdon, Uxbridge, Middlesex, UB10 OBE; 018 9581 8402.

Co-educational day school, ages 3 to 19, 600 pupils. Set on an elegant country estate with modern facilities, offers bus service from Central London.

International Community School; 4 York Terrace East, NW1; 020 7935 1206.

A small school with over 65 nationalities that has a strong English Language and Special Needs department. Ages 4 to 18.

International School of London; 139 Gunnersbury Avenue, W3; 020 8992 5823.

Co-educational day school, ages 4 to 18, 220 pupils. Offers the International Baccalaureate PYP, MYP and Diploma Programmes.

Marymount International School; George Road, Kingston-upon Thames, Surrey, KT2; 020 8949 0571.

Girls only, day and boarding, ages 11 to 18, 340 girls. Offers International Baccalaureate in addition to American curriculum.

Southbank International School; 020 7229 8230; www.southbank.org.

Co-educational day school, ages 4 to 18, 250 pupils. Approximately 30% of the pupils are American. Offers the IB Diploma, MYP and PYP. Has three campuses.

Southbank Hampstead; 16 Netherhall Gardens, NW3; 020 7431 1200. (Ages 3 – 14).

Southbank Kensington; 36-38 Kensington Park Rd, W11; 020 7229 8230. (Ages 3-11).

Southbank Westminster; 63-65 Portland Place, W1; 020 7436 9699.

(Ages 11-18).

The TASIS England American School; Coldharbour Lane, Thorpe, Surrey, TW20, 019 3256 5252; www.tasis.com.

Co-educational boarding and day, ages 4 to 18, 880 pupils. Large percentage of the students are American. Offers the IB Diploma.

Woodside Park International School; 88 Woodside Park Rd, N12; 020 8920 0600; www.wpis.org.

Small school offering the IB Diploma, MYP and PYP.

French

Ecole Francaise Jacques Prevert; 59 Brook Green, W6, 020 7602 6871; www.ecoleprevert.org.uk.

Co-educational school. (Ages 4 to 10).

Lycée Francais Charles de Gaulle; 35 Cromwell Road, SW7, 020 7584 6322; www.lyceefrancais.org.uk.

Co-educational day school. (Ages 4 to 18).

German

The German School; Douglas House, Petersham Road, Richmond, Surrey, TW10; 020 8940 2510.

Co-educationall day school. German curriculum. (Ages 5 – 19).

Greek

Hellenic College of London; 67 Pont Street, SW1; 020 7581 5044; www.hellenic.org.uk.

Co-educational day school. (Ages 2 to 16).

Japanese

The Japanese School; 87 Creffield Road, Acton, W3; 020 8993 7145.

Co-educational day school. (Ages 6 to 15).

Norwegian

The Norwegian School; 28 Arterberry Road, Wimbledon, SW20;
020 8947 6617.

Co-educational day school. (Ages 3 to 16).

Swedish

Swedish School in London; 82 Lonsdale Road, SW13; 020 8741 1751.

Co-educational day school. (Ages 3½ to 16).

LEARNING DIFFICULTIES OR SPECIAL NEEDS

A limited number of schools offer learning support within a mainstream
environment in the London area; typically, only the American and
International Schools, and even they only support mild learning difficulties.
More common are schools designed specifically for students with learning
difficulties or special needs.

An Educational Consultant is often invaluable when Learning Support
or Special Needs services are required, as most are experienced in finding
placements for students requiring additional support, have contacts at the
various schools and a good knowledge of the level of support each can offer,
whether an Independent, State, or American/International School.

If one is considering a State School, the student will need to be
"Statemented." A Statement is very much like an Individual Education Plan
(IEP) and is, simply put, a statement of the child's needs. While a student
can only be "Statemented" with an address in the UK, Educational
Consultants can sometimes help find placements for children on a
provisional basis until a Statement has been completed.

It is advisable to phone any potential Independent Schools before visiting
and sending in an application, to discuss the school's curriculum and your
child's needs. It is often helpful to speak with the Registrar and Head at an
English School or the Director of Admissions at American or International
Schools.

Whether speaking to a School or an Educational Consultant, it is essential
you share all information about your child and the type of support the child

currently receives. Withholding information can easily result in a student either not being accepted or, even worse, being asked to leave a school. Both are very difficult situations for families.

As a final note, while the type of learning support in the London area may be quite different to what one is used to, it does not mean that quality is compromised. One will find most programs offer a caring environment where students are supported by current and up-to-date methodology.

Publications

John Catt's, *Which School for Special Needs*, published and updated annually. Can be purchased from the John Catt's website: www.schoolsearch. co.uk.

Some schools offering Specialised Learning Support are:

Blossom House; 8 The Drive, Wimbledon, SW20 8TG; 020 8946 7348; www.blossomhouseschool.co.uk. (Ages 3-11 years).

Specialises in speech and language problems and associated difficulties such as fine motor problems or poor organizational skills.

Center Academy; 92 St John's Hill, Battersea, SW11 1HS; 020 7738 2344; www.centeracademy.com . (Ages 8-18 years).

Provides both British and American Curriculums. Full evaluation, testing and counselling services. Additional programmes held after school and on Saturday mornings. Over 23 years of expertise of working with Dyslexia + ADD in the UK.

The Dominie; Mandeville Courtyard, 142 Battersea Park Road, SW11; 020 7720 8783.

A co-educational day school for dyslexic and dyspraxic children for children aged 6 to 13.

Fairley House School; 30 Causton Street, SW1P 4AU; 020 7976 5456. (Ages 6 to 12).

Caters for Special learning difficulties (dyslexia and dyspraxia). This can include problems with receptive and expressive language, with information processing, with auditory and visual recall and with fine and gross motor control.

Hornsby International Dyslexia Centre; Glenshee Lodge, 261 Trinity Road, SW18 3SN. Assessment services: 020 8874 1844, distance Learning courses: 020 8877 3539, attendance training courses: 020 8673 5769. Fax: 020 8877 9737. Also lectures, workshops and seminars.

The Moat School; Bishop's Avenue, SW6 6ED; 020 7610 9018; www.moatschool.org.uk. (Ages 11-16).
Whole school approach for pupils with specific learning difficulties. Structured and individual programmes.

Swiss Cottage School; 80 Avenue Road, NW8; 020 7681 8080.
State maintained school for physically disabled children, ages 2 to 16.

For additional information on other dyslexia centres:
The British Dyslexia Association; 98 London Road, Reading, Berkshire, RG1 5AU; 011 8966 2677, Helpline: 011 8966 8271; www.bda-dyslexia.org.uk.

APPLYING TO AMERICAN UNIVERSITIES

If your child has attended English schools through 'A' level exams and wishes to attend an American university, few English schools will have prepared him/her for the required S.A.T. exams or be able to help him/her select the best university for his/her needs. A service available in London that might be of help is the **US-UK Educational Commission** (also known as the Fulbright Commission); Educational Advisory Service, Fulbright House, 62 Doughty Street, WC1N 2LS; 020 7404 6994 (open Monday 13:30 to 19:00 and Tuesday to Friday 10:30 to 16:00). Nearest tube: Russell Square. This organisation principally advises students concerning university study in the US. They hold an annual university day and have a comprehensive reference library of information on US colleges. Additionally, they supply information concerning American colleges in the UK. First time enquirers should send s.a.e. with a request for an information pack. Comprehensive library of US College catalogues are also available.

BRITISH, INTERNATIONAL OR AMERICAN?

What school system is right for you? After much debate, we decided that the best way to convey the differences was to ask two parents to express their own, personal feelings on the subject; one whose children are in an American school and one whose children are in an English school. We hope that their views will prove helpful.

The American School System

For those living in London, there are some fine American schools in the area. If your children have started in the American system, or if they plan to return to it, it may be preferable for them to continue in the American tradition. There are major curriculum differences between the American and English systems resulting in adjustments for the children when they come to London and again when they leave. The American schools eliminate this problem since they strictly adhere to the school programme in the United States as well as the calendar year.

The turnover in the American schools is about one-third each year, about the same as the turnover of Americans living in London. The advantage of this is that a child entering the school for the first time does not feel 'new' as there are many others in the same situation. A disadvantage is that a child may have to say goodbye to some of his friends. American schools are very aware of the adjustments the children are required to make and the social programmes provided at the schools reflect an understanding of this problem.

As is the case in public schools in the United States, self- expression and creativity are encouraged in American schools overseas.

A high school student who is planning to return to the States for college will be able to take the necessary tests and receive college guidance.

American schools have a high percentage of Americans attending but many nationalities are represented. Consequently, there is a deeper learning adventure through shared experiences of classmates who have lived all over the world.

The English School System

The English school system is a traditional one and justifiably famous for its strong discipline and emphasis on the basics of education; reading, writing and maths. Proper education begins at an early age, children begin reading at four and learning French, and sometimes Latin, well before secondary school. A highly structured approach is standard, which might strike some as a bit stifling, but one can be assured that the child will be well equipped for handling work that is more complex later.

In and around London, there are numerous fine English schools; some large, some small, and each has its own philosophy. One can choose a school that is predominantly English or one that caters to the needs of the international community. Some are emphatically academic; some offer a well-rounded curriculum with excellent programmes in sports and/or music. Some schools are co-educational, but many of the finest schools remain single-sex schools.

Most English schools require students to wear a uniform. While this may seem costly initially, the outfits are usually sturdy and practical. Uniforms also ensure that your child will be reasonably well 'turned out' and eliminate all competition to be 'best dressed'. Most mothers love uniforms.

Perhaps the most intangible advantage of sending your child to an English school is that of having a decidedly English experience. Your child will participate in English life and have English friends. You, as parents, will have greater exposure to English families and to 'local' life. Your child may develop exemplary manners, learn to keep a stiff upper lip in difficult situations and speak with an English accent, but most importantly, your child (and you) will gain invaluable experience of the life and culture of the community in which you live.

Cooking, Food and Drink

CONTENTS

The best way to approach cooking in a foreign country is to focus on all the marvellous new tastes and new ingredients available and not on the few ingredients that cannot be easily or inexpensively obtained. The British weigh their ingredients, so purchasing an inexpensive kitchen scale will simplify cooking with British recipes.

The British are well known for many things, but food was never high on the list. Modern British cooking, however, has changed that unpopular perception. Purchase any one of the excellent cookbooks by modern British cooks, such as Nigella Lawson, Jamie Oliver or the River Café, and you will be pleasantly surprised. Reliable classics include *Delia Smith's Cookery Course* or *Mary Berry's Complete Cookbook*.

Many British recipes list ingredients in both imperial and metric measurements. If you are not used to these measurements, a calculator may be one of your most important cooking tools. British ovens are often smaller than you may be used to so make sure that your pans fit the oven before you start!

MEASUREMENT CONVERSIONS

Liquid Measures		
	UK (Imperial / Metric)	US Imperial
Teaspoon	5 ml	1/6 oz
Dessertspoon	10 ml	1/3 oz
Tablespoon	15 ml	½ oz
Gill	150 ml	5 oz
Cup	10 oz / 290 ml	8 oz / 250 ml
Pint	20 oz / 585 ml	16 oz / 470 ml

Dry Measures			
	UK Imperial	UK Metric	US Imperial
Flour	5 oz	140 g	1 cup
Sugar	1 oz	25 g	2 tbsp
	8 oz	225 g	1 cup
Brown sugar	6 oz	170 g	1 cup
Breadcrumbs or nuts	4 oz	115 g	1 cup
Yeast	1/4 oz	7 g	2 ½ tsp
Butter	1 oz	25 g	2 tbsp
	8 oz	225 g	1 cup
	4 oz	100 g	1 stick (8 tbsp)

When measuring dry ingredients such as flour or sugar for a British recipe, remember to weigh the items as the ingredients will be listed in ounces or grams. (Remember, eight ounces of two different ingredients may have distinctly different volumes.)

Once you start saving British recipes from magazines and newspapers, having a set of British measuring utensils and a scale on hand will make cooking much less time consuming.

Further Conversions

Grams to Ounces	Multiply grams by 0.03527
Ounces to Grams	Multiply ounces by 28.35
Quarts to Litres	Multiply quarts by 0.95
Pounds to Grams	Multiply pounds by 453.6
Pounds to Kilograms	Multiply pounds by 0.4536
Kilograms to Pounds	Multiply kilograms by 2.205
Stones to Pounds	Multiply stones by 14
Centigrade to Fahrenheit	Multiply C by 1.8 and add 32
Fahrenheit to Centigrade	Multiply F by 5, subtract 32 and then divide by 9

Cooking Temperatures

Celsius	Fahrenheit	Gas Mark	Description
110	225	1/4	Very slow
125	250	1/2	Very slow
140	275	1	Slow
150	300	2	Slow
165	325	3	Moderate
180	350	4	Moderate
190	375	5	Moderate / Hot
200	400	6	Moderate / Hot
220	425	7	Hot
230	450	8	Hot
240	475	9	Very hot

For fan-assisted ovens you should either turn the heat down slightly or decrease the cooking time.

DRINKING WATER

The quality of tap water is regulated by EC and UK legislation. Bottled mineral water is not required to be as thoroughly and regularly tested as tap water, and are more likely to contain higher levels of bacteria. London tap water is very hard and some people may find it unpalatable. Water purifiers are a popular alternative to buying bottled water and range from small activated carbon filters attached to a jug to plumbed-in filter systems.

The evidence of hard water may be seen on the inside of your kettle, on showerheads and on other household appliances in the form of limescale. Limescale should be removed periodically with a commercial limescale remover (available at supermarkets) or by using a boiled mixture of one-half cup white vinegar and one-half cup water. Remember to rinse appliances well after they have been cleaned. It is always a good idea to empty a kettle after each use to avoid re-boiling water, which can concentrate the hardness. This practice is especially important when using boiled water to make baby formula.

For more information on the quality of your drinking water contact your local water authority (the address is on your water bill). In Central London: **Thames Water Utilities**; P.O. Box 436, Swindon, SN38; 016 4520 0800.

If you are interested in using bottled water from a company that rents water coolers and provides reusable bottles, look for a company that is a member of the **British Water Cooler Association (BWCA)**. One good option is **Culligan Water**; Culligan House, 73-74 Capitol Way, NW9; 0800 212 353; www.culligan.co.uk.

BAKING PRODUCTS

Flour

Plain Flour	A soft wheat flour. Used as a pastry flour and for thickening sauces and gravies.
Superfine Plain Flour	Light white flour used in British recipes for cakes with a delicate texture.
Self-raising Flour	Raising agent already included, requiring no

additional baking powder.

Strong Flour White flour of high gluten content for breads and puff pastry.

Malted Wheat Flour Brown flour with malted wheat grains for a distinctive texture and nutty flavour.

Wholemeal Flour Whole wheat flour for baking and breads.

Baking Powder

British baking powder is half the strength of that used in North America. If you are using an American recipe, remember to double the amount.

Yeast

Dry yeast in the UK is sold in 7 gram / 1/4 ounce sachets. To substitute dry yeast in a North American recipe, use only half the amount required.

Sugar

The British have several varieties of sugar, some of which are better to cook with than others. Here is a description of the most common types of sugar found in supermarkets:

Caster Sugar A finer granulated sugar that dissolves easily and is ideal for baking or desserts.

Demerara Sugar A coarse, crunchy, brown sugar. It is good in coffee or over cereals but is not a substitute for brown sugar in baking.

Icing Sugar Also known as confectioner's sugar.

Muscovado Sugar A soft, dark sugar used in cooking fruit cakes, baked bean casseroles and barbeque sauces.

Soft Light and Dark Brown Sugar	Used mainly in baking.

Vanilla Sugar	A white sugar flavoured with vanilla; primarily used in custards and puddings.

Gelatine

Gelatine (or gelatin) comes powdered and in packets called "sachets". Some specialty shops also sell gelatine in leaves which need to be dissolved in hot water. The amount of gelatine in sachets varies from brand to brand. As a guideline, 15 grams (1 tablespoon) should set 480 ml (16 oz) of liquid. The contents of one package of Knox Unflavoured Gelatine is the equivalent of 15 grams, 1 tablespoon or ½ ounce.

Did you know?...The American generic term derived from the brand name "Jello" is called "jelly" in the UK because it comes in a concentrated gel. It may not work as a substitute in North American recipes and other baking.

Flavoured gelatine called "*Quick Jel*" comes in sachets and is perfect for adding to fruit flans. It saves having to make a full quantity of jelly and sets much quicker.

Chocolate

Most cooking chocolate comes in one of three basic forms:

Bitter	A dark bittersweet chocolate used for rich icings and cakes and as a covering for sweets.

Plain	Similar to semi-sweet chocolate.

Cake Covering Chocolate	Chocolate icing or frosting.

DAIRY PRODUCTS

Milk

Milk can be purchased in supermarkets and grocers' shops or it can be delivered to your door in plastic containers or returnable glass bottles that are all one size: an Imperial pint (20 ounces). To arrange milk delivery in your area, check the **Yellow Pages**™ for your local dairy or see *Chapter 11: Services* for recommendations. All milk in the UK is pasteurised but not all types are homogenised, so check the label.

Cream

Cream in the UK has a higher fat content than in some other countries.

Half Cream	Used like American half and half.
Single Cream	18% butterfat, slightly thicker than half cream.
Double Cream	48% butterfat. Poured over fruits and desserts. If whipped too much, double cream turns to butter.
Sour Cream	18% butterfat.
Crème Fraiche	39% butterfat. Also comes in a half-fat version. Similar to sour cream but slightly thicker and less acidic.
Spooning Cream	30% butterfat. Not suitable for coffee or whipping. Spoon over fruit and desserts.
Whipping Cream	40% butter fat. Suitable for recipes that call for heavy or whipping cream.

Clotted Cream	A specialty from Devon and Cornwall. Very thick; used on fruits and desserts and on scones for "cream teas".
Fromage Frais	A lightly whipped, lower-fat equivalent of double cream that can be used when cooking. Fromage frais ("fresh cheese") is a good source of calcium and is often given as snacks to children.

Cheese

English cheeses range from Gloucester (pronounced GLAW-ster), which is mild, to Blue Stilton, which is blue-veined and has a strong, sharp flavour. In between those extremes, there is Lancashire (LANK-a-sheer) which grates easily and is good in cooking, and Leicester (LES-ter) which is similar to Cheddar. English, Scottish and Irish Cheddars are wonderful all-purpose cheeses that range from mild to mature. Danish Havarti can be substituted for Monterey Jack.

Butter and Margarine

Butter and margarine are widely available in several different varieties. Butter is supplied by different dairy regions in the UK, Ireland and Europe and the difference in taste is a matter of personal preference. Margarine made from 100% polyunsaturated fats is sold in grocery stores along with butter/margarine blends.

Eggs

Most eggs are brown and are not refrigerated in supermarkets. They do not need refrigeration because they are so fresh; the "use by" date stamped on each individual egg is the 21st day after the egg was laid. Both free-range and organic eggs are readily available.

TO MARKET, TO MARKET
Fruits and Vegetables

There is a wide and wonderful assortment of fresh fruits and vegetables available year round in Britain. You are likely to find a good selection at your local grocery store and market. With the increase in popularity of organic produce, you will find areas within larger stores dedicated to these products.

Beef

Most beef is English but "Scotch beef" is available at butchers and supermarkets for a higher price and is considered to be of better quality.

A roast, on or off the bone, is called a "joint". Ground beef is called "mince". Minced steak is the leanest. If you are accustomed to beef from corn-fed cattle, UK beef may taste slightly different as most UK cattle are grass-fed rather than corn-fed.

Steaks for grilling are available in several different cuts, the most common being sirloin, fillet (FILL-it), rib eye and rump. For a pot roast, look for topside, silverside or brisket cuts.

Lamb

British spring lamb is a real treat and unsurpassed for taste. A less expensive alternative is frozen New Zealand lamb. Lamb is available in chops, racks, cutlets, leg roasts and shoulders.

Pork

Pork roast as well as chops, tenderloin and spareribs (called American or Chinese spareribs) are all cuts that are easily found in supermarkets.

"Gammon" is one of the best and most expensive of hams. It is uncooked when purchased. York ham is also of high quality. A wide variety of bacon is available smoked or unsmoked. The most common bacon in the UK is "back bacon". Similar to Canadian bacon, it is larger and meatier than "streaky bacon", which is usually thinner and streaked with fat (similar to American bacon). UK sausages (especially breakfast sausages), tend to have a high cereal content, and come in many different flavours and varieties.

Poultry

A wide variety of poultry is available, including free-range chicken, local corn-fed chicken and French cord-fed chicken, (of which the most famous is from Bresse). In larger supermarkets, you can find turkey, duck and game birds (such as grouse and pheasant in season). If you prefer, ask for grain-fed, free-range or organic chickens.

Fish

Fish (usually cod, haddock or halibut) and chips is one meal that the British made famous. The availability of fresh local fish is never far away. Plaice, skate, brill, flounder, bass, bream, haddock and cod just to name a few!

The best quality of lemon sole and Dover sole can be purchased after April. Salmon, from Scotland and Ireland, is best in June, July and August.

> *Did you know?...When buying fresh fish, look for brightness, prominent eyes and red gills. The fishmonger will scale, clean and fillet a fish if asked.*

There is a large range of shellfish available from local fishmongers and specialist food halls, whilst more and more supermarkets now have their own fish and shellfish counters. Look for prawns, crabs, mussels, scallops, lobsters, oysters (in season), langoustines, cockles, whelks and winkles. You may find that most prawns are sold cooked because they are imported; raw prawns can be very expensive.

For a list of recommended delicatessens, butchers and fishmongers, see *Chapter 11: Services.*

Department and Specialty Stores

Department stores offer a large range of foods and products in their food halls. An international assortment can be found at **Harrods, Selfridges, Fortnum & Mason** and **Harvey Nichols. Marks & Spencer Simply Food** is Britain's finest chain for ready-prepared, high-quality food. Although the food is more expensive in these department store halls, they are wonderful for specialty items, prepared meals, and foreign products. Several offer home delivery.

Farmers' Markets

Farmers' markets provide an opportunity to purchase locally produced food at its freshest, seasonal peak. Almost all of the produce and goods you will find at a farmers' market has been produced, grown, baked or prepared by the individual stallholder, so you are always assured of the quality and freshness of the items. The selection of items available at a farmers' market will vary depending on season and location, but you can usually expect to find a good assortment of fruits, vegetables, meat, eggs, dairy products, and speciality products such as homemade preserves, breads and cakes that are not typically found in your local supermarket.

The popularity of farmers' markets in this country continues to grow as a means of encouraging consumers to buy local food and thus help support British farmers. There are markets in many different areas of London. Some of the more popular ones are listing in *Chapter 12: Shopping*. For more information or a complete list of locations and schedules, call London Farmers' Markets on 020 7833 0338 or visit their website at www.lfm.org. uk. You can also contact the **National Association of Farmers' Markets** on 0845 458 8420 or visit their website at www.farmersmarkets.net.

Farms

For the freshest fruit, pick your own. There are several "pick-your-own" farms around the M25 motorway. It is advisable to ring each farm for directions, opening times and available crops. Additional items like farm fresh eggs, bread and honey may also be available. A day of picking your own fruit and vegetables is a great family outing. Listed below are some of our local favourites:

E.Brill & Sons; Peterley Manor Farm, Beaconsfield; 014 9486 3566.

Aldborough Hall Farm; Aldborough Road North, Aldborough Hatch, Essex; 020 8597 6540.

Garson Farm; Wintersdown Road, West End, Esher, Surrey; 013 7246 4389; www.garsons.co.uk.

Hewitts Farm; Chelsfield, Orpington, Kent; 019 5953 4666.

Parkside Farm; Pick Your Own, Hadley Road, Enfield, Middlesex; 020 8367 2035; www.parksidefarmpyo.co.uk.

Easily accessible from the M25; 20 different types of crops — all for picking.

Local Purveyors

Do try your local butcher, fishmonger, baker and greengrocer to find more personal service and begin to feel a part of your neighbourhood. See *Chapter 11: Services* for a selection of local purveyors.

Organic and Health Food

The Soil Association is the UK's leading campaigning and certification organisation for organic food and farming. They have an excellent website that contains detailed information on all aspects of organic food and farming. The site also includes a complete list of retail outlets in London and throughout the UK that sell organic food products.

The Soil Association; 40-56 Victoria Street, Bristol BS1; 011 7314 5000; www.soilassociation.org.

See *Chapter 11: Services under Food Deliveries* – Organic groceries for some recommendations.

Supermarkets

ASDA, Sainsbury's, Tesco, Somerfield, Morrison's and **Waitrose** all have a large choice of competitively priced supermarkets throughout Britain, especially in London. They offer a wide range of international products and many remain open for long hours or 24 hours a day, to meet busy consumer lifestyles.

Stores can be incredibly crowded and run out of items late in the day, before a holiday, or on the Saturday before a Bank Holiday. Few shops have packers or personnel to take your groceries to your car. Most stores provide plastic carrier bags, and you will often have to bag your own groceries. Most chains have reward cards designed to give frequent shoppers special offerings and discounts.

Many local purveyors and larger supermarkets like **Sainsbury's**, **Tesco** and **Waitrose**, also offer home delivery bringing a whole new level of convenience to busy consumers. You can place your order by phone or online. In addition to the range of standard grocery items, several also offer a broad selection of wine, flowers, music, books, recipes and gift items. Delivery procedures vary, but in most cases, you will be able to specify a particular time frame to suit your needs.

MEAL DELIVERY

On the nights you are too tired to cook, it helps to have some restaurant delivery options on hand. Many restaurants do "take-away" but few offer delivery. Check your local **Yellow Pages**™ for a complete listing or simply call your restaurant of choice and ask.

Room Service Deliveries; 020 7644 6666; www.roomservice.co.uk. Delivers to most areas of central London; offers a choice of over 40 restaurants with varied cuisines.

INTERNATIONAL FOODS AND SPECIALTIES

There are several books available (such as *The Essential Guide to London's Best Food Shops* by Antonio Carluccio (2003) that provide detailed listings of markets and speciality food stores located in many areas of London. It may be worth purchasing one to become acquainted with your neighbourhood's offerings, or to locate specific ingredients.

The following list contains a very small selection of these shops.

American

Harvey Nichols; 5th Floor, 109 Knightsbridge, SW1; 020 7235 5250; www.harveynichols.com.

Fortnum and Mason; 181 Piccadilly, W1; 020 7437 3278; www.fortnumandmason.com. Delivery available.

Panzer's Delicatessen; 13-19 Circus Road, NW8; 020 7722 8596; www.panzers.co.uk. Delivery available.

Partridges; 2-5 Duke of York Square, SW3; 020 7730 0651 and 17-23 Gloucester Road, SW7; 020 7581 0535; www.partridges.co.uk.

Rosslyn Deli; 56 Rosslyn Hill, Hampstead, NW3; 020 7794 9210; www.delirosslyn.co.uk.

Chinese
Loon Fung Supermarket; 42/44 Gerrard Street, W1; 020 7437 7332.
WingYip; 395 Edgeware Road, NW2; 020 8450 0422.

French
Bagatelle; 44 Harrington Road, SW7; 020 7581 1551; www.bagatelle-boutique.co.uk.

Fileric; 12 Queenstown Road, SW8; 020 7720 4844.

Villandry; 170 Great Portland Street, W1; 020 7631 3131.

Greek
Athenian Grocery; 16A Moscow Road, W2; 020 7229 6280.

Italian
Carluccio's; 28A Neal St., Covent Garden, WC2 (and other locations); 020 7240 1487; www.carluccios.com.

Giacobazzi's Delicatessen; 150 Fleet Road, NW3; 020 7267 7222.
   Freshly made tortellini, lasagna, pizza and other Italian specialities.
La Picena; 5 Walton Street, SW3; 020 7584 6573.

Lina Stores; 18 Brewer Street, W1; 020 7437 6482.

L Terroni & Sons; 138-40 Clerkenwell Road, EC1; 020 7837 1712.

Kosher

Golders Green in north London has a wide range of stores offering Kosher fare.

Menachem's; 15 Russell Parade, NW11; 020 8201 8630.

Panzer's Delicatessen (see listing under "American" above).

La Boucherie Kosher Ltd.; 4 Cat Hill, East Barnet, Hertfordshire EN4; 020 8449 9215 and 145 High Street, Barkingside, Ilford, Essex, IG6; 020 8551 9215.

Gourmet

Mortimer & Bennett; 33 Turnham Green Terrace, W4; 020 8995 4145; www.mortimerandbennett.co.uk.

The Pie Man Food Co.; 16 Cale Street, SW3; 020 7225 0587 and 20 Stratford Road, W8; 020 7937 3385; www.the-pie-man.com.

Villandry (see listing under "French" above)

Flaneur; 41 Farringdon Road, EC1; 020 7404 4422.

Also try department store food halls such as **Harrods, Harvey Nichols, Selfridges** and **Marks & Spencer**.

PUBS AND OFF-LICENCES

Pubs

Pubs and licensed restaurants are entitled to serve drinks "on" the premises to individuals over the age of eighteen. Pubs actually fulfil both requirements — you can stay for a drink or buy a bottle to take away with you — a useful thing to know if you are travelling and/or picnicking. London pub hours vary, although most pubs are open all day. Traditional hours are 11:00-23:00; however, new legislation is allowing certain pubs to remain open later. Beware of shorter hours in the countryside and on Sundays in London.

Children

Pubs must have a special permit to allow children on-site. Only pubs that have a separate dining area or room that doesn't contain a bar counter serving drinks, are entitled for such a permit. The permit may also specify hours when children are allowed. Children are not allowed in pubs after 21:00. Therefore, if accompanied by children, it is appropriate to ask whether or not they are welcome.

Off-Licences

Liquor stores or wine shops are known as "off-licences". These shops are licensed to sell beer, wine and spirits for consumption "off" the premises. Most supermarkets also sell alcoholic beverages. Additionally, almost every neighbourhood has its own local off-licence incorporated within a small convenience store that sells everything from crisps to deodorant.

FOOD GLOSSARY

US	UK
Arugula	Rocket
Almond paste	Marzipan
Bacon	Streaky bacon, or rasher
Baking soda	Bicarbonate of soda
Beet	Beetroot
Beer, dark with bitter taste	Bitter
Beer, golden in colour	Lager
Bread	Bread, split tin, bloomer
Broil	Grill
Cake	Cake, gateau
Can	Tin

Candy	Sweets
Celery root	Celeriac
Chicory	Endive
Chips	Crisps
Cheesecloth	Muslin
Chocolate chips	Chocolate buttons
Cilantro	Coriander
Confectioner's sugar	Icing sugar
Cookie	Biscuit
Cornstarch	Cornflour
Corn syrup	Golden syrup (similar to corn syrup)
Cart, grocery	Trolley
Cupcake	Fairy cake
Dessert	Pudding
Dishwashing liquid	Washing-up liquid
Drugstore	Chemist
Eggplant	Aubergine
English muffin	Muffin, crumpet
Fish stick	Fish finger
Flank steak	Skirt of beef
French fries	Chips
Frosting	Icing
Fruit pie	Fruit tart
Gelatin, unflavoured	Aspic power or gelatine
Green bean	Haricot or green bean
Green onion or scallion	Salad or spring onion
Ground beef	Ground or minced beef
Ham	Ham or gammon
Hamburger bun	Bap
Hot dog	Frankfurter
Hominy grits	Maize meal
Kool-Aid	Squash (a concentrate)
Jello	Jelly

Lemonade	Lemon squash
Liquor	Spirits
Liquor store	Off-licence
Molasses	Black treacle
Napkin	Serviette or table napkin
Peanut oil	Groundnut oil
Peapod	Mange tout
Pie, open, single crust, fruit	Flan or tart
Piecrust	Pastry case or flan case
Pits (cherry, peach)	Stones
Popsicle	Ice lolly
Potatoes, baked	Jacket potatoes
Potato chips	Crisps
Pound cake	Madeira cake
Raisins, golden	Sultanas
Roast (meat)	Joint or roast
Roll	Roulade
Sandwich (with lettuce, tomato)	Sandwich (with salad)
Seeds (fruit)	Pips
Seven-up / Ginger ale	Lemonade
Shrimp	Prawns
Sponge cake	Sponge cake/fingers/pudding
Tea biscuit	Scone
Turnip, yellow	Swede
Zucchini, small	Courgette
Zucchini, large	Marrow

Other Helpful Terms – Kitchen Items

US	UK
Faucets	Taps
Stove-top burners	Hobs
Oven	Cooker

Plastic wrap	Cling film
Garbage bags	Dustbin liners
Wax paper	Greaseproof paper

Other Helpful Terms – Food

Term or Phrase	Interpretation
Bubble and squeak	A patty made from swede and mashed potatoes. Other leftover vegetables may be added.
Bangers and mash	Sausages and mashed potatoes.
Branston or ploughman's pickle	A sweet and sour vegetable chutney.
Children's tea	Children's evening meal.
Puddings (such as spotted dick or plum pudding)	Old-fashioned steamed or boiled cake-like desserts.
Toad in the hole	Sausage baked in a Yorkshire pudding.
Top and tail	Snipping the top and bottom off a fruit or vegetable.

10

Drawn by Saiyeed

Services

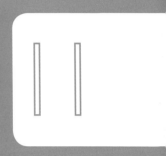

HELPFUL PUBLICATIONS

There are numerous agencies that provide a wide variety of services in London. In some cases, membership, engagement or booking fees can apply. As always, be careful when employing anyone in the household service section, particularly plumbers, electricians, builders or interior designers, so that you do not end up paying more than necessary. Personal recommendations are always best if possible

The following publications are useful sources of information:

Focus; 020 7939 0050. For household and domestic help.

Jean Oddy & Co.; 020 7625 7733; www.jeannoddy.com.
A wonderful resource for locating a wide range of reliable services free of charge.

The Lady; 020 7379 4717; www.lady.co.uk.

A weekly magazine of interesting editorials, holiday accommodations and job opportunities.

Time Out; www.timeout.com/london.

Time Out publishes a weekly magazine and numerous books and reference guides covering all aspects of London and beyond (Restaurants, Children, Shopping, Antiques, Travel (within London and beyond). The guides are available at most bookstores and newsagents.

Yellow Pages; 118 247, www.yell.com.

Telephone and online directory with addresses and phone numbers for businesses and services throughout the UK.

The following list is by no means exhaustive, but should help get you started when trying to locate a particular service provider. Local newspapers, shops and libraries can also be excellent sources of useful local information.

ANTIQUE AND FINE FURNITURE REPAIRERS AND RESTORERS

China Repairers; The Coach House, Kings Mews, N2; 020 8444 3030; www.chinarepairers.co.uk. Repairs all types of ceramics.

Edwardian Antiques; 108 Fortune Green Road, NW6; 020 7794 9820.

Repairs and restoration for all styles of furniture. Also makes replicas of furniture from the Edwardian period. Sells furniture and mirrors.

Hornsby Furniture Restoration; 35 Thurloe Place, SW7; 020 7225 2888; www.antiqueous.com.

Repairs and restoration of both modern and antique furniture. Also offers services such as French polishing, gilding and re-caning.

Frank Pratt; Baileys Close Farm, Pastor Lane, Breachwood Green, Herts; 01438 833 988.

Steve Tierney; 097 3451 520.

French Polisher - punctual, pleasant and fair priced.

ART AND ARTISTS

The Royal Academy of Arts; Burlington House, Piccadilly, W1;
020 7300 8000; www.royalacademy.org.uk.

Holds an annual sale of affordable art by up-and-coming British artists.

Affordable Art Fair; 020 7371 8787; www.affordableartfair.co.uk.

Well-regarded contemporary art fair. Sales held regularly; visit the website
for details.

Lamar Raine; 140 Abbeville Road, SW4; 020 7622 6520;
www.lamarraine.com.

Artist who does portraits of both people and homes in watercolour and
crayon and hand-cut silhouettes.

Fine Art Commissions Ltd; 79 Walton Street, SW3; 020 7589 4111;
www.fineartcommissions.com.

A company that helps you find the right artist to paint a portrait.

Linda Miller Embroideries; 019 6287 0789;
www.lindamillerembroideries.co.uk.

Linda makes unique, colourful, whimsical machine embroideries using
rayon, silk and metallic threads. Great for unique, special gifts – tell her
what you're looking for and she'll create it. Some of her pieces are held
within the permanent textile and dress collections at the Victoria and
Albert Museum.

ACCOUNTING SERVICES

See *"Chartered Accountants"*.

BAKERIES

Jane Asher Party Cakes & Sugarcraft; 22-24 Cale Street, SW3;
020 7584 6177; www.jane-asher.co.uk.

This is the cake shop to end all cake shops. You can specify your design or pick from a vast portfolio of ideas and you don't even have to visit the store since they offer a mail order service. They also use GM-free and organic produce whenever possible.

Clarke's; 122 Kensington Church Street, W8; 020 7229 2190;
www.sallyclarke.com.

Wonderful breads, cakes and tarts. Clarke's also has a well-regarded restaurant at the same address.

Baker & Spice; 47 Denyer Street, SW3; 020 7589 4734;
www.bakerandspice.com.

Wide selection of breads baked in an old brick oven. A selection of prepared foods and catering services are also available. Multiple locations.

Beverly Hills Bakery; 77 E. King Henry's Road, SW3; 020 7586 0070;
www.beverlyhillsbakery.com.

Wide selection of muffins, as well as cookies and pies. Gift basket delivery service available.

The Chelsea Cake Shop; 66 Lower Sloane Street, SW1; 020 7730 6277;
www.chelseacakeshop.co.uk.

Custom-designed cakes for special occasions.

Konditor & Cook; 10 Stoney Street, SE1; 020 7407 5100;
www.konditorandcook.com.

This bakery features fancy fondant-covered cakes in vibrant hues of fuschia, violet and lime. A unique and personalised cake service. Full menu of gourmet takeaway available. Multiple locations.

Patisserie Valerie; 44 Old Compton Street, W1; 020 7437 3466; www.patisserie-valerie.co.uk.

Founded in 1926, this is one of the most famous of the many French patisseries in London. They also serve one of the best breakfasts in town (English breakfast and lunch are served all day in the café). Multiple locations.

Paul; 29 Bedford St., Covent Garden; 020 7836 5321; www.paul.fr.

English branch of the Parisian patisserie with traditional breads, sandwiches, tarts and biscuits. Multiple locations.

Poilane; 46 Elizabeth Street, SW1; 020 7808 4910; www.poilane.com.

Famous Parisian boulangerie and patisserie, particularly known for its sourdough bread. The bread is also available at certain London supermarkets, including **Waitrose** and **Selfridge's** food hall.

BEAUTY SERVICES

Alternative and Complementary Treatments

Neal's Yard Therapy Rooms; 2 Neal's Yard, WC2; 020 7379 7662; www.nealsyardremedies.com.

A well-known therapy centre offering a range of treatments from Alexander technique, lymphatic drainage to shiatsu.

Barbers

Adams of London; 12 St. George Street, W1; 020 7499 9779.

'Enry 'Iggins; 7 Flask Walk, NW3; 020 7435 6007, and 69 Chalk Farm, NW1; 020 7482 4481; www.enryiggins.co.uk.

Flittner; 86 Moorgate, EC2; 020 7606 4750.

George F. Trumper; 20 Jermyn St, SW1; 020 7734 1370, and 9 Curzon Street, W1; 020 7499 1850; www.trumpers.com.

Traditional barber since 1875, fragrances and grooming products, ties and cufflinks. Very professional service.

Truefitt & Hill Gentlemen's Grooming; 71 St. James Street, SW1; 020 7493 8496; www.truefittandhill.co.uk.

Children's Haircutters
Daisy and Tom; 181 King's Road, SW3; 020 7349 5800; www.daisyandtom.com.

Professional Hairstylist (Tracey); 07973 504 552.
Specialising in haircuts for babies and children up to 12 years in the comfort of your own home.

Trotters; 34 King's Road, SW3; 020 7259 9620, and 127 Kensington High Street, W8; 020 7937 9373; www.trotters.co.uk.

Hair Salons and Spas
Most hair salons offer services to men, women and children.
Aveda Spa and Hair Salon; 174 High Holborn, WC1; 020 7759 7350; www.urbanretreat.co.uk. Great services and a café.

Beauty by Nicole Fenton; 3A Kensington Church Walk, W8; 020 7937 8618.

Bliss; 60 Sloane Avenue, SW3; 0207 584 3888; www.blissworld.com.
Fabulous pampering.

Body Experience; 50 Hill Rise, Richmond, Surrey, TW10; 020 8334 9999; www.bodyexperience.co.uk.
Day spa for men and women. Voted one of the top five spas in UK.

Charles Worthington; 34 Great Queen Street, WC2; 020 7831 5303;

www.charlesworthington.co.uk. Multiple locations.

Elizabeth Arden Red Door Hair and Beauty Spa; 29 Davies Street, W1; 020 7629 4488; www.reddoorspas.com.

Gina Conway Salon and Gallery; 612 Fulham Road, SW6; 020 7331 7633, and 62 Westbourne Grove, W2; 020 7229 6644; www.ginaconway.co.uk.

The Green Room; 23 Long Acre (inside The Body Shop), WC2; 020 7379 9600; www.thegreen-room.co.uk.
A full-service salon using Body Shop products.

Jean Marie; 68 Gloucester Road, SW7; 020 7584 6888.

Jo Hansford; 19 Mount Street, W1; 020 7495 7774; www.johansford.com.
Colour specialists.

John Frieda; 75 New Cavendish Street, W1; 020 7636 1401; www.johnfrieda.com. Multiple locations.

Mad Lillies; 34 Heath Street, NW3; 020 7435 3869, and 8 Duke Street, W1; 020 7935 3383; www.madlillies.co.uk.

The Sanctuary; 12 Floral Street, WC2; 0870 7703350; www.thesanctuary.co.uk. Aromatherapy, facials, massage and treatments.

Toni & Guy; 49 Sloane Square, SW1; 020 7730 8113; www.toniandguy.co.uk. Multiple locations.

SPACE.NK; 127-131 Westbourne Grove, W2; 020 7727 8002; www.spacenk.co.uk.
A wide selection of facials, aromatherapy, massage and treatments. Multiple locations.

Unlisted London; 59 Egerton Gardens, SW3; 0870 225 5007; www.unlistedlondon.com.

   Beautiful salon near Harrods, but specialises in providing beauty services in your home.

Urban Retreat at Harrods; 5th Floor, 87 Brompton Road, SW1; 020 7893 8333; www.urbanretreat.co.uk.

Nails

Jannat; 101 Crawford Street, W1; 020 7723 1163.

NYNC; 17 South Molton Street, W1; 020 7409 3332; www.newyorknailcompany.com.

Princess Nails; 131, Moore Park Rd, Walham Green Court, SW6; 020 7385 9288.

BED AND BREAKFASTS AND HOTELS

Chilton Hospitality; 020 8696 0089; www.chilton-hospitality.co.uk.

   Upmarket bed and breakfast company.

The Dorset Square Hotel; 39-40 Dorset Square, NW1; 020 7723 7874; www.dorsetsquare.co.uk.

The Franklin Hotel; 28 Egerton Gardens, SW3; 020 7584 5533; www.franklinhotel.co.uk.

Harrington Hall; 5-25 Harrington Gardens, SW7; 020 7396 9696; www.harringtonhallhotel.co.uk.

The Pelham Hotel; 15 Cromwell Place, SW7; 020 7589 8288; www.firmdalehotels.com.

The Vicarage Hotel; 10 Vicarage Gate, W8; 020 7229 4030; www.londonvicaragehotel.com.

BURGLAR ALARMS AND LOCKSMITHS

Banham Security; 233 Kensington High Street,W8; 020 7622 5151; www.banham.com.

Central Monitoring Services (CMS); 020 7627 0344.
For alarm activation and monitoring.

Chubb Electronic Security; 96¬-100 Clifton Street, EC2; 020 7247 4321; www.chubb.co.uk.

Tara Alarms; 33 Ebury Bridge Road, SW1; 020 7730 0932.
Central London only.

BUTCHERS

Canonbury Butchers; 220 St. Paul's Road, N1; 020 7359 4311.

> *Did you know?... **Selfridge's** food hall sells great meat at supermarket prices.*

Chadwick's Organic Butchers; 208 Balham High Rd, SW12, 020 8772 1895.

J A Steele; 8 Flask Walk, NW3; 020 7435 3587.
Superb selection; including free range products.

Kent & Sons; 59 St. John's Wood High Street, NW8; 020 7722 2258; www.kents-butchers.co.uk.
Offers a wide range of convenient, ready-to-cook items such as breaded veal escallopes and chicken or lamb kebabs. Excellent service and an outstanding selection of the highest quality.

Organic Butchers
J. Seal's Butchers; 7 Barnes High Street, SW13; 020 8876 5118.

Sells grass-fed Aberdeen Angus beef, grass-fed lamb from Dorset, free-range pork, chicken, game in season, and organic turkeys and geese at Christmas.

The Ginger Pig; 10 Moxton Street, W1; 020 7935 7788. Also at the Borough Market.

Superbly organic hung beef, lamb, mutton and great cuts of fine pork. They make pork pies and hamburgers, cure and smoke their own bacon and produce a huge range of their own punchy sausages.

Lidgate; 110 Holland Park Avenue, W11; 020 7727 8243.

Delivers throughout London. Founded in 1850, the shop specialises in naturally reared meat, including organic meat from Prince Charles' Highgrove estate. Also sells a wide variety of homemade sausages, quiches and award-winning pies.

Organic World; 23 Friars Stile Road, Richmond, TW10; 020 8940 0414.

Offers a wide range of organic meat and poultry, game when in season and frozen wild rabbit and venison throughout the year. In the summer, they have a good selection of marinated meats and poultry for barbecuing. And, at Christmas, Bronze turkeys are on offer.

Randall's Butchers; 113 Wandsworth Bridge Road, SW6; 020 7736 3426.

Outstanding selection and excellent service. Offers first-quality organic and free-range beef, lamb and poultry. A wide variety of game is offered in season, as well as haggis, homemade sausages, venison and wild boar. Kelly Bronze turkeys are available at Christmas. A cheese counter at the back offers British and continental cheeses.

W. J. Miller; 14 Stratford Road, W8; 020 7937 1777.

A fine selection of first-class organic meats. Also offers Middle Eastern specialties such as baklava, cow's milk feta cheese and marinated olives. A festive offering is Victorian Royal Roast — a goose stuffed with duck stuffed with pheasant, then chicken, partridge and quail, all boned!

Wholefood Butchers; 24 Paddington Street, W1; 020 7486 1390.

CAR CLEANING AND SERVICING

American Carwash Company; 35 Great Eastern Street, EC2; 020 7739 6345; www.americancarwash.co.uk.

Car cleaning and valet service. Multiple locations.

Did you know?... Many larger supermarkets offer quick and inexpensive car washes in the car park while you shop?

Andrew Brock Automobile Engineer; 31a Shawbury Road, SE22; 020 8299 0299.

Efficient and trustworthy car servicing.

Car Valet, (Ismail Cucala); 078 0893 9510.

Ismail is honest and hard working. He comes to you so no wait at the car wash!

Fly Away Car Storage; Heathrow Airport; 020 8759 1567 or 0870 013 4786.

A unique service for travellers using the car park at Heathrow Airport. The company will collect, store and return your car for your return. They will also wash and service your vehicle while you are away.

Kleencars; 206 Ladbroke Grove, W10; 020 8968 5748 (weekends: 012 2384 5645 or mobile: 078 8507 7882 (Mr. Michael Elkins); www.allminis.com. Car cleaner, repairs and holiday storage.

Whitney's, (talk to Phil); 5 Steele Road, Park Royal, NW10; 020 8965 2095.

Body work for cars. How often have you had scratches, dents on your car, taken it in and been quoted exorbitant sums? Phil is honest, turns around the car in one week and is exceptionally competitive on price.

CARPENTERS AND PAINTERS

Tom Baker; 077 5159 6952.

Internal and external decorator. Particularly good with wallpaper and paint effects.

EZ Builders; 079 0523 0243; www.ezbuilders.co.uk.

Painters, decorators and carpenters.

> Did you know?... In the UK, a "decorator" means a painter, plasterer and/or wallpaper hanger, not an interior designer.

John Gilgan; 020 8883 8496.

Fantastic carpenter.

Robert Harris (Woodcote Painting Contractors Ltd.); Canterbury Work, Canterbury Rd, NW6; 020 7328 5063

Mark Skrzypczak; 079 5004 9168.

A wonderful builder; particularly skillful in carpentry. Absolutely reliable and reasonably priced.

CARPET AND UPHOLSTERY CLEANERS

Designcare; Unit 1, 94 Mount Pleasant, Bricket Wood, St Albans AL2 3XD; 020 8964 2266.

Carpet and sofa cleaning; extremely professional and there is not a stain that they cannot remove. Ask for Nigel.

Look New Dry Cleaners & Carpet Care; 12 Market Place, NW11; 020 8455 2207.

Shirts, dry cleaning and carpet care with collection and delivery depending on your location.

Mickey Humphries; 079 5740 0441 or 020 8761 1407.

Mickey has a wonderful attitude, and gets deeply imbedded dirt and stains out of carpets. Makes them look and smell fresh.

Pilgrim Payne & Co. Ltd.; 290-294 Latimer Road, W10; 020 8960 5656.

Carpet, upholstery and curtain cleaning with great care and attention.

Safeclean; 11 Ashburne Parade, W5; 0800 136 369; www.safeclean.co.uk.

This company uses only environmentally friendly products to clean carpets and upholstery.

CATERERS

Delectable Feasts / Fiona Dalrymple; 103-109 Lavender Hill, SW11; 020 7585 0512; www.delectablefeasts.co.uk.

Provides professional catering and party planning for brunches, lunches, hampers, afternoon teas, parties and banquets.

Finns; 4 Elystan Street, SW3; 020 7225 0733.

Prepared meals made daily; caters for dinner parties.

Jackson Gilmour Ltd.; Unit 12, The Tramsheds, Coomber Way, Croydon; 020 8665 1855; www.jacksongilmour.com.

Fantastic, attentive service; no event is too big or too small.

New Quebec Quisine Ltd.; 17 Enterprise Way, Triangle Business Center, NW10; 020 8960 8654; www.newquebecquisine.co.uk.

Innovative, healthy cuisine specialising in outdoor dining and catering.

The Pie Man Food Co.; 16 Cale Street, SW3; 020 7225 0587, and 20 Stratford Road, W8; 020 7937 3385; www.thepieman.co.uk.

Pieter Maritz Catering; 342 Old York Road, SW1; 020 8870 8750 or 077 9294 4609.

Superb and flexible for parties of any size. His skills range from modern eclectic to ethnic (French, Mexican, Indian, Morrocan, etc). Excellent food; dinner guests always find their way to the kitchen for his phone number.

Rosie Dickinson, 28 Wellington Close, Bicester, Oxon, OX26 4TQ; 018 6932 3209.

Fabulous canapés and hors d' oeuvres; wonderful to deal with. Top quality staff and great clean up.

Searcy Tansley; 124 Bolingbroke Grove, SW11; 020 7585 0505, www.searcys.co.uk. Event catering and hire for groups of 50 or more.

CHARITY SHOPS

Second-hand goods and clothing can be donated to local charity shops. There are many throughout London; these are just a few. Consult the Yellow Pages for the shops nearest you:

- **Notting Hill Housing Trust**
- **Oxfam**
- **Salvation Army**
- **Sue Ryder Care.**

CHARTERED ACCOUNTANTS

A C Bookwise; Fir Tree House, 4 The Brow, Chalfont-St-Giles, Bucks, HP8 4JD; 01494 875 635 or 079 7675 1908. Contact John or Celia Maguire. Computerised bookkeeping and accounts.

Buzzacott Livingstone; 12 New Fetter Lane, EC4; 020 7556 1200; www.ustax.co.uk.

Grashoff & Co.; 35 Whellock Road, W4; 020 8995 4748; infor@handbook.co.uk.

Badger Hakim; 10 Dover Street, W1; 020 7493 3166; www.badger-hakim. co.uk. Prepares both US and UK tax returns; reasonably priced.

Summers & Co.; 6 Jacob's Well Mews, W1; 020 7935 0123.

CHEESE SHOPS

La Fromagerie; 2-4 Moxon Street, London W1; 020 7935 0341, and 30 Highbury Park, N5; 020 7359 7440; www.lafromagerie.co.uk.

Neal's Yard Dairy; 6 Park Street, SE1; 020 7645 3554, and 17 Shorts

Gardens, WC2; 020 7240 5700; www.nealsyarddairy.co.uk.

The dairy has a selection of its own cheeses and also offers a decadent cheese selection from various cheese makers throughout the UK.

Paxton & Whitfield Ltd.; 93 Jermyn St, SW1; 020 7930 0259; www.paxtonandwhitfield.co.uk.

Since 1797, this shop continues to specialises in sourcing and maturing exceptional cheese, and complementing wine.

CHRISTMAS TREES

See *"Garden Centres and Nurseries"* for more recommendations.

Cut Christmas trees can be bought at nurseries, flower shops and many local open air markets.

British Christmas Tree Growers Association; 020 8946 2695; www.bctga.co.uk.

This is the trade association for those who grow specialist Christmas trees in Great Britain and Northern Ireland. Visit the website for a number of locations where you can chop down your own Christmas tree. Many sites have attractions for children and refreshment facilities.

Clifton Nurseries, Ltd; 5A Clifton Villas, W9; 020 7289 6851; www.clifton.co.uk. Delivery and removal of Christmas trees.

Down to Earth; 87 Kentish Town Road, NW1; 079 5617 6482; www.pauldowntoearth.com. Leading gardener and landscape specialist.

Santa Fir Christmas Store; Guildford Road, Cranleigh, Surrey; 014 8326 8296.

CLOTH NAPPY SERVICES

Nappynet Limited ("The Snappy Nappy Service"); 52 Earls Court Road, W8; 020 7937 4099.

Nappy Ever After; 96 Chalton St., NW1; 020 7383 5115;
www.nappyeverafter.co.uk.

A cotton nappy laundry service for Central and North London.

National Association of Nappy Services; 0121 693 4949;
www.changeanappy.co.uk.

A not-for-profit organisation wthat sets the standards and guidelines for the industry. Visit the website for nappy washing services closest to you.

Number 1 for Nappies; 019 9271 3665; www.numberonefornappies.co.uk.

Real Nappy Helpline; 0845 850 0606.

COMPUTERS AND PHOTOCOPYING

For basic computer supplies check the Yellow Pages at www.yell.com. Alternatively, visit Tottenham Court Road in WC2, where there are a number of electronics and computer shops. If bringing a computer to the UK from your home country, make sure it has the correct power supply. See *Chapter 1: Moving* under electrical differences for details

For computer use by the hour and printing facilities, check with your local library.

For photocopying services, **Kall Kwik** (www.kallkwik.co.uk), **Prontaprint** (www.prontaprint.co.uk) and **Kinkos** (www.kinkos.co.uk) have multiple outlets throughout London. Many newsagents have photocopiers within their shop for customer use.

PC World; 087 0546 4464; www.pcworld.co.uk.

A chain of computer stores that can satisfy almost every computer need. Some have in-store technicians to answer questions regarding computer problems.

COMPUTER SERVICES AND REPAIRS

Apple Store; 235 Regent Street, W1; 020 7153 9000;
www.apple.com/uk.

Honeylight Computers Ltd; 1 Parkgate House, 3-9 Broomhill Road, SW18; 020 8871 4187; www.honeylight.co.uk.
Computer services and repairs.

Netural (Yaron Samuel); 087 0441 0046 or 079 7319 0201.
Computer network repairs, upgrades and sales. Yaron is terrific at analyzing your computer needs and determining how best to improve your system. He has a can-do attitude, is very knowledgeable, professional, and stands by his product.

Real Time; Andrew Fernandez, Cobden House, Park Lane, Richmond, Surrey, TW9 2RA; 020 8948 4123 or 079 7344 3752; andrew@realtime.uk.com.
Computer consultancy firm to assist with all home computer needs and troubleshooting. At the time of printing, their hourly rate was approximately £70.

DOMESTIC HELP, CHILDCARE AND HOUSE CLEANERS

The Clean Team; 116 Boundary Road, NW8; 020 7625 5999.
A professional team of cleaners who use their own cleaning products and equipment.

Hampstead Helpers; 7B Heath Street, NW3; 020 7435 3637.
Regular housework, one-off cleans (spring cleaning, moving), after-party cleans and professional ironing service. Fully insured.

Home Organisers; Unit 3, Investment House, 28 Queen's Road, Weybridge, Kent; 01932 844 321.
Babysitting services, including emergency help service.

Workbusters; 2 Olaf Street, W11; 020 7243 5656. Domestic cleaners.

DRY CLEANERS AND LAUNDRIES

A. F. Lustre; 384 Kings Road, SW3; 020 7352 9652.
Delivery service and Sunday hours.

American Dry Cleaning Company; 0800 716 625;
www.americandrycleaningcompany.com.
Offers a laundry service as well as a repair service for handbags, clothes
and shoes. Collection and delivery. Very reasonably priced. Multiple locations.

Jeeves of Belgravia; 020 8809 3232; www.jeevesofbelgravia.co.uk.
Laundry, dry-cleaning, shoe mending and clothing repair. Collection and
delivery. Multiple locations.

Just Shirts; Unit 5C, Heron Industrial Estate, Alliance Road, W3;
020 8992 2777; www.justshirtsoflondon.co.uk.
Shirt service and dry cleaning within 24 hours. Collection and delivery
anywhere in London.

Perkins; 92a Holland Park Road, W11; 020 7221 6927.
Laundry, dry-cleaning and alterations. Collection and delivery. Multiple
locations.

Shirt Master; Unit 2, Parkside Business Estate, Rolt Street, SE8;
020 8469 2339. Free pick up and delivery of dry-cleaning.

Shirt Stream; 5-7 Pelham Street, SW7; 020 7584 1524;
www.shirtstream.com.
Dry-cleaning and shirt service within 24 hours. Free pick-up and delivery
throughout London. Multiple locations.

Swan Dry Cleaners; 152 Arthur Road, SW19; 020 8947 3807.
Provides a general dry-cleaning service and also repairs and alterations.

ELECTRICIANS

Arkady Granik; 077 4777 7608.

Premium electrician who is very reliable and will persevere until the job is done.

EZ Builders; 079 0523 0243; www.ezbuilders.co.uk.

Paul Millard; 86 Woolwich Road, Upper Belvedere, Kent, DA17 5EN; 013 2244 6322.

Highly recommended – trustworthy and reliable. He keeps up the new standards and codes of practice and does not dig holes in your walls unless it is absolutely necessary.

Peter Kessler; 079 7629 8608.

Always the gentleman, honest, reliable, thorough, and a great problem solver.

Canac Building Services (James Cannon); 077 5387 5533 or 079 3261 0828.

Very reliable, responsive and professional. Handles any task from complex wiring jobs to replacing light bulbs that are out of reach.

PW Reynolds; 50A Chatterton Road, Bromley, Kent, BR2 9QE; 020 8466 1001. Highly recommended.

EXTERMINATOR (Pest Control Services)

Safeguard Pest Control; Unit 6, Churchill Business Park, The Flyers Way, Westerham, Kent, TN16 1BT; 01959 565 777.

Elimination and prevention of mice, rats, wasps, fleas, flies, ants, squirrels, and cockroaches.

FISHMONGERS

You can purchase very fresh fish and seafood at the food halls in **Selfridges**, **Harrods** and **Harvey Nichols**.

Chalmers and Gray Fishmongers; 67 Notting Hill Gate, W11; 020 7221 6177.

Cope's Seafood Company; 700 Fulham Road, SW6; 020 7371 7300.
Fishworks; 89 Marylebone High Street, W1; 020 7935 9796;
www.fishworks.co.uk.

Hampstead Seafoods; 78 Hampstead High Street, NW3; 020 7435 3966.

Sandys; 56 King St, Twickenham, Middlesex TW1; 020 8892 5788.

FLORISTS

Some department stores have flower departments (**Harrods, Harvey Nichols, Marks & Spencer**). Most of the shops listed below offer Interflora services. There are also flower markets around London — see *Chapter 12: Shopping.*
Angel Flowers; 60 Upper Street, N1; 020 7704 6312;
www.angel-flowers.co.uk.

Aurora; 41 Englands Lane, NW3; 020 7722 3929; www.auroraflowershop.com.

Flowerstalk; 513 Finchley Road, NW3; 020 7431 5353, and 230 West End Lane, NW6; 020 7431 97454; www.flowerstalk.co.uk.

Jane Packer Flowers; 32-34 New Cavendish Street; 020 7935 2673;
www.jane-packer.co.uk.
Offers same-day delivery within a five-mile radius of the store. Also in **Selfridges'** food hall.

Kensington Flowers; 3 Launceston Place, W8; 020 7937 0268;
www.kensingtonflowers.co.uk.

Mary Jane Vaughan Design in Flowers; 609 Fulham Road, SW6;
020 7385 8400; www.maryjanevaughan.co.uk.

Molly Blooms; 787 Fulham Road, SW6; 020 7731 1212;
www.mollyblooms.co.uk.

Moyses Stevens; 157-158 Sloane Street, SW1; 020 7841 7600;
www.moyses-stevens.co.uk.

New Covent Garden Market; Nine Elms Lane, SW8; 020 7720 2211;
www.cgma.gov.uk.
   Bulk sales of fruit, vegetables and flowers to the trade. Largest wholesale
market in the country. Individuals may enter by paying a parking fee (£4)
and may buy flowers and produce at the vendors' discretion. Market hours:
Monday to Friday 03:00 to 11:00; Saturday 04:00 to 09:00.

Paula Pryke; The Flower House, Cynthia Street, N1; 020 7837 7336;
www.paula-pryke-flowers.com.

Pot Pourri; 255 Chiswick High Road, W4; 020 8994 2404;
www.potpourriflowers.co.uk.

Pulbrook & Gould; 127 Sloane Street, SW1; 020 7730 0030;
www.pulbrookandgould.co.uk.

The Flower Van; Michelin Building, 81 Fulham Road, SW3; 020 7589 1852.
   Sells simple, seasonal quality flowers. Delivery available.

Wild at Heart; 49A Ledbury Road, W11; 020 7727 3095;
www.wildatheart.com. Multiple locations.

FOOD DELIVERIES
Groceries
Dairy Crest; 55 Sleaford Street, SW8; 0870 600 0822;
www.milkdeliveries.co.uk.
   Delivery of milk and dairy products. Multiple locations.

Marks & Spencer; 020 7935 7954; www.marksandspencer.com.

Non-food items can be ordered online. They will also deliver in-store food purchases to your home (selection and order form is on their website). Multiple locations.

The Minerale Water Company; P.O. Box 2798, NW10; 020 8450 8082; www.minerale-water.co.uk.

Delivery service of a wide range of grocery items, baby items as well as mineral water, juices, soft drinks, wine and spirits. Customer service is their specialty.

Nappy Express; 128 High Road, N11; 020 8361 4040; www.nappyexpress.co.uk.

Next-day delivery of nappies, baby products, toiletries, food, cleaning products, laundry products, etc.

Sainsbury's; www.sainsburys.co.uk. Full-service grocery store. Multiple locations.

Tesco; www.tesco.com.

Full-service grocery store, wine, flowers, music, books and gift items. Multiple locations.

Skyco; 11 Twynersh Ave, Chertsey, Surrey; 019 3256 5559; www.skyco.uk.com.

International food club with an emphasis on North American products.

Waitrose; www.ocado.com.

Full-service grocery store that focuses on premium-quality products and outstanding customer service. Large selection of organic products.

Groceries – Organic

Abel & Cole; 16 Waterside Way, Plough Lane, SW17; 020 8944 3780;

www.abelcole.co.uk.
Cartons of organic foods delivered weekly.

Alara Wholefoods; 58 Marchmont Street, WC1; 020 7837 1172.
Sells organic fruit and vegetables, with fresh shipments every Monday.

Farmaround; The Old Bakery, Mercury Road, Richmond, North Yorkshire, DL10 4TQ; 020 7627 8066; www.farmaround.co.uk.
Organic produce by the box from farms in Kent and Sussex delivered to your door.

Fresh & Wild; 69-75 Brewer Street, W1; 020 7434 3179; www.freshandwild.com.
A good selection of organic and health food ingredients, including vitamins and herbs. Also has an on-site juice bar. Multiple locations.

The Grain Shop; 269a Portobello Road, W11; 020 7229 5571.
Organic baker and take-away.

Holland & Barrett; www.hollandandbarrett.com.
A chain of health food stores with over 37 locations in Greater London.
Neal's Yard; Covent Garden, WC2; 020 7379 7222.
A "green" shopping complex that includes a bakery, a dairy, alternative medicines, a health shop and a soup and salad bar.

Organic Delivery Company; Unit A59, New Covent Garden Market, Nine Elms Lane, SW8, 020 7739 8181, www.organicdelivery.co.uk.
Specialises in organic and gourmet products.

Pamona; 179 Haverstock Hill, NW3; 020 7916 2676.
Delivers in-store purchases or pre-arranged orders within a three-mile radius.

Planet Organic; 22 Torrington Place, W1; 020 7436 1929;
www.planetorganic.com.

One-stop supermarket selling a complete range of organic produce, environmentally friendly household cleaners, body care products and cosmetics. Deli, cheese and bakery counter, coffee and juice bar and fresh fish counter. Multiple locations.

Portobello Wholefoods; 266 Portobello Road, W10; 020 8968 9133.

Organic fruits, vegetables and fresh bread, vitamins, homeopathic remedies and essential oils.

Sheepdrove Organic Farm; Lambourn, Berkshire; 014 8871 659;
www.sheepdrove.com.

Top-quality organically produced meats. Orders are packed in insulated boxes and shipped overnight.

The Fresh Food Company; The Orchard, 50 Wormholt Road, W12;
020 8749 8778; www.freshfood.co.uk.

Organic meat, fruit, vegetables, dairy, wines and beers. Home delivery and mail order.

Swaddles Green Farm; Hare Lane, Buckland St. Mary, Chard, Somerset;
0845 456 1768; www.swaddles.co.uk.

Organic meats, soil fertilisers and a catalogue of eco-friendly products available, delivered weekly.

GARDEN CENTRES AND NURSERIES

From the most elaborate garden to the simplest flower box, London is in bloom most of the year. The following are a few suggestions for putting some colour into your life.

B&Q; 0845 609 6688; www.diy.com.

A wide selection of DIY gardening needs. Delivery available. Multiple locations.

C Rassell Ltd; 80 Earl's Court Road, W8; 020 7937 0481.

Garden plants and shrubs, window boxes and hanging baskets made to order.

Camden Garden Centre; 2 Barker Drive, St. Pancreas Way, NW1; 020 7387 7080; www.camdengardencentre.co.uk.

A full-service garden centre with a large selection of outdoor and indoor plants, as well as books, grills and patio furniture. Knowledgeable and helpful staff. Delivery available.

The Chelsea Gardener; 125 Sydney Street, SW3; 020 7352 5656.

Comprehensive garden centre selling everything from shrubs and plants to gardening furniture and books. Also has excellent selection of houseplants and a florist department.

Clifton Nurseries; 5A Clifton Villas, W9; 020 7289 6851; www.clifton.co.uk.

An excellent all-purpose garden centre. Services also include garden design and delivery.

Crocus; 0870 787 1413; www.crocus.co.uk.

A gardening website that specialises in plants. They offer the largest selection in the UK.

The English Garden Company (Neil Fletcher); 017 0764 5069 or 079 5686 9986.

Neil's company does beautiful work all over London and beyond. A very creative, reliable and responsive team; will provide you with a service contract.

Fulham Palace Garden Centre; Bishop's Avenue, Fulham Palace Road, SW6; 020 7736 2640; www.fulhamgardencentre.com.

Good selection of plants, pots and shrubs. Garden landscaping and delivery available.

Hampstead Garden Centre; 163 Iverson Road, NW6; 020 7328 3208.

Full-service garden centre. Large selection of outdoor plants with smaller offerings of garden furniture and indoor plants.

Homebase; 0845 077 8888; www.homebase.co.uk.

All your DIY gardening needs. Delivery service available. Open seven days a week. Multiple locations.

Royal Horticultural Society; 80 Vincent Square, SW1; 020 7834 4333; www.rhs.org.uk.

Has a comprehensive reference library available to non-members.

HAIR SALONS

See *"Beauty Services"*.

HANDYMAN

Handy Andy; 079 6628 4068.

David Welch; 078 0272 5259. Picture hanging.

Red Box Ltd.; 15 Young Street, W8; 020 7381 1539; www.redboxlondon.com.

Various home maintenance and repair services. Specialises in small jobs and certified for plumbing, heating and electrical jobs. Primarily works in West London postcode area to provide a high level of service response.

Steve Cook; 020 8575 6380 or 078 4198 8745.

Very highly recommended from several League members. He will hang pictures, assemble furniture and complete minor repairs and improvements from painting to changing out-plugs on lamps to fixing your broken toilet handles! Punctual and honest; at time of print charged approximately £20-£25 per hour.

INSURANCE

Direct Line; 0845 246 3761 (car) or 0845 246 8703 (home); www.directline.com.

Comprehensive insurance company that will offer policies for travel, home, car and other areas.

Ellis David Limited; 020 7354 3881; www.ellisdavid.com.

Insurance brokers with an American accent, they offer the added benefit of car coverage in North America at no extra cost.

Did you know?... British Gas offers insurance coverage for major appliances whether or not you have a gas contract with them. They will repair major appliances, (e.g., dishwasher, oven, freezer, microwave). Monthly insurance packages are available for as many or as few appliances as you like. Contact 0845 950 0400.

Francis Townsend and Hayward; 0845 345 9000; www.francistownsend.co.uk.

Insurance brokers who can handle most requirements, including contents insurance for rented accommodations.

Norwich Union; 0800 888 112 (car) or 0870 5143 108 (home); www.norwichunion.com.

Comprehensive insurance company offering policies for car, home, health and travel.

INTERIOR DESIGNERS

Most major department stores carrying decorating materials will advise and assist you with draperies, upholstery and other work. Fabric and wallpaper are sold by the metre. Liberty's fabrics are world famous and of a consistently high quality. John Lewis and Peter Jones also carry quality fabrics and are known for their superior haberdashery.

+---+
| **Metric Equivalents:** |
| |
| **Metric**   **Imperial** |
| 1 centimetre (1 cm)   0.33 inches |
| 2.5 cm   1 inch |
| 30 cm   1 foot |
| 90 cm   1 yard |
| 1 metre (1 m)   39.4 inches |
+---+

Metric	Imperial
1 centimetre (1 cm)	0.33 inches
2.5 cm	1 inch
30 cm	1 foot
90 cm	1 yard
1 metre (1 m)	39.4 inches

April Russell Interior Design and Decoration; Flat 45, 45-49 Warwick Square, SW1, 020 7821 7888; www.aprilrussell.com.
Design and make up of curtains and upholstered furniture.

David Wright Interior Design; The Studio, 44 Ramsden Road, SW12; 020 8675 6752.

Fiona Campbell, Ltd; 259 New King's Road, SW6; 020 7731 3681; www.fionacampbelldesign.co.uk.

Kensington Design (Sonita Kember); 12 Stratford Road, W8; 020 7938 2000; www.kensingtondesign.com.

Percy Bass Ltd.; 184 Walton Street, SW3; 020 7589 4853; www.percybass.com.

Cole & Son (Wallpapers) Ltd; Ground Floor 10, Chelsea Harbour Design Centre, Lots Road, SW10; 020 7376 4628; www.cole-and-son.com.
Specialises in hand-printed wallpapers and own range paints.

Colefax & Fowler; 39 Brook Street, W1; 020 7493 2231, and 110 Fulham Road, SW3; 020 7244 7427; www.colefax.com.
Best known for fabrics and wallpapers, yet it is a renowned decorating firm that also sells antiques. Also stocks Jane Churchill fabric, wallpaper and paint.

Conran Shop; Michelin House, 81 Fulham Road, SW3; 020 7589 7401, and 55 Marylebone High Street, W1; 020 7723 2223; www.conran.com. Made to measure blinds, curtains, rugs and furniture.

Fox Linton; 219 & 219B Chelsea Harbour Design Centre, Lots Road, SW10; 020 7368 7700; www.foxlinton.com.
This collaboration between Mary Fox Linton and Philip Cadle encompasses some of the best names in fabric exclusive to Fox Linton in the UK.

John S. Oliver Ltd.; 33 Pembridge Road, W11; 020 7221 6466.
Produces a unique range of paints that match their hand-made wallpapers.

Nina Campbell; 9 Walton Street, SW3; 020 7225 1011; www.ninacampbell.com. Sells her own fabric and wallpaper.

The Paint Library; 5 Elystan Street, SW3; 020 7823 7755; www.paintlibrary.co.uk.
Wallpaper and paint specialists; complete online service (request samples, buy products, communicate with designers).

KENNELS (QUARANTINE AND BOARDING) AND PET SITTING SERVICES

The regulations governing animal quarantine are evolving and easing with the arrival of pet passports. Please read "Bringing your pet to the UK" in *Chapter 1: Moving* for complete information regarding quarantine kennels and the current quarantine requirements.

Kennels and Catteries

The Animal Inn; Dover Road, Ringwould, Near Deal, Kent; 013 0437 3597; www.quarantine.co.uk.
Cats and dogs. Five minutes from the white cliffs of Dover, this facility is considered state of the art as far as quarantines and boarding kennels go.

Granary Kennels; Hawkridge Wood, Frilsham, Hermitage, Thatcham, Berkshire; 016 3520 1489. Boarding for cats and dogs.

Kents Farm; Kents Lane, North Weald, Essex; 019 9252 2183; www.londonandessex.demon.co.uk.

Boarding and quarantine for cats, dogs and other animals. Located 19 miles from London in the Essex countryside. Offers collection and delivery from London and other counties.

Moss Bank Cats; 6 Oxdrove, Picket Piece, Andover, Hampshire; 012 6436 5560. Very caring.

Leander International Kennels Ltd; Arden Grange, London Road, Albourne, West Sussex; 012 7383 3390; www.ardengrange.com.

Arden Grange has very impressive credentials in the pet food industry and an excellent reputation in caring for and feeding other people's pets at their beautifully appointed kennels and cattery set in the rolling Sussex Downs.

Pet Groomers / Pet Supplies

Animal Crackers; 94 Fleet Road, NW3; 020 7485 1476.

Comprehensive selection of pet food and accessories.

K9 Capers; 24-26 The Imperial Business Centre, Gatwick Road, Crawley, West Sussex; 087 1271 8991, www.k9capers.com.

Professional pet care products and services. Products can be delivered free anywhere in the UK.

Pet Pavilion; Chelsea Farmers Market, 125 Sydney St, SW3, 020 7376 8800, or 174 Kensington Church Street, W8; 020 7221 1888; www.petpavilion.co.uk.

Highly recommended for pet grooming. Also sells pet accessories.

Primrose Hill Pets; 132 Regent's Park Road, NW1; 020 7483 2023.

Sells a wide range of pet food and accessories and includes a small grooming salon.

Pet Sitting Services

Animal Aunts; Smugglers Cottage, Green Lane, Rogate, Petersfield, Hampshire; 017 3082 1529.

They care for your pets in your home. Pet sitting service covers London, Surrey, etc.

Animal Concierge; 077 9900 5558; www.animalconcierge.co.uk.

Works with clients and pets for a very personal and tailored service. Regular services include pet sitting, dog walking, pet sitting, puppy training and small animal care. Also run a VIP Concierge Membership and luxury services such as "Doggie's Day Out", personal shopping and pet parties.

Pets At Home; 80 Bushy Road, Raynes Park, SW20; 020 8944 0006; www.petsathome.com.

They care for your pets in your home. Pet sitting service covers most areas of London and the UK.

MINICAB AND TAXI SERVICES

Unlike black cabs, which are licensed, minicabs cannot be hailed from the street and must be booked by phone. Since they are not regulated, standards may vary. Many minicab services are local, but the following taxi and minicab services have been used and recommended by League members.

Addison Lee; 35-37 William Road, NW1, 020 7387 8888; www.addisonlee.com.

The market leader for moving people and parcels throughout London. Can provide cars with child safety seats upon request.

Airport Cars; 020 8877 3000; www.jetcars.co.uk.

Can be paid in advance with a credit card.

Computer Cab; 020 7432 1432 (if paying in advance by credit card) or 020 7908 0207 (if paying with cash); www.computercab.co.uk.

Computer Cab is London's largest supplier of licensed radio taxis covering the entire London area with five fleets: Comcab, DataCab, Zingo, Call a Cab (suburban) and local taxis (local black taxi cabs).

Gemini Cars; 50 Station Road, Egham, Surrey; 017 8447 1111; www.geminicars.co.uk.

Meadway Radio Cars; 1019-1021 Finchley Road, NW11; 020 7328 5555 or 020 8458 5555; www.meadway.com.

Pronto Radio Cars; 408 Harrow Road, W9; 020 7286 2227; www.prontocars.co.uk.

MONOGRAMMING AND ENGRAVING SERVICES

Harrods; 87-135 Brompton Road, SW1; 020 7730 1234; www.harrods.com

The linen department has monogramming service for items purchased at the store.

Monogrammed Linen Shop; 168 Walton Street, SW3; 020 7589 4033; www.monogrammedlinenshop.com.

Leading linen shop in London with a monogramming service department.

Bennett & Thorogood; Unit 109, Grays Antique Market, 58 Davies Street, W1; 020 7408 1880.

Engravers of precious metals and glass.

MOVERS

The Collectors (Nick Cutler); 020 8961 9398 or 078 6058 3864; www.collectors-london.co.uk.

Reliable and efficient removal service. Specialists in small removals, from one box to a flat or a complete office removal.

Davies Turner Worldwide Movers Ltd.; 49 Wates Way, Mitcham, CR4; 020 7622 4393; www.daviesturner.com.

Moves; Moves House, 141 Acton Lane, NW10, 087 0010 4410; www.moves.co.uk.

Cadogan Tate; Cadogan House, 239 Acton Lane, Park Royal, NW10; 020 8963 4000; www.cadogantate.com.

Sterling International Movers; Hallmark House, Rowdell Road, Northolt, Middlesex; 020 8841 7000; www.sterlingmovers.com.

NEWSPAPER / MAGAZINE DELIVERY

Many newspapers and magazines can be delivered to your home. See your local newsagent to make arrangements.

Paper Delivery

Renown Distributors Ltd.; 17-23 Battersea Bridge Road, SW11; 020 7223 3199.

Newspaper and magazine delivery to Central London. Residential and corporate. Reliable early morning delivery. Competitive, flexible service.

PACKAGE DELIVERY, COLLECTION AND COURIERS

DHL Worldwide Express; 0870 110 0300; www.dhl.com.

Federal Express International; 0800 123 800; www.fedex.com/gb. Door-to-door service.

Mail Boxes Etc.; 56 Gloucester Road, SW7; 020 7581 9999; www.mbe-london.co.uk.

Packaging and delivery of parcels and documents worldwide using various courier services. Also has stationary and mailbox services in-store. Multiple locations.

The Packing Shop; 6-12 Ponton Road, SW8; 020 7819 6600; www.thepackingshop.co.uk.

They will collect, pack and ship packages world-wide. Specialty is fine arts and antiques.

PARTY PLANNERS AND SUPPLIES

Fait Accompli; 212 The Plaza, 535 Kings Rd, SW10; 020 7352 2777.

Specialises in organising parties and events.

Gorgeous Gourmets; Unit D, Gresham Way, Wimbledon, SW19; 020 8944 7771; www.gorgeousgourmets.co.uk.

Catering equipment for banqueting or small parties.

HSS Hire; 0845 728 2828; www.hss.com.

Very comprehensive list of items for professional or personal hire, including party supplies (china, glassware, linen, furniture, etc.).

Non Stop Party Shop; 694 Fulham Road, SW6; 020 7384 1491; www.nonstopparty.co.uk.

A retail store that offers balloon decoration, party accessories and costumes. Multiple locations.

Oscar's Den; 127-129 Abbey Road, NW6; 020 7328 6683; www.oscarsden.co.uk.

A retail store that offers balloon decoration, party accessories and costumes. Delivery service for party supplies.

Party Party; 3 & 11 Southhampton Road, NW5, 020 7267 9084; www.partypartyuk.com.

Two retail stores; one offering balloon services (including delivery) and the other offering various party supplies, accessories, gifts and costumes.

Party Planners (Lady Elizabeth Anson); 56 Ladbroke Grove, W11;

020 7229 9666. Will arrange everything for any social function.

Party Professionals; 33 Kensington Park Road, W11; 020 7221 3438.
Will tastefully organise everything for any event from intimate dinners to large gatherings.

PHOTOGRAPHERS

Contre-Jour; 40 Martell Road, West Dulwich, SE21; 020 8670 1234; www.contre-jour.co.uk.
Families, children and weddings. Will travel throughout Europe and the UK.

Natural Portraits (Steve Boreham); 01932 563 318; www.naturalportraits.net.

PIANO TURNER

Jacque Samuel Pianos; 142 Edgware Rd, W2; 020-7723-8818.

PICTURE FRAMING

Campbell's of Walton Street; 1a Stronsa Rd, W1; 020 8743 3666.
Exceptional service. Picture restoration, cleaning and framing.

Ingrid Barron Gallery; 61 South End Road, NW3; 020 7435 7770.
Specialises in original works of art and makes quality frames on the premises.

PLUMBERS / BOILER MAN

1-2-1 Services (Michael & Andy); 86 Finchley Court, Ballards Lane, Finchley, N3; 020 8343 1918.
This duo team knows their boilers! Honest and reliable.

Azee Dee Heating & Plumbing (David Tanner); 141 Studland Road, W7; 077 7492 0922.

BLM Plumbing and Heating; 76 Brunswick Park Rd, N11;
020 8361 8877; blmplumbandheat@aol.com.

EZ Builders; www.ezbuilders.co.uk.

Peter Crisp; 079 5693 8695.

He is courteous, honest, thorough, fantastic problem solver, and he has a
concierge group of related builders to tackle any job you need.

Pimlico Plumbers Ltd.; Pimlico House, 1 Sail St, SE11; 020 7928 8888.

PROBLEM SOLVERS AND LIFESTYLE MANAGEMENT

Buy:Time UK (Claire Brynteson is THE woman); 70 Dinsmore Road,
SW12; 0870 486 2624 or 079 7682 6852; www.buy-time.co.uk.

She is a lifestyle manager. She'll swoop in and organize closets or do
whatever needs doing. You buy blocks of time.

Personal Time Saver; 809 Howard House, Dolphin Square, SW1;
020 7828 2977 www.personaltimesaver.co.uk.

Problem solving for busy people. Can provide a wide range of
services from running errands, party organisation and access for deliveries
in your absence.

> *Did you know?...Used
> postage stamps, mobile
> phones and inkjet cartridges
> are collected by the charity
> Guide Dogs for the Blind. Visit
> www.guidedogs.org.uk or call
> 011 8983 8298 for details.*

RECYCLING

Most communities offer recycling for
some or all of the following: glass, cans, plastics,
newspapers, magazines, rags and Christmas
trees, with many now providing door-side
pick up on designated days. For information
about facilities or door-side pick up in your
area, contact your local council, town hall or public library. See *Chapter 5:
Utilities* for a listing of local councils. You can also visit www.wasteonline.org.
uk for more general information on recycling and waste in London.

RENTALS

Baby Equipment

See *Chapter 8: Children.*

Bicycles

Mend-A-Bike; 19 The Arches, Munster Road, SW6; 020 7371 5867.

Cycle shop, repairs and rentals.

Simpson Cycles; 114-116 Malden Road, NW5; 020 7485 1706; www.simpsoncycles.co.uk.

Family-run shop for over 50 years. Offers a large range of bicycles and exceptional personal service.

Costumes (Fancy Dress)

Angels Fancy Dress; 119 Shaftsbury Ave., WC2; 020 7836 5678; www.fancydress.com.

All types of costumes for both children and adults. Delivery available.

The Carnival Store; 95 Hammersmith Road, W14; 020 7603 7824; www.carnivalstore.co.uk.

All types of costumes for children and adults; also carries period costumes.

Tools Hire (DIY)

There are many local DIY stores. We have only listed the large chains that can be found throughout London. Look in the Yellow Pages (www.yell.com) for a complete listing.

B&Q; 0845 609 6688; www.diy.com.

A wide selection of DIY and garden needs. Open seven days a week; delivery available. Multiple locations.

HSS Hire; 11 Lille Road, SW6; 020 7381 4433; www.hss.com.

Tools of every kind, catering and event equipment for hire.

Homebase; 0845 077 8888; www.homebase.co.uk.

All your DIY household needs, including a gardening centre. Open seven days a week. Delivery available. Multiple locations.

HATS

Hatitude Hat Hire; 9 St Margaret's Road, SE4; 020 8694 0528; www.hatitude4hats.com.

Designer hats for sale and hire.

Hectic Hat Hire; 242 Munster Road, SW6; 020 7381 5127.

WEDDING AND FORMAL ATTIRE

Moss Bros.; 88 Regent Street, W1; 020 7494 0665; www.mossbros.co.uk. Gentlemen's formal wear for sale or hire. Multiple locations.

One Night Stand; 8 Chelsea Manor Studios, Flood Street, SW3; 020 7352 4848; www.onenightstand.co.uk.

Evening dress hire for women. Appointment required.

SELF-STORAGE

Safestore; 0800 444 800; www.safestore.co.uk. Multiple locations.

The Big Yellow Self Storage; 1000 North Circular Road, NW2, 020 8208 3828; www.bigyellow.co.uk.

SPECIAL APPLIANCE REPAIRS

Abbey Appliances; 9 Lower Place Business Centre, Steele Road, Park Royal, NW10; 020 8200 5758. Kitchen appliance repairs.

Waldebeck American Appliance Services; 41 Pavilion Way, East Cote, Middlesex; 020 8569 0606.

Repairs and sells all American major appliances.

TAILORS / ALTERATIONS
Many dry-cleaning shops offer an alteration service. See *"Dry Cleaners and Laundries"* for recommendations.
The Alteration Station; 29 The Pavement, SW4; 020 7627 0167.

Designer Alterations; 220A Queenstown Road, SW11; 020 7498 4360; www.designeralternations.com. Bridal alterations.

First Tailored Alterations Ltd.; 85 Lower Sloane Street, SW1; 020 7730 1400.

K.S. Tailoring Services; 13 Saville Row, W1; 020 7437 9345.
Open Saturdays for fittings.

Maurice Alteration Service; 3 Nottingham Court, WC2; 020 7836 9401.

Thimble Alterations and Repairs; 24 Thackeray Street, W8; 020 7938 1161.

TAXIS
See *"Minicab Services."*

VETERINARIANS
Abingdon Veterinary Clinic; 85 Earls Court Road, W8; 020 7937 8215.

Brompton Veterinary Clinic; 96 Fulham Road, SW3; 020 7225 2915.
24-hour emergency cover at clinic. In addition to regular veterinary services for dogs and cats, has a grooming service for long-haired cats.

Elizabeth Street Veterinary Clinic; 55 Elizabeth Street, SW1; 020 7730 9102.
Offers emergency veterinary service 24 hours a day, 365 days a year to members of specific clinics. The regular day clinic is very good as well. Appointment required.

Kynance Veterinary Clinic; 8 Kynance Mews, SW7; 020 7584 2019.

Michael Gordon; 35 Alexander Street, W2; 020 7229 2040.

Primrose Hill Pet Clinic; 138 Gloucester Avenue, NW1; 020 7586 8806.

The Village Vet Practice; 11 Belsize Terrace, NW3; 020 7794 4948; www.villagevet.co.uk .

Emergency service 24 hours a day, 365 days a year. Multiple locations.

creativity

Drawn by freja

Shopping

London offers an incredible selection of stores. From shops that have been around for centuries selling traditional British goods, to chic boutiques and the high street, shopping in London will satisfy every shopper's desire.

The following list of shops is not intended to be inclusive; it simply provides some suggestions. *Time Out*'s annual shopping guide to London's best shops and services is also a useful resource.

SHOPPING AREAS

THE HIGH STREET

Virtually every town has its own "High Street" — the main shopping street that fulfils most shopping needs. In addition to clothing and shoe shops, you will usually find chemists, grocery stores, newsagents, bookstores, electronics stores and restaurants.

The biggest high street shopping areas in central London are Oxford

269

Street and Regent Street where you will find the flagship stores of most major UK and many international retailers. Other great shopping areas include Neal Street and the Piazza in Covent Garden, Marylebone High Street (just north of Oxford Street), Westbourne Grove in Notting Hill, the King's Road in Chelsea, and Knightsbridge, which boasts two of London's best department stores (Harrods and Harvey Nichols). A great website that lists all the shops and restaurants for London's most popular streets is www. streetsensation.co.uk.

SHOPPING MALLS

If you are seeking the convenience of a one-stop mall, you'll need to head a bit outside of Central London.

Bluewater; 0870 777 0252; www.bluewater.co.uk.

Just off Junction 2 of the M25 at Greenhithe in Kent. Bluewater has over 300 stores, including a vast number of up-market shops, more than 40 restaurants and a 13-screen cinema.

Brent Cross; 020 8202 8095; www.brentcross-london.com.

Located at the junction of the A406 (North Circular) and the A41.

Lakeside; 017 0886 9933; www.lakeside.uk.com.

Located at Junction 30/31 off the M25, at West Thurrock, Essex.

SALES

The vast majority of London's shops have two large sales each year; one in January and one in July. It is becoming more common for many shops to hold mid-season sales as well. Outside these times, you can find a listing of current sales in and around London in the "Sale Finder" on the website www.gooddealdirectory.co.uk. You can also call 016 3422 6203 to order *The Good Deal Directory*, detailing how to buy brand names for less than the usual high street prices, as well as information on over 3,100 outlets and discount businesses.

SHOPPING

ART AND ANTIQUES

Antique hunting in London is a joy. No matter how elegant or humble the establishment, gracious haggling is always permitted. Dealers are often prepared to come down 10 per cent, which they say is a trade discount. If they do not come down, do not persist, as the price may genuinely be the best they can give.

Antique Fairs

There are too many antique fairs in and around London to list them all. The **BBC** has a great website (www.bbc.co.uk/antiques/local_to_you), that lists antique fairs when you input the region, month and even the day you are planning to visit a fair. The website offers a wealth of additional information on antiques.

For complete listings of regularly scheduled Sunday fairs in London and throughout the UK, check the weekly newspaper *The Antiques Trade Gazette*, the weekly magazine *Time Out: London* or the monthly magazines *The Antique Collector* and/or *The Antique Dealer and Collector's Guide*. All are available at larger newsstands.

Some of the Junior League of London members' favourites are:

- **The Affordable Art Fair** (www.affordableartfair.co.uk) held in Battersea Park in both the autumn and the spring. Sells contemporary art for under £3,000.

- **The Association of Art and Antiques Dealers** (LAPADA) also hosts several fairs a year. Call 020 7823 3511, or visit their website (www.lapada.co.uk) for more information.

- **The British Antique Dealers' Association** (BADA) holds Antiques & Fine Art Fairs. They can be contacted at 020 7589 4128 or visit their website (www.bada.org) for a listing of their fairs.

- **The Chelsea Antiques Fair** held in the Chelsea Old Town Hall in both the autumn and spring.

- **The Decorative Antiques and Textiles Fair** held in Battersea Park generally in January, April and September.

- **The Grosvenor House Art & Antiques Fair** held in June.

- **The Fine Arts & Antiques Fair** held in Olympia in February, June and November.

- **The West London Antiques Fair** held in Kensington Town Hall in January.

Antique Markets

See the listings under "Markets" below.

Antique Shops

If you are looking for a specialist dealer, The **British Antique Dealers Association**, (20 Rutland Gate, SW7; 020 7589 4128; www.bada.org), will send a list of members on request.

A wide selection of expensive antiques can be found on Bond Street, the King's Road, the South Kensington end of Fulham Road and Kensington Church Street (which also has shops specialising in china and glass). Pimlico Road is interesting for unusual and decorative pieces.

Chevertons of Edenbridge; 71-73 High Street, Edenbridge, Kent; 017 3286 3196; www.chevertons.com. Open 09:00–17:30 Monday–Saturday. Great prices and friendly service.

The Millinery Works; 87 Southgate Road, N1, 020 7359 2019; www.millineryworks.co.uk. Open 11:00–18:00 Tuesday–Saturday and 12:00–17:00 on Sunday. Closed Mondays.
Specialises in arts & crafts and furniture.

Auction Houses

Dealers or agents purchase the majority of their stock from auction houses. Therefore, auction houses are a good and fun alternative for antique hunting if you have the time and you remember to view the items carefully (during the preview, which is usually a few days before the sale).

Auction houses offer services to assist their customers. They can provide a detailed summary of a specific piece or they can arrange to have a specialist work with you during the preview. At the viewing, you can purchase a catalogue, which includes descriptions and estimates for each lot. Bidding is easy. First, you register and receive a paddle with a number. When the lot you are interested in comes up, raise your hand. The auctioneer will take your bid. If you are successful, he or she will note your number. It's that simple!

The main auction houses are **Christie's** and **Sotheby's**. Visit their websites or look at listings in the newspaper or magazines for specific auctions. See "Antique Fairs" above for more details.

Bonham's; Montpelier Street, SW7; 020 7393 3900, and 101 New Bond Street, W1; 020 7447 7447; www.bonhams.com.

Christie's; 8 King Street, SW1; 020 7839 9060, and 85 Old Brompton Road, SW7; 020 7930 6074; www.christies.com.

Lots Road Auctions; 71-73 Lots Road, SW10; 020 7376 6800; www.lotsroad.com.

Two sales every Sunday. The lots can be viewed online. The full catalogue is available from 19:30 on Thursdays.

Rosebery's; 74-76 Knight's Hill, SE27; 020 8761 2522; www.roseberys.co.uk. Twelve catalogued sales a year.

Sotheby's; 34-35 New Bond Street, W1; 020 7293 5000 and Hammersmith Road, W1; 020 7293 5555; www.sothebys.com.

Art Galleries

London has many fine art galleries whether your taste is for Old Masters or young contemporary artists. The more expensive dealers are concentrated in St. James and Mayfair; others are scattered throughout the city.

The Society of London Art Dealers website (www.slad.org.uk) has a list of various galleries throughout London as well as upcoming exhibitions and art fairs.

BOOKS

Chain bookstores like **Waterstone's** and **WH Smith** are ubiquitous in London. There are numerous other bookstores with branches throughout London, including **Books Etc.**, and **Borders**, which also offer a good general selection of standard books in print.

But if you're looking for specialty books, maybe something old, out of print, or an art book, you're in luck because London is still peppered with small, independent bookstores. Many sell a mix of new and used books, often devoted to specialist themes to differentiate themselves from the chains. Others are devoted exclusively to dusty and dog-eared, second-hand books or rare first editions and leather-bound gems. The heart of London's book trade is found in the Bloomsbury area, where a number of fine bookshops are clustered around the British Museum. Among them are **Foyle's**, **Gekoski** and **Ulysses**. You also might want to visit Henry Sotheran as well as Cecil Court and Charing Cross Road, where you'll find a number of second-hand and specialist book, poster and print shops devoted to many subjects.

Bertram Rota; 31 Long Acre, WC2; 020 7836 0723; www.bertramrota.co.uk.

Specialises in modern first editions, books on architecture and the applied arts, and private press printing and livres d'artiste.

Blenheim Books; 11 Blenheim Crescent, W11; 020 7792 0777.

Gardening books for the beginner through to the professional.

Biblion; 1-7 Davies Mews, W1; 020 7629 1374; www.biblion.com.

A must see for any book lover with a vast collection of antiquarian booksellers located under one roof. You can spend hours here sampling the merchandise. Visit their website, where nearly three million books are listed by more than 500 dealers. This is the UK's largest website by far for rare, antiquarian and second-hand books.

Books for Cooks; 4 Blenheim Crescent, W11; 020 7221 1992; www.booksforcooks.com.

A vast array of cookbooks is stacked floor to ceiling. The knowledgeable staff will help with suggestions or special orders. There is a small kitchen where they test recipes and offer courses, but you'll need to book early.

Comic Showcase; 63 Charing Cross Road, WC2; 020 7434 4349.

Specialises in adult comics and books by well-known cartoonists.

Daunt Books; 83 Marylebone High Street, W1, 020 7224 2295; www.dauntbooks.co.uk.

Unique arrangement of travel guides, novels and non-fiction arranged by country. Also includes good general selection. Multiple locations.

The Economist Bookshop; 15 Regent Street, SW1; 020 7839 1937.

Specialises in social sciences.

Forbidden Planet; 179 Shaftesbury Ave, WC2; 020 7420 3666; www.forbiddenplanet.com.

Specialises in science fiction, fantasy and horror with a range of comics, magazines, books and collectibles. Multiple locations.

Foyle's; 113-119 Charing Cross Road, WC2; 020 7437 5660; www.foyles.co.uk.

A massive one-of-a-kind store. If you are looking for that "hard to find" book, this is the place.

Gay's the Word; 66 Marchmont Street, WC1; 020 7278 7654; www.gaystheword.co.uk.

London's exclusively gay and lesbian bookshop offering fiction, biography, travel literature and sex manuals.

Gekoski; Pied Bull Yard, 15A Bloomsbury Square, WC1; 020 7404 6676; www.abebooks.com/home/RAGEKOSKI/.
Sells rare and first editions of 19th century and modern literature.

Hatchard's; 187 Piccadilly, W1; 020 7439 9921; www.hatchards.co.uk.
Excellent selection; bookseller since 1797.

Henry Sotheran; 2 Sackville Street, W1; 020 7439 6151; www.sotherans.co.uk.
The longest established antiquarian booksellers in the world (York, 1761). Has a handsome ground floor room lined with glass-fronted cabinets packed with antiquarian books, supplemented by a downstairs print gallery.

Keith Fawkes; 1-3 Flask Walk, NW3; 020 7435 0614.
Hampstead's oldest antiquarian bookshop.

Maggs Brothers; 50 Berkeley Square, W1; 020 7493 7160; www.maggs.com.
Arguably the most prestigious antiquarian bookseller in London, selling pre-20th century manuscripts and first editions, with an outstanding selection in literature and travel.

Murder One; 76-78 Charing Cross Road, WC2; 020 7539 8820; www.murderone.co.uk.
Specialises in crime and mystery books.

Shipley, Specialist Art Booksellers; 70 Charing Cross Road, WC2; 020 7836 4872; www.artbook.co.uk.
A fine collection of new, old, rare and scholarly books on art.

Silver Moon Women's Bookshop (within Foyle's); 113-119 Charing Cross Road, WC2; 020 7440 1562; www.silvermoonbookshop.co.uk or www. foyles.co.uk. Largest women's-interest bookshop.

Stanford's; 12-14 Long Acre, WC2; 020 7836 1321; www.stanfords.co.uk. Excellent range of travel literature, guide books and very helpful staff. Maps and globes are also a specialty.

Talking Books; 11 Wigmore Street, W1; 020 7491 4117; www.talkingbooks. co.uk. Massive selection of audio books on CDs and MP3CDs.

Travel Bookshop; 13-15 Blenheim Crescent, W11; 020 7229 5260; www.thetravelbookshop.com.

Guidebooks, travelogues, literature, history and biography on countries around the world. Also has photographic titles, maps, atlases and an eclectic range of second hand, rare and antiquarian books.

Ulysses; 40 Museum Street, WC1; 020 7831 1600.

Collection of modern first editions and 20th century classics. This shop is full of rare and second-hand books.

CLOTHING
Size Charts

The tables below should be used as an approximate guide, as the actual sizes may vary according to the manufacturer, as well as the country of origin. Small sizes are generally difficult to obtain. It is advisable to try the clothing on to ensure the correct size. Children's clothes in the UK are usually based on the child's age using a calculated average weight and height.

Women's Clothing

UK	8	10	12	14	16	18	20	22	24
France	36	38	40	42	44	46	48	50	52
Germany	34	36	38	40	42	44	46	48	50
Italy	40	42	44	46	48	50	52	54	56
Australia	10	12	14	16	18	20	22	24	26
Japan	9	11	13	15	17	19	21	23	25
US	6	8	10	12	14	16	18	20	22

Women's Shoes

UK	3	3½	4	4½	5	5½	6	6½	7	7½
Continental Europe	35½	36	37	37½	38	38½	39	40	41	42
Australia	4	4½	5	5½	6	6½	7	7½	8	8½
Japan	21½	22	22½	23	23½	24	24½	25	25½	26
US	5½	6	6½	7	7½	8	8½	9	9½	10

Men's Clothing

UK	32	34	36	38	40	42	44	46
Continental Europe	42	44	46	48	50	52	54	56
Australia	42	44	36	37	38	39	41	42
Japan	--	S	--	M	L	--	LL	--
US	32	34	36	38	40	42	44	46

Men's Shirts or Collar Sizes

UK	14	14½	15	15½	16	16½	17	17½
Continental Europe	36	37	38	39	41	42	43	44
Australia	36	37	38	39	41	42	43	44
Japan	36	37	38	39	41	42	43	44
US	14	14½	15	15½	16	16½	17	17½

Men's Shoes

UK	7½	8	8½	9	9½	10	10½	11
Continental Europe	41	42	43	43½	44	44½	45	45½
Australia	7½	8	8½	9	9½	10	10½	11
Japan	26	26½	27	27½	28	28½	29	29½
US	8	8½	9	9½	10	10½	11	11½

Socks

UK	9½	10	10½	11	11½	12	12½
Continental Europe	39	40	41	42	43	44	45
US	9½	10	10½	11	11½	12	12½

DEPARTMENT STORES

The list below contains a mixture of large department stores with multiple branches and smaller, specialty department stores.

Argos; 087 0600 8784; www.argos.co.uk.

Locations throughout London and the UK. A catalogue store stocking a wide range of consumer products goods, including furniture, kitchen appliances, children's toys, sports equipment and electronics. Delivery available.

BHS; 252-258 Oxford Street, W1; 020 7629 2011; www.bhs.co.uk.

Offers relatively inexpensive clothing and home goods. Multiple locations.

Debenhams; 334-348 Oxford Street, W1; 084 4561 6161;
www.debenhams.com.
General purpose department store. Multiple locations.

Fenwick of Bond Street; 63 New Bond Street, W1; 020 7629 9161;
www.fenwick.co.uk.
Up-market clothes and accessories.

Fortnum and Mason; 181 Piccadilly, W1; 020 7734 8040;
www.fortnumandmason.com.
Offers Old World charm and atmosphere. The ground floor houses a formal food hall stocked with specialty teas, fabulous hampers and a genteel setting for an afternoon tea. Goods sold include classic women's and men's clothing, furniture, home goods and made-to-order hampers.

Harrods; 87-135 Brompton Road, SW1; 020 7730 1234;
www.harrods.com.
London's most famous emporium. Unequalled grandeur fills their food halls. Known for their twice yearly sales and amazing range of goods (exotic animals to medieval instruments). Offers over 60 fashion departments, including an excellent selection of designer shoes. The dress code is strict: anyone arriving wearing shorts, torn jeans or carrying a rucksack may be asked to leave.

Harvey Nichols; 109-125 Knightsbridge, SW1; 020 7235 5000;
www.harveynichols.com.
Offers a fabulous array of designer collections and exquisite home furnishings. Don't miss the drinks bar and café on the fifth floor, which sits alongside the food hall.

John Lewis; 300 Oxford Street, W1; 020 7629 7711; www.johnlewis.com.
Known for their curtain department and household items selection. Also boasts an electronics section and a good range of stylish, functional clothing.

Its famed "never knowingly undersold" policy means prices, as a rule, are very reasonable.

House of Fraser; 318 Oxford Street, W1; 087 0160 7258; www.houseoffraser.co.uk.

A wide range of services is available in many of the stores, including hair salons, beauty treatment rooms, nail bars, restaurants, coffee bars and a complimentary personal shopping service for both men and women.

Liberty; 210-220 Regent Street, W1; 020 7734 1234; www.liberty.co.uk.

Housed in two adjoining Tudor-style buildings, Liberty is famous for its Liberty print fabrics, Art Deco period furniture and a unique selection of home goods and designer fashions.

Marks & Spencer; 458 Oxford Street, W1; 020 7935 7954; www.marksandspencer.com.

Known for its food hall (Simply Food) specialising in ready-meals, and staple products like socks and underwear. Also carries women's, men's and children's fashions focusing on good value at the right price. Multiple locations.

Peter Jones; Sloane Square, SW1; 020 7730 3434; www.peterjones.co.uk.

Affiliated with The John Lewis Partnership. Carries many of the same lines as John Lewis.

Selfridges; 400 Oxford Street, W1; 087 0837 7377; www.selfridges.co.uk.

Large and varied selection of cutting-edge, but not intimidating, fashions, including children's. Boasts London's largest cosmetics hall, a spectacular toy department, and a gourmet food hall. Offers a number of in-store restaurants that range from sprawling family-oriented affairs to hip coffee bars.

DO IT YOURSELF (DIY)
See *Chapter 11: Services*.

GARDEN CENTRES AND NURSERIES
See *Chapter 11: Services.*

GROCERIES

The major supermarkets are **Sainsbury's, Tesco, Waitrose, Asda** and **Morrison's/Safeway**. You can also buy groceries from smaller, independent stores peppered throughout London, as well as in the food halls of most major department stores. The best food halls are in **Fortnum & Mason, Harrods, Harvey Nichols, Selfridges**, and branches of **Marks & Spencer.** While variety is limited in these venues, the quality is quite good.

Most supermarkets offer online shopping. Some of the most popular include www.sainsburys.co.uk, www.tesco.com and www.waitrose.com (some post codes can get delivery only through Waitrose's partner, Ocado (www.ocado. com). Groceries are usually delivered to your door within a one or two hour pre-arranged time slot.

MARKETS

With over 70 markets in London, it is not uncommon to stumble upon one while taking a stroll. The markets vary greatly in size, the variety of goods on offer and the overall feel. And in a city as expensive as London, you can find some true gems and save a significant amount of money by market shopping.

Below are some of the most popular markets in London but search out others not mentioned here. If markets are intriguing to you, a very good resource guide is *The London Market Guide* by Andrew Kershman.

Antique Markets

There are antique markets all over London where groups of dealers, specialising in a variety of antiques or collectibles at all different price levels, display their goods. Consult "Markets" for outdoor street markets specialising in antiques. The following indoor markets contain numerous permanent stalls that deal in smaller items such as silver, prints and ceramics.

Admiral Vernon; 141-149 Portobello Road, W11; 020 7727 5242; www.portobello-antiques.co.uk.

Only open on Saturday. The busiest arcade on Portobello Road, with over 200 private dealers. It features 17th-19th century porcelain, advertising art and antique textiles.

Alfie's Antique Market; 13-25 Church Street, NW8; 020 7723 6066; www.alfiesantiques.com.

Closed Sunday and Monday. London's largest antique market; a fabulous maze of treasures in a historical street market. Source of some real bargains. The basement is packed with antique textiles, 19th century furniture, jewellery and accessories, while on the upper levels you might find French country furniture or 1960s furniture and lighting.

Antiquarius; 131-141 King's Road, SW3; 020 7351 5353; www.antiquarius.co.uk.

Closed Sunday. The oldest and most famous antiques centres in London. It has a village-like charm and a vast array of antiques. Good for browsing; features glassware, classic luggage, silverware and costume jewellery.

Bermondsey Market (New Caledonian Market); Long Lane and Bermondsey Street, SE1. Open 04:00-14:00 Fridays. Best before 09:00.

Specialises in paintings, silver and jewellery.

Bond Street Antiques Centre; 124 New Bond Street, W1; 020 7493 1854.

Closed Sunday. Internationally renowned for silver and jewellery, vintage watches and objects d'art.

Camden Passage; Camden Passage, Upper Street, N1. Open 10:00-14:00 Wednesdays and 10:00-17:00 Saturdays.

Specialises in prints, silver, 19th century magazines, jewellery and toys.

Chelsea Antique Market; 245-253 King's Road, SW3; 020 7352 5689.

Closed Sunday. A great place for finding unusual antiques. Prices tend to be higher than in other markets in London, although more-modestly priced pieces can be found.

Gray's Antique Market & Grays in the Mews; 58 Davies Street and 1-7 Davies Mews, W1; 020 7629 7034; www.graysantiques.com.

Closed Saturday and Sunday. The front hall has an enormous collection of antique jewellery and silverware dealers. The Mews is a bit cheaper but offers no less desirable collectibles, particularly, tinplate toys.

London Silver Vaults; Chancery House, Chancery Lane, WC2; 020 7242 3844; www.thesilvervaults.com.

Closed Sunday. World's largest collection of antique silver. These subterranean vaults are home to over 40 dealers offering every imaginable kind of silver item, from antique to modern. They also offer a wealth of knowledge (many are second- and third-generation dealers). Prices range from £10 to £100,000+, so you should find something to suit you.

Portobello Road Market; see "*General Markets*" below.

General Markets

Brick Lane Market; Brick Lane, E1. Open 06:00-13:00 Sundays.

Furniture, old books, jewellery, watches, food, bicycles, handbags — offers something for everyone. The market itself changes from week to week so look for new stalls on adjacent streets.

Brixton Market; Electric Avenue, SW9. Open 08:00-17:30 Monday to Saturday; 08:00-15:00 Wednesday.

All kinds of wonderful Afro-Caribbean food from goat's meat to plantains.

Camden Market; Buck Street, Camden High Street and Camden Lock, NW1; www.camdenlock.net. Open 10:00-18:00 Tuesday to Friday and

09:00-18:00 Saturday and Sunday.

Camden Market is really made up of six markets selling everything, including antiques, furniture, health food, retro clothing, jewellery, arts and crafts. Saturday is the busiest day since the entire market is open. Many shops and stalls are open every day. Teens and those who like to re-live the '70s punk lifestyle will be at home here.

East Street Market; East Street, SE17. Open 08:30-16:00 Tuesday to Sunday.

On Sundays there are over 250 stalls selling fruit, vegetables, flowers, clothes, and electrical and household goods.

Greenwich Market; Greenwich High Road, SE10; www.greenwich-market.co.uk. Open 07:30-17:30 Thursday and 09:30-17:30 Friday to Sunday and Bank Holiday Mondays. Antiques and collectibles are Thursday and Friday only. Most shops, cafes and restaurants are open seven days a week.

Leadenhall Market; Whittington Avenue, EC3; 07:00-16:00 Monday to Friday.

It's not a traditional London market, but Leadenhall Market, whose retailers include upscale clothing shops and foodie paradises, is worth visiting alone for the beautiful Victorian arcade in which it's situated.

Petticoat Lane Market; Middlesex Street, E1; 09:00-14:00 Sunday.

Leather goods, clothes, watches, jewellery and toys.

Portobello Road Market; Portobello Road, W10; www.portobelloroad.co.uk.

Shops are open six days a week. Market is open 08:00-18:30 Monday to Wednesday, Friday to Saturday and 08:00-13:00 Thursday. Over 2,000 stalls of hip new and vintage clothes, jewellery, old medals, paintings, silver, objects d'art, great food, flowers and ambience. Saturday is by far the busiest day (and the only day for antiques); so if you go, arrive early and be prepared

12

to face the crowds.

Shepherd's Bush Market; Goldhawk Road, W12. Open 09:30-17:00 Monday to Saturday; 09:30-13:30 Thursday.

West Indian food, Asian spices and cheap electrical and household goods.

Walthamstow Market; Walthamstow High Street, E17. Open 08:00-18:00 Monday through Saturday.

Claims to be Britain's longest daily street market, with 450 stalls selling cheap clothing, fruit and vegetables, as well as household items.

Fruit, Vegetable and Flower Markets

Berwick Street Market; Berwick Street and Rupert Street, W1. Open 09:00-17:00 Monday to Saturday.

Offers the best and cheapest selection of fruit and vegetables in central London. There are also good cheese, fish, bread, herb and spice stalls and inexpensive household goods.

Borough Market; 8 Southwark Street, SE1; www.boroughmarket.org.uk. Open 12:00-18:00 Friday; 09:00-16:00 Saturday.

This superb farmers' market, nicknamed London's Larder, has been trading here since 1756. There are some good cut flowers, as well as quality coffee, fruit, vegetables, fishmongers and butchers. A number of traders offer organic produce and gourmet food selections.

Columbia Road Flower Market; 4 Columbia Road (between Gosset Street and the Royal Oak pub), E2. Open 08:00-14:00 Sundays only.

Without question this is the prettiest street market in town. Flowers, shrubs, bedding plants and other horticultural delights are spread in all directions, while the shops stock flowers, garden accessories, and even gifts and furniture. Visit in December to pick up a Christmas tree, poinsettia and a wreath.

Spitalfields Market; 65 Brushfield Street, E1; www.visitspitalfields.com/osm.html. Open 10:00-16:00 Monday to Friday and 09:00-17:00 Sunday.

Crafts and antiques stalls are set up through the week, but on Friday and, particularly, Sunday, the market comes alive with a dozen or so organic producers selling relishes, pickles, herbs and spices, breads and cakes, and fruit and vegetables.

OUTLET SHOPPING

There are many shopping outlets throughout the UK, and every one has a variety of shops offering discounts up to 70% off the retail price of the products they sell. Visit www.shoppingvillages.com for a complete listing of outlet locations, opening hours, and new shops or special offerings.

Bicester Village; Pingle Drive, Bicester, Oxfordshire (Junction 9 off of the M40); 018 6932 3200; www.bicestervillage.com.

Top-quality merchandise from over 60 designer and famous brand-named shops.

Burberry Outlet; 29-53 Chatham Place, E9; 020 8985 3344.

Clarks Village Factory Shopping; Farm Road Street, Somerset; 0145 884 0064; www.clarksvillage.co.uk. Nearly 60 shops.

Costco; Hartspring Lane, Watford, Herts; 019 2322 5449; www.costco.co.uk.

Sells high-quality, nationally branded and selected private-label merchandise at low prices to businesses purchasing for commercial use or resale, and also to individuals who are members of selected employment groups.

Great Western Designer Outlet Village; Churchward Village, Swindon (Junction 16 of the M4); 017 9350 7600.

Offers discounts every day for end-of-season merchandise and high street surplus stock. Also has a kids play area and a crèche.

Merchants Quay; Brighton Marina Village, East Sussex; 012 7381 8504; www.brightonmarina.co.uk. Famous-name outlets, selling a wide range of products including clothing, lighting, cosmetics and toiletries, shoes, bedding and luggage.

Discount China

Home to the world's greatest pottery manufacturers, Stoke-on-Trent offers visitors hundreds of pottery shops to choose from. Over 1,500 potteries have operated here since the early 1700s and many are still in operation today, offering china and crystal at significant discounts. These include *Aynsley®, Hartley and Sons®, Royal Doulton®, Minton®, Portmeirion®, Royal Crown Derby®, Royal Worcester®, Spode®, Waterford®, Wedgewood®* and many, many more. Visit the website (www.thepotteries. org) for a complete listing of all potteries, their locations, latest news and other attractions in the area.

Discount Crystal

Dartington Crystal Ltd.; Linden Close, Great Torrington, Devon; 018 0562 6262; www.dartington.co.uk.

Edinburgh Crystal; Eastfield, Penicuik, Midlothian; 019 686 75128; www.edinburgh-crystal.co.uk.

Royal Brierley Crystal; The New Royal Brierley Experience, Tipton Road, Dudley, West Midlands; 012 1530 5600; www.royalbrierley.com.

Tudor Crystal; Stewkins, Stourbridge, West Midlands; 013 8439 2525; www.tudorcrystal.com.

VAT

A Value Added Tax (VAT) of 17.5% is added to most goods and services purchased in the UK. In certain circumstances, VAT paid to a UK merchant may be reclaimed.

You are only eligible for a VAT refund if you are visiting the UK and you intend to take the purchased goods out of the UK within three months after purchase. To reclaim the VAT on items purchased, you must have the retailer fill out the export documentation. If you live in the UK or in any country within the European Union, you do not qualify for a VAT refund. If you have lived in the UK for more than a year and would like to purchase goods before returning to your home country, different VAT rules may apply to you (since you may be considered a departing UK resident).

For more details, contact **HM Revenue and Customs** at www.hmrc.gov.uk.

Continuing Education

CONTENTS

13

The opportunities for continuing education in London are immense. Since it is not possible to list the thousands of programmes offered in London every year, this chapter focuses on those courses that are well known and repeatedly attended by members of the Junior League of London.

The cost of courses varies greatly and some mentioned here are quite costly. Do not hesitate to ask about the cost of a course while enquiring about dates and availability.

COURSE LISTINGS

Don't let this listing of courses limit you. There are a plethora of courses offered throughout Greater London. *Floodlight* and *Hotcourses* are the standard references for courses offered in London (www.floodlight.co.uk and www.hotcourses.co.uk). *Floodlight* guides are published three times a year: the March edition lists summer courses, the July edition lists part-time and short courses offered throughout the academic year, and the October edition lists full-time courses. *Hotcourses* (formerly known as *OnCourse*), publishes *Hotcourses Magazine, Hotcourses University and Career Guide* and *Hotcourses World Study Guide.* These publications can be found at most bookshops and newsagents, and can also be ordered through Central Books on 0845 458 9911.

Adult Education Courses

Contact your local council for information on hundreds of adult education classes, ranging from pottery, car mechanics and language courses to degrees in social work. The fees are usually very reasonable because they are government subsidised and classes are held at various locations in your neighbourhood.

ART HISTORY

Prices vary depending on the duration of the course and the institution. Many courses follow a semester or school-year schedule; therefore it is advisable to book well in advance to secure a place. Additionally, many course offerings change based on current interest. For the most current curriculum content and schedule, call the school and ask for a brochure.

Intensive Courses

Christie's Education; 153 Great Titchfield Street, W1; 020 7665 4350; www.christies.com. Christie's aim is to give students a firm and practical foundation of knowledge in the arts of the Western world.

One-year diploma courses or certificate courses (three terms of 10 weeks each) are offered for the following:

> • Early European Art — Antiquity to Renaissance
> • Fine and Decorative Arts — Renaissance to the present
> • Modern and Contemporary Art and Design — late 19th century to the present.

Evening and short courses are also offered. These classes meet once a week for a specified number of weeks and cover a variety of specialised subjects.

The New Study Centre; 21 Palace Gardens Terrace, W8; 020 7229 3393.

Courses are held at the Royal Entomological Society, 41 Queen's Gate, SW7. The decorative arts course is divided into four self-contained parts (which can be taken separately): 16th and 17th century, 18th century I, 18th century II, 19th and 20th century. Other short courses and day visits to country houses are also available.

Sotheby's Institute in London; 30 Bedford Square, WC1; 020 7462 3232; www.sothebys.com.

The Institute runs over 30 courses in all aspects of fine and decorative art at both undergraduate and post-graduate levels (Masters of Art). Internationally recognised courses offer unique first-hand examination of works of art with privileged access to auction rooms. Full-time courses are available in a large range of topics. Acceptance is by application and interview.

Sotheby's also offers a variety of evening, daytime and short courses to the public covering various topics within art business, fine and decorative art, contemporary art and East Asian art.

Day, Evening and Short Courses

The Art Study Circle; (Sara Hebblethwaite), 020 8788 6910.

Art history lectures given weekly in an informal setting by experts in their fields. Some lectures tie-in with current exhibitions in London and include visits.

See also **Christie's** and **Sotheby's** above.

COOKERY

Books for Cooks; 4 Blenheim Crescent, W11; 020 7221 1992; www.booksforcooks.com.

Special 3-hour workshops focusing on various topics, tips and cuisines. Imperative to book in advance since workshops fill up quickly.

Le Cordon Bleu Cookery School; 114 Marylebone Lane, W1;
020 7935 3503; www.cordonbleu.edu.

Offers career training, short and part-time courses, practical and demonstration classes. Because this school is world famous, there is often a waiting list for its diploma and certificate courses. Cookery demonstrations are open to the public but require advance booking.

Leith's School of Food and Wine; 21 St. Alban's Grove, W8;
020 7229 0177; www.leiths.com.

Associated with Leith's restaurant, the school offers diploma and certificate courses in food and wine for all levels, and a variety of short cookery courses.

Tante Marie School of Cookery; Woodham House, Carlton Road, Woking, Surrey, GU21; 014 8372 6957; www.tantemarie.co.uk.

Offers both certificate and diploma courses as well as occasional short-course demonstrations. A wide range of cuisine is covered.

Constance Spry Ltd.; Moor Park House, Moor Park Lane, Farnham, Surrey GU9 8EN; 012 5273 4477; www.constancespry.com.

Offers a wide variety of one-day cooking demonstrations held in conjunction with flower arranging courses (see "*Flower Arranging*"). Several week-long summer courses in entertaining are also available.

FLOWER ARRANGING

Jane Packer Flower School; 32-34 New Cavendish Street, W1;
020 7486 1300; www.jane-packer.co.uk.

Offers a four-week career course and a three-day introductory course in flower arranging. Also offers evening, one-day and half-day courses in a variety of subjects including dried flowers, Christmas decorations and wedding flowers.

Kenneth Turner; 1 Hall Road, Hemel Hampstead, Herts, HP2;

014 4283 8181; www.kenturnerflowerschool.com.

One, two and three-day courses available on a variety of flower arranging subjects.

Paula Pryke Flowers; The Flower House, Cynthia Street, N1;

020 7837 7336; www.paula-pryke-flowers.com.

One-day, half-day and multi-day courses are available on a variety of themes.

Constance Spry Ltd.; Moor Park House, Moor Park Lane, Farnham, Surrey, GU9 8EN; 012 5273 4477; www.constancespry.com.

One-day flower workshops and two-day short courses covering a variety of flower arranging subjects.

GARDENING AND INTERIOR DESIGN

The British take great pride in their gardens and the following courses are very comprehensive.

The English Gardening School; The Chelsea Physics Garden, 66 Royal Hospital Road, SW3; 020 7352 4347; www.englishgardeningschool.co.uk.

Offers one-year diploma courses in garden design, practical horticulture, horticulture drawing, plants and plantsmanship. Also offers short courses of varying length, on a wide range of topics such as garden design, Christmas wreaths and flower arranging. There are also distance-learning courses in design and horticulture available.

The Inchbald School of Design: Garden Design; 32 Eccleston Square, SW1; 020 7630 9011; **Interior Design**, 7 Eaton Gate, SW1; 020 7730 5508; www.inchbald.co.uk.

Offers a one-year diploma course, a 10-week certificate course and an MA course in garden design (basic principles of design, plant knowledge, the role of fine art in design, garden architecture and business skills) or in interior design and decoration. Part-time and Saturday classes are also offered in garden design and interior decoration.

KLC School of Design; 503 The Chambers, Chelsea Harbour, SW10; 020 7376 3377; www.klc.co.uk.

Offers a variety of full-time, part-time, short and open learning courses are available in interior design and garden design.

LANGUAGES

Institut Francais; 14 Cromwell Place, SW7; 020 7581 2701; www.institut-francais.org.uk.

The official French government centre of language and culture in London offers courses at all levels; part-time or full-time, weekdays or weekends. Enrolment in a course provides access to the Institute's cultural centre, multimedia library and the children's library.

University of Westminster; 309 Regent Street, W1; 020 7911 5000; www.wmin.ac.uk.

Offers courses in most European languages one evening a week from late September through May.

Oxford House College; 28 Market Place, W1; 020 7580 9785; www.oxfordhousecollege.co.uk.

Offers many language courses ranging from general English (to improve speaking, reading, writing and listening) to business-oriented skills to improve career prospects.

MUSEUM AND GALLERY LECTURES

Most museums and galleries offer regular free lectures and tours. Call or review individual websites for a schedule of events (See *Chapter 16: Culture* for museum listings). Many also offer the opportunity to receive e-mails of upcoming events. Information on talks and lectures, as well as new exhibits, can be found in the weekly magazine *Time Out: London*.

UNIVERSITY AND COLLEGE COURSES

There are numerous courses available: undergraduate, graduate, part-time and full-time. Check to see whether the course might be credited to any degree you are planning to complete. Tuition fees vary and if you have lived in the UK for a minimum of five years, or hold certain other residency equivalencies, you will qualify for "home student tuition", which is generally half the price of the overseas student fee. Check with the school.

The Open University; Walton Hall, Milton Keynes, MK7 6AA; 019 0827 4066; www.open.ac.uk.

Offers university courses to any resident of the European Union and Switzerland over 18 years of age. Methods of instruction include television courses, tutorials and correspondence work.

The University of London; Birkbeck College, Malet Street, WC1; 020 7631 6000; www.bbk.ac.uk.

Offers certificate and diploma courses, as well as one and two- term courses to anyone over 18 years of age. Classes usually meet two hours a week for 24 weeks.

WINE

Christie's Education; 153 Great Titchfield Street, W1; 020 7665 4350; www.christies.com.

Offers an "Introduction to Wine Tasting" course (primarily focusing on French wines) one evening a week for five weeks; available six times per year. Occasional "one-off" master classes on fine and rare wines, wines of the New World and seminars abroad.

Sotheby's Wine Department; 34-35 New Bond Street, W1; 020 7293 6423; www.sothebys.com.

Separate courses covering varietals and regional wines, running one evening a week for five weeks; offered twice each year. Occasional "one-off" wine seminars are also available.

Drawn by Katie

Sports and Leisure

CONTENTS

14

Sports and games are a huge part of British life. Many sports were invented, developed or unified by the British — golf, skiing, tennis and football to name a few. Just about every sport is enjoyed somewhere, from the most popular "sport" of angling (with over 2.2 million participants), to the more arcane sports of lawnmower racing and curling. Team games traditionally have a higher profile. Association football, rugby football and cricket are the most popular. Golf, racing and motor sports also have large followings.

BRIEF BRITISH SPORTING VOCABULARY GUIDE

Athletics   Track and Field.

Cricket   A very popular summer sport. The basic concept
                       of cricket is similar to that of baseball, however
                       the game play and rules are very different.

The Derby	Pronounced "dar-bee". A very famous and prestigious flat horse race held in June every year at the Epsom Downs Racecourse in Surrey.
FA Cup	The main football knock-out competition, open to all clubs in England and Wales (amateur and professional).
Fixture	Game, match, contest.
Football	Association football (soccer) or rugby football, but usually refers to the former. NFL football is known as "American football".
Grand National	The world's best-known horse race over fences, run at Aintree, Liverpool in early April.
Hockey	Field hockey. Ice hockey is known as ice hockey.
Netball	Women's sport. Foundations come from basketball, although the ball is smaller, the ring is smaller and higher, and there is no backboard. Seven-player teams.
Pitch	Field of play.
Premiership	An elite league of the best 20 football clubs in England and Wales. There is also a Premiership league in rugby union that consists of the top 12 rugby football clubs in the U.K. Generally, this term refers to the football league.
Racing/Horse racing	Race Meeting.

Rounders	A version of softball usually played at school.
Rugby	Amateurs play "rugby union", which is 15-a-side; professionals play "rugby league", which is 13-a-side and a faster game.
Six Nations	Premier Northern Hemisphere rugby competition between England, Wales, Scotland, Ireland, France and Italy. Held in January or February.
Test Match	An international rugby or cricket match, lasting either one or four days.
The Open	The British Open Championship in golf.
Royal Ascot	The world's most famous horse-race meeting typically held the third week of June. Attended by Her Majesty the Queen.
Touts	Scalpers. Expensive and dubious sources of hard-to-find tickets.

SPECTATOR SPORTS

Tickets to see the biggest sporting events are quite difficult to obtain, with the most sought after being Wimbledon (tennis), the FA Cup Final (football), Six Nations fixtures (rugby union), Test cricket matches (cricket) and the Formula One British Grand Prix (car racing). Unless you are affiliated with a club, have very good connections, or you are prepared to pay vastly inflated prices on the black market, the best way to attend one of these events may be to encourage your employer to purchase a corporate hospitality package, or to somehow acquire an invitation to another corporate box or tent. Try **The Sporting Traveller** (017 3724 4398; www. thesportingtraveller.com) or **Matchpoint** (020 8332 7384; www.matchpoint.

co.uk), which both offer deals for all these events. **Ticketmaster** (020 7316 4709; www.ticketmaster.co.uk) is another option. Regardless of where tickets are found, the best advice is to purchase them early.

FOOTBALL

Association football, also known as soccer, is the national game, and every visitor should experience at least one match. The season runs from August until April, ending with the drama and passion of the FA Cup Final in May. Among other events, FA Cup Finals are normally played at **Wembley Stadium** (alternative locations are being used while it is under construction). Sixty-five per cent of tickets are allocated to season ticket holders of the two clubs contesting the Final. The remainder of the tickets are for the football league, its members and hospitality packages. These are always available for a price — expect to pay at least £500 per ticket (see the agencies listed above).

Premier League / Nationwide League

The FA Premier League consists of the top 20 professional football teams in England. Several of the teams are located in London (go to www.premierleague.com for a current listing). Tickets to see habitual premiership teams like Arsenal, Chelsea and Tottenham Hotspur are hard to obtain, particularly for high-profile matches. Other teams' tickets may be easier to get hold of, such as Charlton, Fulham and West Ham United. Tickets for "derby" matches against local London rivals or matches against well-known teams such as Manchester United must be booked several weeks in advance. It should be possible to purchase tickets a few days ahead for other games. Most football clubs allow for bookings via the telephone or online. For fixtures and tickets, try **Ticketmaster** or the individual club websites (for example: www.fulhamfc.co.uk, www.whufc.co.uk and www.spurs.co.uk). Alternatively, try one of the London clubs in Nationwide Division One (just below the Premier League). It is usually easier to acquire tickets and many times offers a more representative taste of the national game. **Crystal Palace Football Club** (www.cpfc.co.uk) in south London has a reputation for being especially family friendly.

Going to the Game – Some Handy Hints

- Professional football matches take place on weekends and on weekday evenings. The traditional kick-off times are 15:00 on Saturday and 19:45 during the week. Always be sure to check the day before the match since the time printed on your ticket can change at short notice due to TV schedules and police requests.

- Most football clubs welcome children, but book seats in the designated family areas, which will be non-smoking and specially stewarded.

- Expect opposing supporters to be strictly segregated. If ever offered a match ticket, check where the seats are located. Avoid sitting with the away supporters unless you and your family are diehard fans of the away team. Equally, you may be asked to leave by the stewards if you are seen to be supporting the away team in a home area.

- Take public transport to the game if at all possible. Roads around the ground may be blocked and parking may be virtually impossible.

- Do not try to take food or drink with you, as it will probably be confiscated. Not only do clubs prefer you to buy food from the concession stands, cans and bottles are regarded as a safety hazard. Beer is available inside the stadium before the match, but cannot be taken to your seat. The bar will close as soon as the match is underway. This applies to corporate boxes as well.

- Dress warmly. Unless in a corporate box, there will be no heating and seats may not be under cover. Matches are usually played rain or shine.

14

RUGBY FOOTBALL

There are two types of rugby played in England — rugby union (15-a-side) and rugby league (13-a-side). There are various national and international leagues and competitions for both sports. Look at www.rfu.com (rugby union) or www.therfl.uk.co.uk (rugby league) for more details.

In London and the south, rugby union is far more popular. The English national team plays at Twickenham in West London, where Test Matches are played. There is also a Premiership league in which the top 12 professional teams compete. In general, rugby matches have a more relaxed and friendly atmosphere than football matches and opposing supporters are not separated. Tailgate parties in the carpark before and after matches are a long-standing Twickenham tradition.

The Six Nations tournament, held in January/February, is the premier northern hemisphere rugby union competition among the national teams of England, Wales, Scotland, Ireland, France and Italy. Twickenham hosts the three home matches in this tournament for the England team.

Tickets for Twickenham are notoriously hard to obtain for matches against Australia, New Zealand, South Africa and the Six Nations competition. For those contests, unless you are a playing or coaching member of a rugby club, your best bet is to book a hospitality package, which will include a ticket, lunch, tea and drinks. These are not cheap, and most are bought for corporate entertainment. Try ticket agency **Keith Prowse** (020 8795 2222). For other matches, tickets may be obtained through the team's website or via **Ticketmaster**.

If you would like to see a domestic rugby union match, there are several professional clubs based in and around London: the Saracens in Watford (www.saracens.com), London Irish in Reading (www.london-irish.com) and Harlequins, just down the road from Twickenham (www.harlequins. co.uk). Tickets are relatively easy to obtain, except for certain Premiership matches.

There are various semi-pro and club level teams in and around London. Club teams Richmond (www.richmondfc.co.uk) and London-Scottish (www.londonscottish.com) share a home pitch in Richmond. Tickets to matches are inexpensive and available on the grounds before matches. Spectators may stand around the pitch boundaries to watch the match.

GOLF

There are more than 2,500 golf courses in the British Isles and its popularity has increased dramatically with worldwide TV coverage. Many old, established member-only clubs now allow "pay and play" on weekdays and some weekends. Strict club rules and etiquette must be observed. The biggest annual golf event is **The Open Championship**, which is rotated around links (seaside) courses in England and Scotland. Admission tickets and hospitality may be booked online at www.britishopengolf.co.uk or by phone on 012 5378 0000. You will need to book in early spring for general admission tickets.

TENNIS

Tennis is a very old sport in the UK. There are hundreds of clubs around the UK, but its popularity is seasonal due to the inconsistency of weather on outside courts. **The Lawn Tennis Association** (LTA) was founded at Wimbledon and tennis is only played for two weeks of the year on Centre Court and No. 1 Court. It is played in June when the whole nation seems to go tennis-mad, particularly if a British player manages to survive the first week. See www.wimbeldon.org for more information.

Catering at Wimbledon is excellent, yet expensive. Strawberries, champagne, lobster and Pimms are all available within the grounds, but you can also take your own picnic. There is a large, atmospheric grassy picnic area known as "The Hill" with a large screen relaying live action from the show courts.

There are four main ways to obtain tournament tickets:

1. Submit an application into the public ballot for a pair of show court tickets. You will need to send a stamped, self-addressed envelope to **The All England Lawn Tennis & Croquet Club**, PO Box 98, Wimbledon, London SW19 5AE, between 1 August and 15 December the year before you wish to attend. Tickets are awarded randomly to applicants; submitting an

application does not guarantee tickets. Days and courts are randomly assigned, so it is not possible to specify a choice in this method.

2. If your family or club is a member of the Lawn Tennis Association, you may enter the LTA Advantage ballot for tickets. For more details, phone 020 7381 7037 or visit www.lta.org.uk/advantage.

3. Some tickets go on sale on the day of play. Queues can be very long. Expect to queue overnight for show court tickets or several hours before the grounds open for Ground Tickets. There are approximately 6,000 Ground Tickets available each day, which entitle access to the No. 2 Court unreserved seating and the standing enclosure on Courts 2 through 19.

Alternatively, many Londoners choose to visit Wimbledon in the late afternoon / early evening, when show court tickets are resold for charity once their original holders (often corporate hospitality guests) have left for the day.

4. If all else fails, there is always corporate hospitality. Expect to pay at least £500 per person for the day. Try:

Keith Prowse; 4th Floor, Elvin House, Stadium Way, Wembley, Middlesex HA9 0DW; 020 8795 2222; www.keithprowse.co.uk.

Sportsworld Group; New Abbey Court, Stert Street, Abingdon, Oxon OX14 3JZ; 012 3555 5844; www.sportsworld.co.uk.

HORSE RACING
Cheltenham National Hunt Festival

The most important jump racing meeting on the calendar occurs at Cheltenham Racecourse each March. The National Hunt Festival, a combination of steeplechase and hurdle racing, features four major Championship races (in addition to Grade 1 contests and Handicap races) over the course of four days, culminating with the Cheltenham Gold Cup race. Apply for tickets and book accommodation from 30 September. A discount scheme is offered for early purchases. Contact the Cheltenham Racecourse; Prestbury Park, Cheltenham, Gloucestershire; 012 4251 3014; www.cheltenham.co.uk.

Grand National

The Grand National, held at Aintree Racecourse in Liverpool each April, is perhaps the most famous steeplechase in the world: a 4.5 mile race over 30 challenging fences. Tickets are relatively inexpensive and plentiful 015 1522 2929; www.aintree.co.uk).

Ascot

Race meetings are held at Ascot Racecourse in Berkshire year-round — jump racing in the winter and flat racing in the summer. Royal Ascot, held in June, is perhaps the most famous meeting. The Queen, who is an avid owner, always attends. Foreign nationals may obtain tickets for the Royal Enclosure at Royal Ascot by application to their embassy or high commission. Morning dress, smart dress or national dress for men, and hats and skirts for ladies must be worn. Alternatively, you can buy tickets for other enclosures from Ascot Racecourse; Ascot, Berkshire; 0870 727 1234; www.ascot.co.uk.

The Derby

The Derby, a classic flat race for three-year-old horses, is run every June at Epsom Downs Racecourse in Surrey. This race is a tradition that dates back to 1779. Go to www.epsomderby.co.uk for ticket information.

MOTOR RACING

The Formula One British Grand Prix is held in July at the Silverstone Circuit in Northamptonshire, located 115km north of London. Tickets are available on the venue's website (www.silverstone-circuit.co.uk) or by telephone on 0870 458 8290. Purchasing early is recommended to ensure availability. The track website provides the full calendar of British motor races for the year.

CRICKET

Cricket is the English summer national game, and is famously said to be incomprehensible to foreigners. In fact, it is easy to follow once the basic terms are understood. Many believe that there is nothing more peaceful than spending an afternoon beside a village cricket green lounging on a picnic rug, reading the weekend papers and sipping a cup of tea or glass of wine. You can experience the excitement and atmosphere of a one-day international or a five-day Test Match at either the **Oval Cricket Ground,** Kennington; 020 7582 6660 or **Lord's Cricket Ground,** St. John's Wood; 020 7616 8603. Alternatively, contact the **English Cricket Board** on 0870 533 8833 (www.ecb.co.uk) for additional information, fixtures and tickets.

BASKETBALL

The **British Basketball League** (www.BBL.co.uk) consists of 11 teams throughout the UK whose season runs September through April. London's team, the London Towers, play home fixtures at the **Crystal Palace National Sports Centre**, off Anerley Hill, Upper Norwood, SE19; 020 8776 7755; www.london-towers.co.uk. Check the website for fixtures and tickets.

ICE HOCKEY

London's professional ice hockey team, the London Racers, play in the **Elite Ice Hockey League** (www.eliteleague.co.uk). The season runs from September through March. The Racers home games are played in Leyton, E10; 020 8533 3154. Go to www.londonracers.com for fixtures and ticket information.

BASEBALL / SOFTBALL

Baseball and softball as spectator sports are a bit unsettled in London. **BaseballSoftballUK** (BSUK) manages the various leagues and formats of both baseball and softball throughout the United Kingdom. The season runs from May through September and there are leagues to satisfy all levels of play (women, men and juniors alike). Current information on baseball and softball spectator and participant opportunities can be found at www.baseballsoftballuk.com.

Although there are no professional teams, the **London Warriors Baseball Club** (www.londonwarriors.com) has existed since 1979 and plays at Finsbury Park. The team plays in the Rawlings National League, the top amateur league in the country.

An affiliated club, the **Sidewinders** (www.sidewinders.co.uk), compete in the Premier Division of the British Baseball League and are based in Enfield, north of London.

FITNESS AND SPORTS FACILITIES

Sport England (www.sportengland.org.uk) is an organisation that delivers the Government's sporting objectives in the UK. Its mission is to work with others to create opportunities for persons to get involved in sport, and to stay and succeed in sport. Sport England works through nine regional offices that can provide a vast array of information on sporting activities throughout England. Visit the Sport England website to research sport opportunities in a specific area.

The Corporation of London (www.cityoflondon.gov.uk) also has a good listing of various sport and leisure facilities throughout London. Since the website contains a vast amount of information regarding London in general, use the search function to find information on the various sport facilities.

Most boroughs have a variety of public recreational facilities, such as pools, tennis courts, aerobics classes and parks. Some councils run a residents' discount scheme, such as **Westminster's ResCard** (www.westminster.gov.uk/leisureandculture) and **Camden's Leisure Card** (www.camden.gov.uk/ccm/navigation/leisure/camden-leisure-card), which entitles members to reductions on certain gym memberships and other activities. Contact your local council for location, activities, costs and availability. A full listing of councils can be found at: www.direct.gov.uk/Dl1/Directories/LocalCouncils/fs/en.

Listed below are some of the facilities that are frequented by League members and their families. Check your local residents' magazine or newspaper for the most up-to-date information on new club openings.

Private Health Clubs and Gyms

There are many health clubs and gyms located throughout London. Membership rates and services provided vary according to the quality and location of the club. Many clubs have off-peak memberships that cost less than a full membership and, in general, allow you to use the club on weekdays from 09:00-17:00. Additionally, many have flexible payment schedules to accommodate instalments on a monthly basis. Telephone the specific club for membership rate information.

> *Did you know?...London health clubs and gyms are generally expensive to join and often demand a guarantee of at least one year's commitment. When thinking about joining a gym, always ask for at least a fortnight's trial, and if necessary shop around to find the right one for you.*

Clubs with Multiple Locations

Cannons Sports Clubs; 020 7283 0101; www.cannons.co.uk

Many locations across the City, making it handy for after-work visits. Some have pools, some do not. Good value.

David Lloyd Leisure Clubs; www.davidlloydleisure.co.uk.

Many locations across London. Offers full gym: machines, pool, exercise classes and children's facilities.

Esporta; 011 8912 3500; www.esporta.com.

Fitness centre chain with more-spacious facilities than most. Some locations (e.g., the Riverside Club in Chiswick) are more like country clubs with tennis courts, outdoor swimming pools and plenty of children's facilities. London branches include Wandsworth, Chiswick, Kingston, Islington, Swiss Cottage and Wimbledon.

Fitness Exchange; London Bridge City, Tooley Street, SE1; 020 7403 1171; www.fitness-exchange.net.

Seven clubs in the City, one in the West End and one in Clapham. Pool, squash, aerobics, fitness training, jacuzzi, sauna, steam room, beauty facilities, physiotherapy and restaurant.

Fitness First; www.fitnessfirst.co.uk.
Many locations across London. Offers full gym facilities and classes.

Holmes Place; www.holmesplace.co.uk.
An upper-end chain with many branches throughout Greater London. Be warned that facilities can vary enormously between branches while prices tend not to stay the same. Most have pools; a few have indoor running tracks, separate men's and women's gyms, crèches and restaurants. Varied studio programme includes aerobics, spinning, Pilates and yoga.

Jubilee Hall Clubs; www.jubileehallclubs.co.uk.
Includes: The Armoury Hampstead, The Gym Covent Garden, Westminster Gym and The Columbo Centre (Southwark). Range of fully inclusive membership options, including unlimited use of the gym and exercise classes. No joining fee and offers pay-as-you-go programme.

LA Fitness; www.lafitness.co.uk.
Many locations across London. Offers full gym facilities and classes.

Living Well; 0870 600 7001; www.livingwell.co.uk.
A mid-priced national chain. All the basics, not too many frills.

Independent Clubs
The Armoury; 25 Pond Street, Hampstead, NW3; 020 7431 2263; www.jubileehallclubs.co.uk.
Aerobic classes, treadmills, StairMaster, Lifecycle bike, free weights, Cybex equipment, personal training, children's classes and sunbed facilities. Offers a no-initiation, pay-as-you-go programme.

The Berkeley Club and Spa; The Berkeley, Wilton Place, SW1; 020 7201 1699; www.theberkeleyhotellondon.com.
Expensive, but one of the only pools in London with a sliding roof for summer, and a good place to spot film stars staying at the hotel. Full spa

service, aqua aerobics, personal training, Powersport runners, Lifestride treadmill, Lifecycles, Concept II rower and Cybex weight machines.

Champneys Citypoint; 1 Ropemaker Street, EC2Y; 020 7920 6200; www.champneys.com/cityclub_citypoint.asp.

Expensive. Private members' health club and health spa. Pool, squash, gym, Cybex machines, sauna, steam room, solarium, beauty facilities, two dance studios and restaurant.

Springhealth Leisure Club; 81 Belsize Park Gardens, NW3, 020 7483 6800; www.springhealth.net/home/home.htm.

Reasonable rates; heated swimming pool, whirlpool spa, steam room and saunas.

The Dorchester Spa; The Dorchester, 53 Park Lane, W1; 020 7629 8888; www.dorchesterhotel.com.

Precor treadmills, Technogym weight equipment, StairMasters, rowers, Lifecycle bike, Concept II rower, personal training and spa treatments.

The Harbour Club; Watermeadow Lane, SW6; 020 7371 7700; www.harbourclub.co.uk.

Pool with separate baby area, tennis (indoor / outdoor), aerobics, fitness training, restaurant, beauty facilities, crèche and a variety of children's activities, including gymnastics, karate, ballet, tennis and swimming.

The Peak; Carlton Tower Hotel, Cadogan Place, Sloane Street, SW1; 020 7858 7008.

Beautifully located in an atrium of the hotel, offers a pool, yoga and Pilates classes, full fitness studio, restaurant and bar. A variety of treatments are available.

Cycling

Cycling on the streets of London is legal but can be dangerous. Cycle routes and lanes are marked throughout the city for safer riding. A map of cycle routes is available at your local council office and libraries. Please note that lights on your cycle should be used after dark if you are cycling on the street, and that cycling on pavements (sidewalks) is illegal.

Parks — On marked bicycle paths.

Road Cycling — On Sundays, South Carriage Drive and Constitution Hill and the Mall near Buckingham Palace are closed to cars.

Off-Road Cycling — Parts of Wimbledon Common and Richmond Park.

Road Safety Unit, Royal Borough of Kensington and Chelsea, The Town Hall, Hornton Street, W8; 020 7361 3170. Children's cycling safety classes offered through schools.

London Cycling Campaign (LLC); 020 7234 9310; www.lcc.org.uk.
Seeks to increase cycling in Greater London. Many of the activities happen at the local borough level. To contact your local group, choose your London borough from the website. The LLC also provides very good cycling maps of London.

Dance and Fitness Classes
Alan Herdman Studios; 17 Homer Row, W1; 020 7723 9953; www.alanherdmanpilates.co.uk.
Practices the Pilates technique, including body conditioning and corrective exercise.

Bikram Yoga; www.bikramyoga.com.
Centres located in Chalk Farm, Chiswick, Fulham, City (Old Street) and Queen's Park. Bikram yoga is 26 asana postures designed to scientifically warm and stretch muscles, ligaments and tendons, in the order in which they should be stretched. Otherwise known as "hot yoga", as it is practiced in a 37°C (104°F) room. Centres offer special prices for first timers.

British Military Fitness; 020 7751 9742; www.britmilfit.com.

For something different, try military-style training in London's parks! Classes are conducted by army or marine instructors most days in Hyde Park, Battersea Park, Clapham Common and Hampstead Heath, among others, for varied-ability ranges.

Danceworks; 16 Balderton Street, W1; 020 7629 6183; www.danceworks.net. A variety of dance, aerobic and Pilates classes.

English National Ballet; 39 Jay Mews, SW7; 020 7581 1245.

Adult ballet class one evening a week. Ten-week courses are available for beginners and those at intermediate levels.

 The Life Centre; 15 Edge Street, W8; 020 7221 4602; www.thelifecentre.com/centre. Classes include yoga, Pilates and tai chi.

Light Centre; 9 Eccleston Street, Belgravia, London, SW1; 020 7881 0728; www.lightcentrebelgravia.co.uk.

Offers range of classes: yoga, Pilates, tai chi, meditation and capoieira. Also provides therapies.

Pilates Institute; 0870 111 0166; www.pilates-institute.com.

This organisation will provide you with a list of qualified Pilates teachers in and around London.

The Pineapple Dance Studio; 7 Langley Street, WC2; 020 7836 4004; www.pineapple.uk.com.

A variety of dance classes for beginners to professionals.

Triyoga; 6 Erskine Road, Primrose Hill, NW3; 020 7483 3344; www.triyoga.co.uk.

Vast array of yoga and Pilates classes for all standards and ages. Also offers post-natal yoga and baby massage classes.

Yogabase; 255-257 Liverpool Road, Islington N1; www.btinternet.com/~yogabase/index.html.

Iyengar, Astanga and Hatha yoga. All classes are held on a drop-in basis and the fee is paid directly to the teacher.

GOLF

There are very few golf courses in central London, although there are some hidden driving ranges. The courses and ranges below are all open to the public (and you do not need a handicap to play) but offer preferential rates and booking times if you become a member. Do not expect golf carts; they are rare in the UK.

Note that at smarter and more traditional golf clubs, shirts with collars are obligatory for both sexes, and ladies' shorts should be at knee length. Some clubs also require men to wear knee-high socks with shorts. Ask your host beforehand if in doubt.

Driving Ranges / Golf lessons

Alex Saary; 077 9967 6307; alexsaary@zoom.co.uk.

Excellent young, professional golf instructor based in West Sussex. Specialises in your short game, golf psychology and fitness, but highly recommended all around.

Ealing Golf Range; Rowdell Road, Northolt; 020 8845 4967.

Large driving range; very convenient to the A40 motorway. Tuition (lessons), pro shop, bar and new short-game area.

Knightsbridge Golf School; 47 Lowndes Square, SW1; 020 7235 2468; www.knightsbridgegolfschool.com.

An underground driving range in a converted squash court! Good reputation for tuition. KGS members receive a discount on greens fees at Stoke Park Golf Club in Buckinghamshire.

14

Regent's Park Golf School; Outer Circle, Regent's Park, NW1; 020 7724 0643; www.rpgts.co.uk.

Short driving range, small pitching area, tuition and shop.

Top Golf; Bushey Mill Lane, Watford, Hertfordshire; 019 2322 2045; www.topgolf.co.uk.

Outside of London, but worth it for the heated bays, food delivery service and the microchips inside each ball, which tell you exactly how far and where each ball is hit. Tuition, putting course, shop, café and children's parties.

Golf Courses

All courses listed below welcome non-members on a casual basis.

Central London Golf Centre; Burntwood Lane, Wandsworth, SW17; 020 8871 2468; www.clgc.co.uk.

Young, informal club with a nine-hole course and driving range. Club hire available and tuition offered, including a recommended group beginner's course.

Chiswick Dukes Meadow Golf Course; Chiswick, W4; 020 8995 0537. Driving range and an all-par-3, nine-hole golf course. Instruction available, but no club hire.

Richmond Park Golf Course; Roehampton Gate, Priory Lane, SW15; 020 8876 3205; www.richmondparkgolf.co.uk.

Two 18-hole golf courses.

Stockley Park Golf Course; The Clubhouse, Stockley Park, Uxbridge, Middlesex; 020 8813 5700.

"Pay and play" European PGA 18-hole golf course.

HIKING

See "*Walking*".

ICE HOCKEY

If you are interested in non-professional UK ice hockey leagues (for example: women's teams, juniors or recreational play), take a look at the Ice Hockey UK website (www.icehockeyuk.co.uk), the internationally recognised governing body for the game within the UK.

ICE SKATING

For the winter holiday period (late November – early January), a number of venues throughout London will set up ice rinks. Some of these are Marble Arch, the Natural History Museum, Hampstead Heath, The Tower of London, Hampton Court Palace and Kew Gardens. Check various websites or *Time Out: London* for the annual locations.

Alexandra Palace Ice Rink; Alexandra Palace Way, Wood Green, N22; 020 8365 2121; www.alexandrapalace.com.

The palace offers a wide range of activities suitable for all ages; including skate training and tuition. They offer children's parties (which even include 15 minutes of tuition time) and private hire. Booking is essential.

Queen's Ice and Bowl; 17 Queensway, W2; 020 7229 0172.
Open year-round. Skate hire on premises.

Broadgate Ice Rink; Broadgate Circle, EC2; 020 7505 4068; www.broadgateice.co.uk.
Small circular outdoor rink is open late October to early April. Skate hire and lessons available.

Somerset House; The Strand, WC2; 020 7845 4600; www.somerset-house.org.uk/icerink.
Late November to January/February only. Skating lessons for adults and children offered.

MARTIAL ARTS

The Budokwai; GK House, 4 Gilston Road, SW10; 020 7370 1000;

www.thebudokwai.com.

Offers a range of instruction in judo, karate, aikido and jiu-jitsu; judo classes for children; toddler gym classes and paint groups.

Kamon Wing Chun at the Pineapple Dance Studios; 7 Langley Street, WC2; 020 7836 4004; www.kamonwingchun.com.

Kevin Chan teaches this very direct and practical version of kung-fu, called Wing Chun. Visit the website for more information and for classes offered at other locations.

PERSONAL TRAINERS

Personal fitness trainers are an increasingly popular alternative/addition to the use of health club facilities. They can provide a programme to meet your individual fitness needs within your time schedule. Many health clubs offer personal trainers to members for an additional fee.

Brian Brown; 079 7389 6102.

Over 15 years' experience in the fitness industry. Specialises in pre- and post-natal and weight-loss programmes in the Kensington and Chelsea area.

British Military Fitness (See *"Dance and Fitness"* classes above).

RIDING

Equipment usually can be hired from the stables for a small fee. Hard hats are compulsory in the UK. Most stables require children to be at least four or five years of age to ride.

Hyde Park Riding School; 63 Bathurst Mews, W2; 020 7723 2813; www.hydeparkstables.com.

Riding by the hour offered for beginner through advanced levels. Tuition offered for adults and children. Pony camp for children during weekday afternoons.

Kingston Riding Centre; 38 Crescent Road, Kingston-Upon-Thames, Surrey, KT2; 020 8546 6361; www.kingstonridingcentre.com.

Lessons available. Famous for their "Pimm's Hacks" through Richmond Park on summer evenings.

London Equestrian Centre; Frith Manor Farm, Lullington Garth, N12; 020 8349 1345.

Large equestrian centre with 30 school horses and ponies. There is also a restaurant.

Wimbledon Village Stables; 24A/B High Street, Wimbledon, SW19; 020 8946 8579; www.wvstables.com.

Offers short courses, lessons and hacks (rides across Wimbledon Common).

ROWING

There are many boat clubs along the Thames that train and compete in crews for regattas and "head" races, the most famous of which are the **Henley Royal Regatta** in Oxfordshire held in July, and the **Head of the River Race on the Thames** in March. Most also have active social programmes and are an excellent way to meet people.

Thames Rowing Club; Putney Embankment, SW15; 020 8788 0798; www.thamesrc.demon.co.uk. A large, successful club with men's, women's and juniors' sections. Beginners welcome.

RUGBY (Touch Rugby)

Touch Rugby. Men's, women's and mixed leagues of various levels competing at many venues in and around London. Emphasis is on the social aspects of the game. Individuals may sign up to be placed on a team. Go to www.in2touch.com/uk to learn more about the various leagues and venues.

RUNNING

British Military Fitness; www.britmilfit.com (see *"Dance and Fitness"* classes above). Running club in Clapham Common on Wednesday evenings and in Hyde Park on Thursday evenings.

Serpentine Running Club; www.serpentine.org.uk.

The club covers all aspects of running from a beginner's running guide to triathlon training. Check the website for information on joining the club, club events, where to run in London and much more.

SAILING

Little Ship Club; Bell Wharf Lane, Upper Thames Street, London, EC4; 020 7236 7729; www.little-ship-club.co.uk.

Unique sailing club based in the City of London with restaurant, bar and guest rooms. Holds sailing trips and rallies at clubs across Southern England, plus **Royal Yachting Association (RYA)** training and lots of social events. New members welcome to visit on Tuesday nights — no boat of your own is required. Membership required to use facilities.

Ranelagh Sailing Club; The Embankment, Putney, SW15; 020 8788 4986; www.ranelagh-sc.co.uk.

Friendly club offering year-round sailing on the Thames.

Sail UK; 209 Blandford Road, Hamworthy, Poole, Dorset, BH15; 0120 266 8410; www.sailuk.net. Offers sailing lessons on the Solent.

SHOOTING

West London Shooting School; Sharvel Lane, West End Road, Northolt, Middlesex, UB5; 020 8845 1377; www.shootingschool.co.uk. Sporting clays.

Holland & Holland; Ducks Hill Road, Northwood, Middlesex, HA6; 019 2382 5349; www.hollandandholland.com/shooting-ground. Sporting clays.

SWIMMING

Your local council provides a list of local public pools and/or leisure centres. A list of all swimming pools and their facilities in Greater London may be obtained from Sport England (0845 850 8508; www.sportengland.

org.uk). Also see *"Private Health Clubs and Gyms"*.

TENNIS

There is a range of options for the tennis enthusiast in London. You can either enjoy the luxurious facilities of a private club or take advantage of the public courts in the parks, which can be extremely good value.

Public / Open Courts

Battersea Park; SW11; 020 8871 7542; www.battersepark.org.

Floodlit courts available all year. Only members may reserve courts; non-members must appear in person to check immediate availability. No racquet hire available. Individual and group coaching available.

Hyde Park Tennis Centre; South Carriage Drive, Hyde Park, W2; 020 7262 3474.

Six hard courts. Racquet hire available. Private tuition available.

Regents Park Golf and Tennis School; Outer Circle, Regent's Park, NW1; 020 7724 0643; www.rpgts.co.uk.

Floodlit courts available to hire by the hour.

Regents Park Tennis Centre; York Bridge, Inner Circle, Regent's Park, NW1; 020 7486 4216.

Twelve hard courts in a lovely setting. Tuition, café, changing rooms.

Private Tennis Clubs

The Campden Hill Lawn Tennis Club; 9 Aubrey Walk, W8; 020 7727 4050; www.chltc.co.uk.

Six hard indoor courts and six artificial grass courts outside.

David Lloyd Tennis Centre; 1 Southall Lane, Hounslow, Middlesex, PW5; 020 8573 9378.

Tennis (10 indoor and nine outdoor courts), squash, badminton, pool, aerobics, fitness training, crèche, restaurant and beauty facilities.

Globe Lawn Tennis Club; 190A Haverstock Hill, NW3; 020 7435 0248.
Boast several tennis courts and also provide coaching.

The Harbour Club (see *"Private Health Clubs and Gyms"*).

Magdalen Park Tennis Club; 38 Magdalen Road, Wandsworth Common,
SW18; 020 8874 8313.
Very friendly and social with a nice clubhouse. Eight hard courts; six are
floodlit. Juniors welcome. New members are advised to visit at weekends
12:00-16:00 and ask for a committee member.

WALKING

Inside London

In addition to the parks listed below, there are a number of established
routes and guided tours to try:

The Thames Path is a 290 km-long (180 miles) National Trail that follows
the course of the Thames River, from Thames Head near Kemble in the
Cotswolds, to the Thames Barrier in east London. As well as passing through
central London, it also takes in historic places such as Oxford, Henley,
Windsor and Greenwich. Various guides are available for this trail online or
in bookstores.

Saturday Strolls, The Inner London Ramblers Association (ILRA) runs
regular free guided walks in the London area. They are 5-7 miles long and
start and finish at public transport points within Travelcard zones. No booking
required — just show up at the designated station entrance. Call the ILRA
hotline on 020 7370 6180 or visit their website (www.innerlondonramblers.
org.uk) for a list of upcoming walks. There is also a comprehensive listing of
interesting walks throughout London on the website for individual use.

Outside London

Within as little as one hour from central London by train or car, you can walk in beautiful countryside on many public footpaths and trails. Two easily accessible trails by train are the **North Downs Way** in Kent (www. kent.gov.uk has more information and guides) and the **1066 Country Walk** in Sussex (read The 1066 Country Walk by Brian Smailes (2000) or visit www.1066country.com).

Try the following for more ideas and information on hiking and walking in the UK:

Ramblers Association; 020 7339 8500; www.ramblers.org.uk.

The Ramblers Association is the largest charity in the UK working for walkers. Their website contains a list of national parks, forests and "Areas of Outstanding Natural Beauty" in the UK, plus general information and advice on walking, routes and accommodation. The association produces a handbook, Walk Britain, which contains useful information for walkers. The Ramblers have various local groups meeting in and around London. Visit their website for details.

The Long Distance Walkers Association; www.ldwa.org.uk.

An association of people with a common interest in walking long distances in rural, mountainous or moorland areas. The website has information on all of the UK's long distance paths.

PARKS

The Royal Parks

The Royal Parks (www.royalparks.gov.uk) look after eight parks throughout London owned by the Crown.

Bushy Park; Richmond, TW12; 020 8979 1586. 450 hectares/1,099 acres lying north of Hampton Court Palace. Contains the famous Chestnut Avenue with its Arethusa "Diana" Fountain.

The Green Park; SW1; 020 7930 1793. 16 hectares/350 acres; a peaceful refuge, popular for sunbathing and picnics in good weather; paths used by runners.

Greenwich Park; SE10; 020 8858 2608. 73 hectares/183 acres with views of the Thames, Docklands and the City of London from its hilltop; contains the Old Royal Observatory, the Royal Naval College, the National Maritime Museum and the Queen's House; sanctuary for deer, foxes and birds.

Hyde Park; W2; 020 7298 2100. 140 hectares/350 acres that provide facilities for many different leisure activities and sports as well as being a focal point for public events of all sizes. Contains the Diana, Princess of Wales Memorial Fountain.

Kensington Gardens; W2; 020 7298 2100. 111 hectares/275 acres adjacent to Hyde Park; contains Kensington Palace and the Diana, Princess of Wales Memorial Playground; popular with sunbathers and runners; cycling is permitted on designated paths.

The Regent's Park; NW1; 020 7486 7905. 197 hectares/487 acres that provide the largest outdoor sports area in London; also contains the Open Air Theatre (home of the New Shakespeare Company in the summer), London Zoo and many cafés and restaurants.

Richmond Park; Surrey, TW10; 020 8948 3209. Largest open space in London (1,000 hectares/2,500 acres); home to a huge array of wildlife; varied landscape of hills, woodland gardens and grasslands. Popular for cycling on unpaved terrain.

St. James's Park; SW1; 020 7930 1793. 144 hectares/360 acres of parkland located in the heart of London, (bordered by three royal palaces); live concerts twice a day in the summer; children's playground; cafe.

Community Parks

There are numerous other parks in and outside of London, a selection of which are listed below. Most parks are open from dawn until dusk.

Alexandra Park and Palace; Musgrove Hill; Wood Green, N22. An 80 hectares/200 acre public park surrounding a palace—has sporting facilities (including an ice rink) and plenty of attractions for children including a playground, boating lake and small animal enclosure. Children's shows and workshops in the summer. Nature reserve with woodlands, dense scrub, meadow and pond. The "Parkland Walk" is a shady walk that follows an old rail bed.

Battersea Park; Albert Bridge Road, SW11; www.batterseapark.org. Bordered on one side by the Thames River, the 83 hectares/200 acre park contains a boating lake, children's zoo, deer park, playground, Old English Garden, tree and nature trails, the Peace Pagoda and an herb garden. Also bike hire for the whole family.

Crystal Palace Park; Thicket Road, Penge, SE19. A 140 hectares/350 acre park with boating and bands during the summer. The maze, farmyard, lake and play area are all popular with children.

Golders Hill Park; North End Road, Golders Green, NW11. A 63 hectares/159 acre area within Hampstead Heath. Playground and small zoo (deer, goats, ducks, etc), putting green, good café and beautiful gardens.

Hampstead Heath; Parliament Hill, NW3; www.cityoflondon.gov.uk/ Corporation/living_environment/open_spaces/hampstead_heath.htm. 316 hectares/791 acres of ponds, woodlands, trails and museums. Famous for kite flying on "Parliament Hill" with a beautiful view of central London. Swimming ponds, swimming pool, wading pool, tennis courts, concerts in summer at Kenwood House, cafes, playgrounds, animal enclosures, horseback riding, cycling, walking paths and more. Visit the website for special events and a map.

Highgate Woods; Muswell Hill Road, N6. 28 hectares/70 acres of shady woodland, including an adventure playground, nature hut and trails, and a vegetarian café.

Holland Park; W14. 21 hectares/52 acres containing the Kyoto Japanese Garden, rose gardens, abundant wildlife, an ecology centre, a wildlife pond, tennis courts, golf driving range and an adventure playground. There is an open air theatre and opera in the summer against the backdrop of Holland House.

Primrose Hill; NW3. 24 hectares/61 acres of grassy hill; includes a children's playground and outdoor gymnasium. Fantastic views of London.

Royal Botanic Gardens, Kew; Richmond, Surrey, TW9; www.rbgkew.org.uk. 120 hectares/300 acres that include a lake, an aquatic garden, a pagoda, Kew Palace and Palm House, among many other things. A World Heritage Site.

Theme Parks

Alton Towers; Stoke-on-Trent, Staffordshire, ST10; 0870 520 4060; www.alton-towers.co.uk. Britain's biggest theme park with rides for all ages. Located three hours outside central London. Open 365 days a year.

Chessington World of Adventures; Surrey, KT9; 0870 999 0045; www.chessington.co.uk. Geared toward families with children under 12. Open March through October.

Legoland Windsor; Berkshire, SL4; 0870 504 0404; www.legoland.co.uk.
Set in 60 hectares/150 acres of parkland, contains over 50 interactive rides, attractions and shows geared toward children aged 2-12 and their families. Open March through October.

Thorpe Park; Surrey, KT16; 0870 444 4466; www.thorpepark.co.uk.
Amusement park offering attractions, shows, rides and exhibits for all ages. Open March to November.

Drawn by Liam

Travel

CONTENTS

One of the many great things about living in London is the opportunity to travel throughout the United Kingdom and Europe. London's wealth of transportation offerings coupled with its proximity to continental Europe (affectionately referred to as "the Continent") and other destinations makes it easy to weekend in the country or to pop over to Paris or Milan for a short break.

The ease of travelling to a wide variety of destinations has created a great travel industry in London. Limitless resources exist to assist in planning a getaway locally, within Europe or beyond. There are numerous guidebooks available at bookstores, specialty travel shops and travel agents. The internet also provides a seemingly infinite number of resources in selecting a destination as well as booking transportation and accommodation. Other good resources are *Time Out London* and the weekend newspapers that continually offer ideas and special packages for holidays.

It is normally advisable to arrange holidays well in advance, especially for

> *Did you know?...A popular getaway for UK residents is the "City Break" in which a package deal is offered for a short holiday. City Break specials are offered through travel agents and online services and can also be found in newspapers and travel magazines.*

peak holiday times. Traditional holidays such as Christmas, Easter, bank holiday weekends, and half term are popular times for UK residents to take a holiday. Many Europeans holiday in August, so it may be wise to avoid resort destinations during this busy month, although major European business cities are quieter than normal and will often offer special rates.

If you book a holiday last minute, you may be able to take advantage of falling prices. Airlines and hotels may reduce fares and/or rates in an effort to fill capacity. There are good deals to be found on last minute bookings (e.g., www.lastminute.com), though your first-choice hotel or flight may not be available. The very worst time to book, as a rule, is a few weeks in advance.

PLANNING YOUR TRIP

Despite the number of online resources offered for travel planning, it is still worthwhile to consult travel agencies and brokers for advice on trip planning. These agencies and shops can offer discounts on package deals and are worthwhile to consider especially when planning a major holiday or a journey to a destination with which you are not familiar.

TRAVEL AGENCIES / TOUR OPERATORS

Travel agencies and tour operators can provide assistance with selecting a holiday destination as well as take care of booking arrangements. They are most helpful with booking package tours for a range of holidays from the inexpensive to the luxurious. Package tours will include transportation and accommodation, and can include other items of interest such as transfer from airport to hotel, car hire, sightseeing tours or excursions. Exploring a travel agent's website can be a good way to begin narrowing down the list of potential destinations!

It is recommended that you only use **International Airline Transport**

Association (IATA), **Association of British Travel Agents** (ABTA) or **Air Tours Operators Licence** (ATOL) approved travel agents, tour operators and ticket brokers, as many travellers have been stranded when some of the less-reliable companies suddenly go out of business. The following is a selection of such approved travel agents and tour operators:

- **Abercrombie & Kent**; 0845 070 0613; www.abercrombiekent. co.uk. Specialising in luxury holidays worldwide.

- **FlightCentre**; various locations in and around London; 0870 499 0040, www.flightcentre.co.uk. Targets the cost-conscious traveler and specialises in the cheap flights, holiday packages, domestic travel and ancillary sales. Also offers upscale package holidays.

- **Goodarce & Townsend**; 020 7702 1166; www.goodtown.co.uk. Specialist luxury travel consultancy for destinations worldwide for personal or business travel.

- **Kuoni Travel**; 020 7589 8959; www.kuoni.co.uk. Known for its long haul travel operator services, though offers shorter breaks as well.

- **Simply Travel**; 0870 166 4979; www.simplytravel.co.uk. Offers a selection of villas, hotels and properties that are slightly off the beaten track. Flexible packages; not tied into the typical 7-day routine.

- **Powder Byrne**; 250 Upper Richmond Road, SW15; 020 8246 5300; www.powderbyrne.com. Powder Byrne is a tour operator offering tailor-made, exclusive ski resorts and beach destination packages available year-round.

- **Thomas Cook**; various locations throughout the U.K., 0870 750 5711, www.thomascook.com. Offers a variety of flights, hotels, cruises, city breaks and packages, at a wide range of prices.

- **Trailfinders**; operates 13 travel centres in the UK; 0845 058 5858; www.trailfinders.com. Expertise in creating individual holidays worldwide. Offers discounted airfares, hotels, tours, cruises and vehicle rental.

TICKET BROKERS AND BUCKET SHOPS

Ticket brokers offer charter flights at a discount. Most charter flights are linked to package tours, but ticket brokers will sell tickets on a seat-only basis. Some brokers also offer discounted seats on scheduled (non-charter) airlines.

"Bucket" shops sell unofficially discounted air tickets on charter and scheduled routes at large reductions. A good bucket shop requires only a nominal deposit. If booking a flight through a bucket shop, check with the airline directly to make sure that you are included on the passenger list.

You will find ticket broker and bucket shop advertisements in the travel sections of the Sunday and daily newspapers and in the back of the weekly magazine *Time Out London*.

ONLINE RESOURCES

Planning/Booking

Do-it-yourself travel booking is much easier with the vast number of online resources. A selection of the most popular is listed below. Please note that it is often less expensive to book airfare and accommodation together using these resources rather than booking the items separately.

www.ebookers.com

www.expedia.co.uk

www.lastminute.com

www.opodo.co.uk

www.travelocity.co.uk

Destination Feedback

A website that offers travellers the opportunity to review or post opinions about destinations, hotels and resorts, museums, etc. is www.tripadvisor.

com and is often a good starting point for considering a destination.

GETTING THERE

There are five major international airports in the London area and many railway stations to get you around the UK. A detailed listing of the airports, railway stations and other transportation links is available in *Chapter 6: Transportation*.

By Air

The British Airport Authority (BAA) operates the three largest London airports: Heathrow, Gatwick and Stansted. BAA has a very informative website (www.baa.co.uk) for real-time arrival and departure information, directions, methods of public transport available and more.

Below is a list of the five international airports in and around London. Consult *Chapter 6: Transportation* for a detailed listing of the airports and how to get to/from them.

City of London Airport; Royal Docks, E16; 020 7646 0000; www.londoncityairport.com. Accessible by tube and DLR, bus, and taxi/car.

Gatwick Airport; West Sussex, RH6; 0870 000 2468; www.gatwickairport.com. Accessible by rail, bus, coach, and taxi/car.

Heathrow Airport; Hounslow, Middlesex, TW6; 0870 000 0123; www.heathrowairport.com. Accessible by train, bus, coach, tube or taxi/car.

Luton Airport; Bedfordshire; 0158 240 5100; www.london-luton.co.uk. Accessible by rail, bus, coach, and taxi/car.

Stansted Airport; Essex; 0870 000 0303; www.stanstedairport.com. Accessible by rail, bus, coach, and taxi/car.

Often the best airfares are found on the airline's website. Many airlines will charge you a fee if you book a flight on the telephone, so be sure to inquire about surcharges if you choose to book over the telephone. Always confirm the terms and conditions of any discount fares, which may include a required length of stay and cancellation charges.

Aside from the airlines' websites, the online resources listed above (e.g., **opodo, expedia**) will list a variety of fares to get you to your destination. These general use websites often do not include the discount airlines (e.g., **RyanAir, EasyJet, Monarch**) so be sure to consult those airlines' websites directly. There are some excellent fares to destinations in and around Europe on these low-cost airlines if you are prepared to forego some of the "frills" associated with traditional airlines (e.g., free meal/snack service, seat assignments). Be aware that many of these airlines may use alternative airports, so attention should be paid to the destination airport and consideration given to the onward journey after landing. Each discount airline is different and should be consulted for its specific services.

By Rail

There are numerous railway stations in and around London where you can start your journey. Consult *Chapter 6: Transportation* for a more thorough listing.

Domestic

When booking rail tickets, you can visit the train websites directly, call to reserve tickets, or buy the tickets at the train station. Many trains offer both reserved and unreserved seating. It is recommended that, if you want an assigned seat (where available), book the tickets in advance.

International - The Channel tunnel

The Channel Tunnel, commonly referred to as the "Chunnel", links England and France and has greatly reduced travel time to the Continent. (Using the Chunnel, Paris is less than three hours from London.) The Chunnel is rail-only and cannot be driven through in a car, though there is a "drive-on" service. Two rail operators use the Chunnel for passenger travel:

Eurostar (passengers only); 0870 518 6186; www.eurostar.co.uk. Trains depart London's Waterloo Station (with a stop at Ashford in Kent) directly to Calais, Paris (Gare du Nord and Disneyland Paris), Lille (Europa) and Avignon in France and to Brussels (Gare du Midi) in Belguim. A special ski service also runs to the French Alps. Tickets are priced in a similar way to flights, and to obtain the best deals you will probably need to buy a non-flexible ticket with a Saturday night stay well in advance of your trip. You can add on connecting train journeys throughout France, Belgium and select other countries to your Eurostar ticket.

> Did you know?...The Orient Express operates day and weekend trips around the UK. This is a wonderful way to see the countryside (www.orient-express.co.uk). It also offers trips throughout Europe.

Eurotunnel (passengers and cars); 0870 535 3535; www.eurotunnel.co.uk. Offers a drive-on service from Folkestone in Kent to Calais, France. Offers standard fares, flexible fares and short stay saver fares. Tickets may be purchased online or by phone.

ACCOMMODATIONS

Whether you are seeking to rent a cottage in Wales or a suite in a European city hotel, your first stop should be the travel supplements of the weekend papers. *The Observer* (Sunday), *The Telegraph* (Saturday and Sunday) and *The Times* (Saturday and Sunday) are particularly good, and frequently feature special offers and discounts available exclusively to their readers. Late spring is a particularly good time to look for reduced room rates and upgrade packages for summer holidays because tour operators and cruise lines seek to sell off any unsold capacity. In major business cities, such as Milan, Paris and even London, August is generally the best month to find excellent room rates within cities because the local population has fled to seaside resorts for la vacance.

Resources for locating accommodations within Britain include:
Bed and Breakfast Nationwide; 012 5583 1235; www.bedandbreakfastnationwide.com. Offeres B&B homes throughout the UK.

Country Holidays; 0870 078 1200; www.country-holidays.co.uk.
Offers a wide range of quality cottages throughout the British Isles.

English and Scottish Country Cottages; 0870 078 1100;
www.english-country-cottages.co.uk, www.scottish-country-cottages.co.uk.
More than 3,000 properties from which to choose your ideal cottage holiday
home. Properties for rent vary from converted farmhouses to medieval castles.

Farm Stay UK; 024 7669 6909; www.farmstayuk.co.uk.
Offers opportunities to stay with farming families in rural settings.

Hoeseasons; 015 0250 2588; www.hoseasons.co.uk.
Offers places to stay in coastal and countryside settings throughout
Britain, Ireland and Europe.

Lake and Cottage Company; Cumbria/Lake District; 015 3953 8180;
www.lakelandcottageco.com.
Assists with finding cottages and self-catering holidays in the Lake District.

The London Bed and Breakfast Agency; 020 7586 2768;
www.londonbb.com.
Offers both rooms in family homes and self-catered flats for stays of two
or more nights.

The National Trust; 36 Queen Anne's Gate, SW1; 017 9381 7400;
www.nationaltrust.org.uk.
A non-profit organisation and special interest group which purchases or
is bequeathed historic properties or places of great natural beauty that are
preserved for the nation. Many of these properties are available for holiday
or weekend stays.

Northern Ireland Tourist Board; 59 North Street, Belfast BT1 1NB;
028 9023 1221; www.discovernorthernireland.com.

Assistance with locating accommodations and other general tourism advice.

Visit London; 020 7234 5800; www.visitlondon.com.

Provides information, travel and destination advice, including accommodation assistance, for those interested in travel in and around London.

Visit Britain; 020 8846 9000; www.visitbritain.com.

Offers an accommodation search that will assist in locating various types of accommodation in Britain including hotels, bed & breakfasts, self-catered apartments, campus locations and hostels.

In addition to the more specialist resources listed above, and the general flight plus accommodations websites listed earlier in the chapter, the following websites provide internet access to hotel and other accommodations around the world:

www.hotels.co.uk. Locates hotel rooms worldwide at discount prices.

www.itwg.com. Offers Italian hotels reservation with immediate confirmation and discounted negotiated rates, travel packages dedicated to art, wellness, sport, relax and much more, worldwide car rental at special rates, air tickets for any destination including low-cost flights, ferry tickets for main destinations in the Mediterranean sea.

www.laterooms.com. Late booking database for hotels offering rooms in UK, Ireland, continental Europe and worldwide.

www.octopustravel.com. Online resource for discount hotels, apartments, self-catering, car hire, travel insurance and group travel accommodation.

www.venere.com. Find and book hotels, B&Bs and apartments throughout Europe.

BEFORE YOU TRAVEL

PAYING FOR YOUR HOLIDAY

Be aware that some ticket brokers and travel agents will charge you extra to pay by credit card for holidays and flights. It may be worth doing so, however, because most credit card companies provide refunds if you have paid with their card and your travel agent or ticket broker then goes out of business. Travel insurance may also reduce the risk. (See below for more information on insurance.)

TRAVEL INSURANCE

Package tour operators will often try to sell you holiday insurance, however it is rarely worth buying for a single holiday. Be sure to review the terms and conditions of the insurance offered to see if it will cover the risks about which you are concerned. Be sure to inquire about what coverage will exist if the tour operator goes out of business.

A good option to consider if you travel abroad more than twice a year is annual multi-trip coverage. The **Post Office™**, major banks and credit card companies, as well as companies specialising in travel or insurance offer this product. Visit the **UK Foreign & Commonwealth Office** website (www.fco. gov.uk) to view its tips on what to look for in a policy as well as a list of reputable travel insurers.

HEALTH AND SAFETY

The **UK Foreign & Commonwealth Office** (Travel Advice Unit: 0870 606 0290; see also www.fco.gov.uk) can provide you with up-to-date country-specific advice regarding health and safety issues. **The Department of Health** also offers advice on health issues associated with travel (020 7210 4850; www.dh.gov.uk).

IMMUNISATIONS AND VACCINATIONS

When travelling on business or pleasure, in order to enter certain countries, immunisations may be necessary. It is best to review your itinerary-specific immunisation and other health requirements at least six weeks before you travel. There are several ways to determine which immunisations and vaccinations, if any, you need to before you can travel:

- **Contact your GP.** Under the NHS, some immunisations and vaccinations may be carried out by your GP. Some immunisations, such as for polio and tetanus (and sometimes hepatitis and meningitis) are free of charge at the NHS, while others may require you to pay a fee or may not be easily available to your doctor, who may then refer you to a clinic.

- **Contact Medical Advisory Services for Travellers Abroad** (MASTA), 020 7291 9333; www.masta.org. This not-for-profit organisation offers medical services and advice. For a small fee, MASTA will provide you with a "Health Brief" containing medical advice specifically tailored to your journey specifying which "jabs" (shots) you will need, which can then be taken to one of their local travel clinics. Visit the website to find the clinic nearest you.

- **Go directly to an immunisation clinic.** Appointments can easily be made and the clinics are familiar with the necessary injections. Many international airlines and some large travel agents have immunisation clinics. Keep in mind that if you need several immunisations, it may be worth shopping around as prices vary considerably.

Two suggested travel clinics are:

- **British Airways Travel Clinic**, 213 Piccadilly, W1; 0845 600 2236; www.britishairways.com (search for "travel clinics"). Walk-in clinic.

- **Trailfinders Travel Clinic**, 194 High Street Kensington, W8; 020 7938 3999; www.trailfinders.com. No appointment necessary.

For information regarding immunisations for babies, please see *Chapter*

7: Healthcare (under "Paediatrics") or *Chapter 8: Children.*

HEALTH CARE ABROAD

The UK has reciprocal healthcare agreements with EEA countries and Switzerland, which enables travellers to receive free or low-cost emergency care. Persons carrying a European Health Insurance Card (EHIC) are eligible to receive healthcare that becomes necessary during visits to any of these countries. The EHIC replaced the Form E-111 and is available to persons who are ordinarily resident in the UK, with some restrictions. You can obtain an EHIC by telephone (0845 606 2030), by filling in and posting the application at your local **Post Office**™ or on the internet at www.ehic. org.uk.

Outside the EEA and Switzerland, you will have to pay for treatment. Package tour operators will try to sell you their own travel insurance (which usually has a health-related benefit), but it is rarely worth buying. A better option to consider is annual multi-trip travel insurance, offered by a variety of sources (see discussion earlier in this chapter). Be sure to examine the coverage provision in any insurance policy you consider in order to determine its coverage of health care issues.

15

Drawn by Effie

Culture

CONTENTS

London provides many cultural offerings to its diverse population and visitors, from its wealth of museums, galleries and historical homes and parks, to its broad spectrum of performing arts. This chapter provides a general guide to all that London has to offer; to describe its long and assorted history and the cultures that contribute to it.

MUSEUMS, GALLERIES AND HISTORIC HOUSES

London has a wealth of both publicly and privately owned museums, galleries and other preserved landmarks, due in part to its rich history and colourful past.

Many of the public museums do not charge general admission (though there may be a charge for special exhibitions). As with most museums, contributions from visitors and supporters is a large part of the operational budget. Accordingly, most museums and the like, offer membership or "friend" programs. Becoming a supporter gives you special privileges such as easier accessibility to major exhibitions, discounts on entrance fees, restaurants and gift shops, and invitations to special functions. Privileges vary; contact the institution directly for information. Those museums, galleries or events that require admission often have a website where tickets may be purchased in advance, sometimes at a discounted rate.

It is a good idea to call ahead before heading out to any venue in London. Unexpected closures occur from time to time without prior notice.

London's museums are varied and range from, mass appeal to those with a more specific focus. The following lists some of the most popular museums.

☺ This symbol indicates that the museum or gallery is child-friendly.

Bankside Gallery; 48 Hopton Street, SE1; 020 7928 7521; www.banksidegallery.com.

Home of two historic art societies: the Royal Watercolour Society and the Royal Society of Painter-Printmakers.

Banqueting House; Whitehall, SW1; 0870 751 5178; www.hrp.org.uk.

The Banqueting House, designed by Indigo Jones, is all that remains of Whitehall Palace, the sovereign's principal residence from 1530 until 1698, when it was destroyed by fire. Renowned for its architecture and painting, the building is also famous as the site of King Charles I's execution. Admission charge.

Barbican Art Gallery; Barbican Centre, Silk Street, EC2; 020 7638 4141; www.barbican.org.uk/artgallery.

Located in the Barbican arts complex, this gallery curates and develops internationally renowned exhibitions, offering a varied programme of work from 20th century art and photography to modern design and architecture. Admission charge.

☺ **British Museum**; Great Russell Street, WC1B; 020 7323 8000; www.british-museum.ac.uk.

The British Museum houses a vast collection of human cultural history, including the Rosetta Stone. Free entry, though some special exhibits will charge for admission.

Buckingham Palace; The Mall, SW1; 020 7766 7300; www.royal.gov.uk.

Built in the early 1700s by the Duke of Buckingham, it has served as the British monarch's London residence since the reign of Queen Victoria. Its State Rooms are open to visitors for two months every year (late July – early September). Admission charge.

Cabinet War Rooms and Churchill Museum; Clive Steps, King Charles Street, SW1; 020 7930 6961; http://cwr.iwm.org.uk.

The hidden underground rooms where Churchill and his government lived and worked during World War II. A very in-depth chronology of Winston Churchill's life. Admission charge.

Courtauld Institute of Art Gallery; Somerset House, Strand, WC2; 020 7848 2526; www.courtauld.ac.uk.

The Courtauld collection consists of Old Masters, Impressionist and Post-Impressionist paintings as well as other notable painting and drawing collections, including the Hermitage Rooms. Admission charge.

☺ **The Dickens House Museum**; 48 Doughty Street, WC1; 020 7405 2127; www.dickensmuseum.com.

The only surviving London house in which Dickens lived and wrote some of his best-known works. Original manuscripts exhibited. Admission charge.

Dulwich Picture Gallery; Gallery Road, Dulwich Village, SE21; 020 8693 5254; www.dulwichpicturegallery.org.uk.

Important collection of old masters paintings, including works by Van Dyck, Rembrandt, Gainsborough and Poussin. Visiting exhibitions. The gallery was designed by Sir John Sloane as England's first public art gallery Admission charge.

The Fan Museum; 12 Crooms Hill, Greenwich, SE10; 020 8305 1441; www.fan-museum.org.

Delightful private collection of 2,000 fans from different countries displayed in an 18th century townhouse. Admission charge.

☺ **Geffrye Museum**; Kingsland Road, E2; 020 7739 9893; www.geffrye-museum.org.uk.

English domestic period (17th century to the present) rooms especially arranged for children's enjoyment and participation. Free admission.

Goldsmith's Hall; Foster Lane, EC2; 020 7332 1456; www.thegoldsmiths.co.uk/hall.

Important antique silver and gold plate collection. Largest collection of modern silver and jewellery in Britain. Not open to the public except during exhibitions and on "Open Days" when free guided tours may be booked.

Guildhall; Gresham Street, EC2; 020 7606 3030; www.cityoflondon.gov.uk.

Centre of the City of London's government since medieval times. The gallery exhibits the permanent collection belonging to the Corporation of London and contains the Guildhall Library and Clock Museum. The remains of a Roman amphitheatre and large medieval crypts lie beneath the ancient site. Free admission.

☺ **Hampton Court Palace**; Surrey; 0870 752 7777; www.hrp.org.uk.

The 500-year-old Hampton Court Palace has something to offer everyone. Set in 60 acres of world-famous gardens including its own Maze, the palace showcases its history from the days of Henry VIII to George II. Many special events throughout the year, including an important flower show and summer music festival. Admission charge.

☺ **Hayward Gallery**; South Bank Centre, Belvedere Road, SE1; 020 7921 0813; www.hayward.org.uk.

Temporary exhibitions of historical and contemporary fine and decorative arts of major importance. Admission charge.

Hogarth's House; Great West Road, Hogarth Lane, W4.

A charming early 18th century house which was once the country home of William Hogarth, the painter and engraver. It is now a gallery where most of his well-known engravings are on display. Free admission.

☺ **Horniman Museum**; 100 London Road, Forest Hill, SE23; 020 8699 1872; www.horniman.ac.uk.

Impressive collection of ethnography, musical instruments, decorative arts, natural history and gardens. Free admission.

☺ **HMS Belfast**; Morgan's Lane, Tooley Street, SE1; 020 7940 6300; www.hmsbelfast.iwm.org.uk.

This former battle cruiser serves as a floating museum of 20th century British naval power. Admission charge.

☺ **Imperial War Museum**; Lambeth Road, SE1; 020 7416 5320; www.iwm.org.uk.

Permanent exhibitions of all aspects of wars in which Britain and the Commonwealth have been involved since 1914. Includes weaponry, vehicles, photographs, war paintings and posters. Archival films shown on weekends and holidays. Free admission, though a fee may be charged for special exhibitions.

Institute of Contemporary Arts; The Mall, SW1; 020 7930 3647; www.ica.org.uk.

Changing exhibitions of avant garde art. Admission charge.

16

The Jewish Museum; Raymond Burton House, 129-131 Albert Street, NW1 (Camden); 020 7284 1997; and Sternberg Centre, 80 East End Road, N3 (Finchley); 020 8349 1143; www.jewishmuseum.org.uk.
Extensive collection of Jewish religious antiquities. Admission charge.

Dr Johnson's House; 17 Gough Square, EC4; 020 7353 3745; www.drjh.dircon.co.uk.
Small library with relics located in a furnished house in which Samuel Johnson lived and worked on England's first definitive dictionary from 1748 to 1759. Admission charge.

Keats' House Museum; Keats Grove, Hampstead NW3; 020 7435 2062; www.cityoflondon.gov.uk.
House where John Keats lived from 1818 to 1820, which inspired some of Keats's most memorable poetry. The house and gardens are open to the public year-round. Admission charge.

Kensington Palace State Apartments; Kensington Gardens, W8; 0870 751 5170; www.hrp.org.uk.
Acquired by William and Mary in 1689 when it was called Nottingham House, Kensington, Kensington Palace has been a royal home for over 300 years. Highlights include the restored King's Apartments with a magnificent collection of old masters and the Royal Ceremonial Dress Collection. Admission charge.

☺ **Kew Bridge Steam Museum**; Green Dragon Lane, Brentford, Middlesex, TW8; 020 8568 4757; www.kbsm.org.
Housed in a magnificent 19th century water pumping station, the museum displays major developments in steam engine technology and centres around the station's famous Cornish engines in their original engine houses and its rotative engines, some of which can be seen in action each weekend. Admission charge.

Leighton House; 2 Holland Park Road, W14; 020 7602 3316;
www.rbkc.gov.uk.

Late 19th century home of the artist Lord Leighton, who designed its notable Arab Hall. Contains works by Leighton and other major Victorian artists. Admission charge.

Linley Sambourne House; 18 Stafford Terrace, W8; 020 7602 3316 (Mon-Fri) and 0797 606 0160 (Sat. & Sun.);
www.rbkc.gov.uk/linleysambournehouse.com

Home of cartoonist Edward Linley Sambourne. The impressive contents of the house remain undisturbed from his day and reflect the taste of the "Aesthetic movement" of the late Victorian period. Admission charge.

☺ **London Dungeon**; 28 Tooley Street, SE1; 020 7403 7221;
www.thedungeons.com.

Located on the site of a medieval prison, a "horror experience" of some of the city's grimmest history. Definitely not for the squeamish or those under 10 years old; interesting otherwise. Admission charge.

☺ **London Transport Museum**; 39 Wellington Street, WC2; 020 7565 7299;
www.ltmuseum.co.uk.

Closed until spring 2007 for refurbishment, although the museum is still running a programme of special events. Visit the website for details.

☺ **Madame Tussaud's**; Marylebone Road, NW1; 0870 999 0046;
www.madame-tussauds.co.uk.

The famous collection of wax figures of historic and contemporary celebrities. Admission charge includes admission to the adjacent London Planetarium.

☺ **Museum of Childhood**; Cambridge Heath Road, E2; 020 8983 5200;
www.vam.ac.uk/moc.

The UK's national collection of childhood-related objects dating back to the 16th century. Re-opening in late 2006 after a redevelopment. The new themes for the displays are: "Creativity & Imagination" (interactive displays looking at imagination, inspiration and exploration) and "Moving & Optical Toys" (exploring the science and technology of movement).

☺ **Museum of London**; 150 London Wall, EC2; 0870 444 3852, www.museumoflondon.org.uk.

The world's largest urban museum. Leads the visitor through the chronological development of London's history from prehistory until today. Exhibits include the Lord Mayor's coach and a wealth of archaeological objects and historical reconstructions. Free admission.

Museum of Garden History; St. Mary-at-Lambeth Church, Lambeth Palace Road, SE1; 020 7401 8865; www.cix.co.uk/~museumgh.

The deconsecrated church is used for exhibitions of botanical drawings, antique garden implements, etc, and the churchyard contains an interesting collection of plants and flowers. Voluntary admission charge.

Percival David Foundation of Chinese Art; 53 Gordon Square, WC1; 020 7387 3909; www.pdfmuseum.org.uk.

A unique collection of Chinese ceramics covering more than 1,000 years of production. There is also a library of East Asian and Western books related to Chinese art that were presented to the University of London in 1950 by scholar Sir Percival David. Donations encouraged.

National Archives Museum; Kew, Richmond, Surrey; 020 8876 3444; www.nationalarchives.gov.uk.

The National Archives of England, Wales and the United Kingdom has one of the largest archival collections in the world, spanning 1,000 years of British history, from the Domesday Book of 1086 to government papers recently released to the public. There is also a rolling programme of exhibitions. Free admission.

☺ **National Army Museum**; Royal Hospital Road, SW3; 020 7730 0717; www.national-army-museum.ac.uk.

Extensive display of army mementoes, equipment and colours from various British and colonial regiments from 1485. Free admission.

☺ **National Gallery**; Trafalgar Square, WC2; 020 7747 2885; www.nationalgallery.org.uk.

World-renowned collection of masterpieces from all schools and movements in art. Donations encouraged; admission charge for some special exhibits.

☺ **National Maritime Museum**; Park Row, Greenwich, SE10; 020 8858 4422; www.nmm.ac.uk.

Exhibitions relating to all aspects of Britain's maritime power. The Queen's House and the Royal Observatory in Greenwich Park are also part of the complex. Greenwich Park stretches up the hill behind the museum. Free admission.

☺ **National Portrait Gallery**; St. Martin's Place, WC2; 020 7312 2463; www.npg.org.uk.

Beautiful galleries, arranged by period, with portraits of notable personalities from each era in British history from the Tudors to the present. Donations encouraged; charge for special exhibitions.

☺ **Natural History Museum**; Cromwell Road, SW7; 020 7942 5000; www.nhm.ac.uk.

Innovative exhibitions of zoology, entomology, palæontology, mineralogy and botany. Children love the dinosaur exhibit as well as the life-sized blue whale, creepy crawlies and the earthquake simulator. Donations encouraged.

Old Royal Naval College; King William Walk, Greenwich, SE10; 020 8269 4747; www.greenwichfoundation.org.uk.

Housed in a late-17th century hospital on the Thames, partially designed by Christopher Wren, this is considered to be the great baroque masterpiece of English architecture. The chapel and the Great Hall, together with the grounds of the Old Royal Naval College, are open to the public. Free admission.

Queen's Gallery; Buckingham Palace Road, SW1; 020 7766 7301; www.royal.gov.uk. Changing exhibitions of art and objects from the Royal Collection. Admission charge.

Royal Academy of Arts; Burlington House, Piccadilly, W1; 020 7300 8000; www.royalacademy.org.uk.

An independent fine arts institution which supports contemporary artists and promotes interest in the arts through a comprehensive and ambitious exhibition programme. The Summer Exhibition is a hugely popular show of contemporary art held every year since 1769. Also renowned for many major loan exhibitions. Admission charge.

☺ **Royal Air Force Museum**; Grahame Park Way, Hendon, NW9; 020 8205 2266; www.rafmuseum.org.uk.

National museum devoted to aviation and the comprehensive history of the RAF. The Battle of Britain wing houses a unique collection of memorabilia and machinery dedicated to the people involved in the battle. Donations suggested.

☺ **Royal Hospital Chelsea**; Royal Hospital Road, SW3; 020 7881 5204; www.chelsea-pensioners.co.uk.

A small museum containing artefacts left by deceased In-Pensioners is located within the impressive Wren-designed structure. The entrance hall is dedicated to the memory of the Duke of Wellington, and displays objects associated with him. Visitors may also see the famous Chapel (open for services and concerts) and the pensioners' dining room, and walk in the park. Free admission.

☺ **Royal Mews; Buckingham Palace Road**, SW1; 020 7766 7302;
www.royal.gov.uk.

Splendid collection of state coaches, carriages and the royal horses.
Limited opening hours. Admission charge.

☺ **Science Museum**; Exhibition Road, SW7; 0870 870 4868;
www.sciencemuseum.org.uk.

Comprehensive displays of the history of mathematics, chemistry, physics,
engineering, transport and industry. There are several children's play areas
throughout. The Garden area allows those under six years to experiment
with water, sound and construction. The Launch Pad is a popular hands-on
exhibit for children of all ages. Free admission.

Sir John Soane's Museum; 13 Lincoln's Inn Fields, WC2; 020 7430 0175;
www.soane.org.

Built in the early 19th century by the architect as his private residence.
Contains his collection of art, furniture and antiquities. Excellent tour for
limited numbers for a fee on Saturday afternoons. Donations encouraged.

☺ **Syon House**; Brentford, Middlesex, TW8; 020 8560 0881;
www.syonpark.co.uk.

Syon Park is home to Syon House -- the last surviving ducal residence
complete with its country estate in Greater London. Look around the Duke
of Northumberland's London home, view the magnificent State and Private
Apartments and enjoy the spectacular Great Conservatory and 40 acres of
gardens. Syon Park is also home to various attractions for children: the
London Butterfly House, the Tropical Forest and Snakes and Ladders (an
indoor/outdoor adventure playgound). Admission charge.

Tate Britain; Millbank, SW1, 020 7887 8000; www.tate.org.uk/britain.

The national collection of British art (from 1500 to present day).
Donations encouraged; admission charge for major special exhibitions.

Tate Modern; Bankside, SE1; 020 7887 8888; www.tate.org.uk/modern.

A national gallery, comprised of the national collection of British modern art from 1500 to the present and of international foreign modern art. Entrance is free, but donations are encouraged. Admission may be charged for certain exhibitions.

☺ **Theatre Museum**; Russell Street, WC2; 020 7943 4700; www.theatremuseum.org.uk.

Permanent displays trace the history of the stage since the 16th century. Programmes of special activities and exhibitions, many aimed at children. Free admission.

☺ **Tower of London**; Tower Hill, EC3; 0870 756 6060; www.hrp.org.uk.

Impressive fortification, parts of which date to Norman times; includes the White Tower, the Crown Jewels and an extensive armoury collection. It is the execution site of three queens and home to many legends and myths. Admission charge.

Victoria and Albert Museum; Cromwell Road, SW7; 020 7942 2000; www.vam.ac.uk.

One of the truly great collections of art and design in the world. Fine and decorative arts covering most periods of history from many of the world's richest cultures. Donations encouraged.

Wallace Collection; Hertford House, Manchester Square, W1; 020 7563 9500; www.wallacecollection.org.

Private collection assembled during the 19th century with an emphasis on French 18th century fine and decorative arts. Fine collection of arms and armour. Donations encouraged.

Wesley's House and Chapel; 49 City Road, EC1; 020 7253 2262; www.wesleyschapel.org.uk.

Home of the founder of Methodism; contains a large collection of his personal possessions. Donations encouraged.

William Morris Gallery; Water House, Lloyd Park, Forest Road, Walthamstow E17; 020 8527 3782; www.lbwf.gov.uk.

Childhood home of the designer William Morris. The collection includes furniture, pictures, stained glass, wallpapers and textiles designed by Morris and his contemporaries. Donations encouraged.

Wimbledon Lawn Tennis Museum; Church Road, SW19; 020 8946 6131; www.wimbledon.org.

Offers a glimpse of how tennis has become a multimillion dollar professional sport, played all over the world. The museum includes memorabilia from many famous players, views of Centre Court and a state-of-the-art audiovisual theatre showing highlights of great players in action. Admission charge.

The National Trust

The National Trust is a charity that protects and opens to the public over 300 historic houses and gardens and 49 industrial monuments and mills. The Trust produces a handbook to stately properties throughout the UK and membership entitles you to discounts on many admissions. The properties under National Trust's management often serve as museums. A sampling of properties are listed below. More information may be found at www.nationaltrust.org.uk.

Carlyle's House; 24 Cheyne Row, SW3; 020 7352 7087.

Queen Anne period home of writer John Carlyle and his wife Jane. Paintings, decorative arts, personal effects, manuscripts and Carlyle's library. Admission charge.

Fenton House; Windmill Hill, Hampstead, NW3; 020 7435 3471.

A late-17th century house with walled gardens and an outstanding collection of porcelain and early keyboard instruments. Admission charge.

16

Ham House; Ham Street, Ham, Richmond-upon-Thames, TW10; 020 8940 1950.

Superb 17th century house along the Thames with an important collection of Stuart and early Georgian furnishings. Restored formal gardens. Admission charge.

Osterley Park & House; Jersey Road, Isleworth TW7; 020 8232 5050.

Neoclassical mansion transformed by Robert Adam (1760 to 1780); 140 acres of landscaped park and pleasure grounds. Admission charge to house.

English Heritage

English Heritage is a not-for-profit organisation, partly funded by the government, that seeks to conserve and enhance the historic environment and broaden public access to and understanding of England's heritage. It cares for over 400 historic properties, some which also serve as museums, and opens them to visitors. Membership benefits include free or reduced admission to its properties and events. More information on each of its properties including those highlighted below, may be found at www. english-heritage.org.uk.

Apsley House; 149 Piccadilly, W1; 020 7499 5676.

The home of Arthur Wellesley, the first Duke of Wellington; contains his art collection and military memorabilia. Admission charge.

Chiswick House; Burlington Lane, Chiswick W4; 020 8995 0508.

8th century villa set in extensive grounds; built by Lord Burlington, influenced by Palladio and Indigo Jones. Gardens by William Kent. Admission charge.

Kenwood House; Hampstead Lane, NW3; 020 8348 1286.

Set in splendid grounds beside Hampstead Heath, this outstanding neoclassical house holds one of the most important collections of paintings ever given to the nation, including works by Rembrandt, Vermeer, Turner, Reynolds and Gainsborough. The house was remodelled by Robert Adam from 1764 to 1779, when he transformed the original brick building into a majestic villa for Lord Mansfield. Donations encouraged.

Ranger's House (The Wernher Collection); Chesterfield Walk, Blackheath SE10; 020 8853 0035.

A stunning collection of medieval and Renaissance art purchased by the diamond magnate and philanthropist Sir Julius Wernher (1850-1912). Nearly 700 works of art are displayed within the elegant mansion's early Georgian panelled interiors. Among them are rare, early religious paintings and Dutch old masters, Gothic ivories, bronzes and silver treasures, and a fine jewellery collection of more than 100 Renaissance pieces.

The National Art Collection Fund

A leader among the many worthwhile charities in London is the **National Art Collections Fund**, Millais House, 7 Cromwell Place, SW7; 020 7225 4800; www.artfund.org. This charity is dedicated to keep Great Britain's art treasures in Great Britain by aiding in the purchase of art for galleries and museums. Membership provides entry to many museum and historic properties, and substantial discounts on many exhibitions, talks and travel offers.

THE PERFORMING ARTS

London benefits from a wide range of venues for the performing arts. An essential guide to what is on offer each week is *Time Out London* (www.timeout.com/london), published every Tuesday and available at news agents. It lists current and upcoming events, locations, dates, times, ticket prices, reviews and previews.

Each venue will have its own schemes relating to membership benefits and discount tickets. Some venues offer concessions for certain groups such as students, pensioners, union members, residents of certain neighbourhoods (e.g., Westminster, Barbican). Other venues reserve a set number of tickets for same-day sales, often at a discount. Still others offer membership schemes with benefits that include early booking information and ticket discounts. Check with the specific venue to determine what discount schemes they offer either in advance or for same-day performances.

Comedy

For a thorough list of pubs and clubs that provide stand-up comedy events, visit www.comedyonline.co.uk. Comedy clubs and venues include:

The Bedford; 77 Bedford Hill, SW12; 020 8682 8940; www.thebedford.co.uk.

Hosts the Banana Cabaret Comedy on Friday and Saturday nights, and New Acts night on Tuesdays. Also serves as live music venue and offers dancing classes.

The Chuckle Club; Houghton Street (London School of Economics), WC2; 020 7476 1672; (www.chuckleclub.com). Open Saturdays only.

Comedy Café; 66 Rivington Street, EC2; 020 7739 5706; www.comedycafe.fsnet.co.uk. Open Wednesday through Saturday.

The Comedy Store; 1a Oxendon Street, W1; www.thecomedystore.co.uk. Tickets available through Ticketmaster at 0870 154 4040 or www.ticketmaster.co.uk.

Jongleurs; three locations in London — Camden (Middle Yard, Camden Lock, Chalk Farm Road, NW1), Battersea (49 Lavender Gardens, SW11) and Bow Wharf (221 Grove Road, E3); 0870 787 0707; www.jongleurs.com.

Newsrevue; Canal Café Theatre, Delamere Terrace, Little Venice, W2; 020 7289 6054; www.newsrevue.com.

A fast-paced show of hilarious sketches and songs based on absolutely anything in the news -- politics, sport or celebrities. Performances are Thursday through Saturday.

Up The Creek; 302 Creek Road, Greenwich, SE10; 020 8858 4581; www.up-the-creek.com. Friday and Saturday night comedy shows; disco thereafter.

Dance

For a current list of news and events related to ballet and dance in the UK, visit www.ballet.co.uk.

English National Ballet; 39 Jay Mews, SW7; 020 7581 1245; www.ballet.org.uk.

Internationally acclaimed classical ballet company, employing British and international talent. Tours extensively throughout England, and presents two high-profile seasons in London, at the London Coliseum at Christmas and at Royal Albert Hall in the summer.

The Peacock Theatre; Portugal Street, WC2; 0870 737 0337; www.sadlers-wells.com/peacock/default.asp.

Sister theatre to Sadler's Wells (see below), it hosts a variety of contemporary dance shows.

Rambert Dance Company; 94 Chiswick High Road, W4; 020 8630 0600; www.rambert.org.uk.

The oldest dance company in Britain, committed to presenting a broad range on modern repertoire, tours annually through Britain as well as internationally. Many performances in London occur at Sadler's Wells.

Royal Ballet Company; The Royal Opera House, Bow Street, WC2; 020 7304 4000; www.royalballet.org.

Based at the Royal Opera House, the Royal Ballet is Great Britain's most prestigious ballet company. The Company's repertory showcases the great classical ballets alongside new works both by international choreographers and choreographers from within the Company. Extensive international touring.

359

Sadler's Wells and Lilian Baylis Theatre; Rosebery Avenue, EC1; 0870 737 7737, www.sadlers-wells.com.

Dedicated to contemporary dance ranging from cutting-edge performances to mainstream dance. The Lilian Baylis Theatre serves as a forum to learn and develop skills.

MUSIC

London offers something for those who appreciate music of any kind. World-famous artists as well as up-and-comers perform regularly at venues large and small. Classical performances are offered in a variety of venues. Live music of all sorts is available seven days a week.

Classical

Kenwood House; Hampstead Heath, NW3; 020 8348 1286; www.picnicconcerts.com.

Events held throughout the year; outdoor summer concerts are a specialty and consist of varied genres including classical, rock and popular musical artists.

Royal College of Music; Prince Consort Road, SW7; 020 7591 4314; www.rcm.ac.uk.

Events offered include large-scale orchestral concerts, opera and chamber concerts, as well as jazz and contemporary music features. Many events are free of charge.

Royal Albert Hall; Kensington Gore, SW7; 020 7589 3203; www.royalalberthall.com.

A great variety of musical events in various genres are staged here, including Christmas concerts, "The Proms" (a popular series of performances held throughout the summer) and performances by popular contemporary artists. The Royal Philharmonic Orchestra is the resident orchestra.

St. John's; Smith Square, SW1; 020 7222 1061; www.sjss.org.uk.

This concert hall is situated in a restored Queen Anne church and presents a varied programme of classical music.

Wigmore Hall; 36 Wigmore Street, W1; 020 7935 2141; www.wigmore-hall.org.uk.

A small recital hall, known for its acoustics, offers a variety of performances which are often particularly attractive to music connoisseurs. Attracts leading classical musicians famed for its presentation of chamber music and song.

Contemporary

The major concert venue in London that attracts major artists seeking a stadium audience is Wembley Arena, Empire Way, Wembley; 0870 060 0870; www.whatsonwembley.com. While it is under construction, there is a wealth of smaller venues that attract big-name artists as well as newcomers who are up-and-coming on the London music scene. A small selection follows.

Brixton Academy; 211 Stockwell Road, SW9; 020 7771 3000; www.brixton-academy.co.uk.

The Forum; 9-17 Highgate Road, NW5; 020 7284 1001; www.meanfiddler.com.

London Astoria; 157 Charing Cross Road, W1; 020 7434 9592; www.meanfiddler.com.

Royal Albert Hall — see above under "Classical".

Shepherds Bush Empire; Shepherds Bush Green, W12; 0870 771 2000; www.shepherds-bush-empire.co.uk.

Jazz

100 Club; 100 Oxford Street, W1; 020 7636 0933; www.the100club.co.uk.
Various musical styles offered, including jazz, blues, rock, punk and R&B.

606 Club; 90 Lots Road, SW10; 020 7352 5953; www.606club.co.uk.
Jazz club restaurant.

Jazz Café; 5 Parkway, NW1; 020 7916 6060; www.meanfiddler.com.
Popular with locals and gig-goers.

Ronnie Scott's; 47 Frith Street, W1; 020 7439 0747;
www.ronniescotts.co.uk.
World famous night club presenting jazz music of an international
standard.

Opera

The English National Opera; London Coliseum, St. Martin's Lane, WC2;
0870 145 0200; www.eno.org.
The resident opera company sings its performances in English.

Glyndebourne Festival Opera; Glyndebourne, Lewes, East Sussex;
0127 381 2321; www.glyndebourne.com.
Opera performed in the summer in the grounds of an Elizabethan house.
Famous for black-tie picnics on the lawn. The company tours the UK in
the fall.

Opera Holland Park; Holland Park, W8; 0845 230 9769;
www.operahollandpark.com.
Opera is presented during the summer in a covered outdoor setting.

The Royal Opera; Bow Street, WC2; 020 7304 4000; www.royalopera.org.
Based in the Royal Opera House in Covent Garden, this opera company
conducts a regular program of performances in London.

Royal College of Music – see above under "Classical".

THEATRE

The concentration of London theatre venues, particularly the large, commercial ones, are located in London's West End. However, the smaller-scale productions in the fringe theatres and venues should not be overlooked. The weekly listings magazine *Time Out: London* (www.timeout.com/london) provides comprehensive coverage of all London theatre productions.

Some of the smaller theatres of note are:

Donmar Warehouse; 39 Earlham Street, WC2; 020 7240 4882; www.donmarwarehouse.com.

One of London's leading independent producing theatres which offers an intimate studio theatre seating 250.

Royal National Theatre; South Bank, SE1; 020 7452 3400; www.nationaltheatre.co.uk.

Three theatres (the Olivier, the Lyttelton and the Cottesloe) all under one roof, offering an eclectic mix of new plays and classics.

Shakespeare's Globe; 21 New Globbe Walk, Bankside, SE1; 020 7401 9919; www.shakespeares-globe.org.

Dedicated to the experience and international understanding of Shakespeare in performance, this reproduction of the original Globe theatre offers performances in its open-air theatre from May through October, as well as tours and educational events year-round.

THEATRE TICKETS

Tickets to most West End shows are available from theatre box offices, ticket agencies (e.g., Ticketmaster), major department stores, hotels and online. Useful reference websites are www.londontheatre.co.uk, www.officiallondontheatre.co.uk and www.expressevents.com.

Theatre box offices frequently offer same-day price reductions on standby tickets (either on a limited number of tickets released that morning or for concessions) and returned tickets can often be bought for full price one

16

hour before the show. As a rule, these tickets can be bought from the box office in person only.

Half-price tickets for same-day performances are more readily available at two independent ticket booths:

Tkts; Leicester Square, WC1 (in the clock tower building on the south side of the garden in Leicester Square). Open Monday to Saturday 10:00 to 19:00, Sunday 12:00 to 15:00.

Tkts; Canary Wharf, Docklands, E14 (kiosk located at Canary Wharf Docklands Light Railway Station on Platforms 4/5). Open Monday to Saturday 10:00 to 15:30; closed Sunday.

Most tickets are sold at half price plus a service charge per ticket. Additional shows may also be available at a lesser discount or at full price. Payment is in cash or by credit or debit card; cheques and travellers' cheques are not accepted. Please note that cash is not accepted at Canary Wharf. Daily availability can be viewed at www.officiallondontheatre.co.uk/tkts.

MULTI-ARTS VENUES

London has multi-arts venues that offer world-class programmes in performing and visual arts.

Barbican Centre; Silk Street, EC2; 020 7638 8891; www.barbican.org.uk.

The Barbican presents a diverse programme of performing and visual arts, encompassing all forms of classical and contemporary music, international theatre and dance, visual arts and design, and a cinema programme which blends first-run films with special themed seasons. Its Resident Orchestra is the **London Symphony Orchestra** and its Associate Orchestra is the **BBC Orchestra**.

South Bank Centre (including Queen Elizabeth's Hall, the Royal Festival Hall, the Hayward Gallery and the Purcell Room); Belvedere Road, SE1; 0870 380 4300; www.southbankcentre.org.uk.

Southbank Centre's diverse musical program includes classical and world music, rock and pop, jazz and dance. The venue offers theatrical events, dance performances, houses an art gallery and serves as the home of the **London Philharmonic Orchestra** and the **Opera Factory.**

Drawn by Sharday

Annual Events

There is never a dull moment in London! To assist you in planning an exciting year, we have provided a month-by-month schedule of events, along with advice on when and where to obtain tickets. For those events requiring advance planning and/or ticket purchase, we have added reminders at the time of year when you must send away for tickets.

Please Note: The following information is accurate at the time of publication. It is strongly suggested that you always verify details before making your plans. You should either call the venue directly or contact the following for assistance: **Visit London** at 020 7234 5800 or **Visit Britain** at 020 8846 9000.

Here are a few other helpful hints:

    • Dress codes are often in effect. Ask your host/hostess or someone who has attended the event before for advice.

Did you know?... that if you live in Westminster you may qualify for a "ResCard"? Not many residents of the City of Westminster realise that they are eligible for a whole range of special offers and discounted tickets to sights and cultural venues and activities in the area. These include discounts to Apsley House (the home of the Great Duke of Wellington), the London Dungeon, London Aquarium, National Maritime Museum, Madame Tussaud's and the London Planetarium. You can even obtain a reduced entry to the latest exhibitions at the Hayward and Serpentine Galleries, Tate Britain, some West End shows and cinemas. For information, contact: 020 7460 6972 (www.westminster. gov.uk/rescard). Along with the card, you will receive a regular brochure with details of the discounts available at that time.

• When booking an event, always enclose a self-addressed envelope (s.a.e.) and enquire if it is possible or necessary to book the car park.

• For more popular events, such as Wimbledon, The Queen's Garden Party, Trooping the Colour and Ascot, tickets must be obtained through a lottery or ballot. Entry forms, referred to as ballots, must be submitted by a certain deadline.

• Individual castles, stately homes and numerous other venues offer their own calendar of events. Visit the website, telephone, write or email to request a detailed schedule of events.

JANUARY
Reminders:
1 JANUARY – 28 FEBRUARY: Submit your application for Ballots to Trooping the Colour. *See May and June.*

1 JANUARY: Bookings open for Chelsea Flower Show in May, The Derby in June and the Goodwood Festival in July.

31 JANUARY: Tickets for Beating the Retreat in June are available.

JANUARY STORE SALES
Most stores have major sales beginning in late December and ending in late January.

NEW YEAR'S DAY

1 JANUARY – Bank Holiday

NEW YEAR'S DAY PARADE

1 JANUARY

This is the official birthday for all race horses. Lord Mayor of Westminster's parade begins in early afternoon at Piccadilly and ends at Hyde Park. Entertainment continues in Hyde Park throughout the day and concludes with a fireworks display, marching bands and colourful floats. Free of charge.

ROYAL EPIPHANY GIFTS SERVICE

6 JANUARY

Officers of the royal household give gold, frankincense and myrrh in the Chapel Royal at St James Palace. The gold is changed for coins which are given to charity. Contact: St. James's Palace at 020 7930 4832.

LONDON INTERNATIONAL BOAT SHOW

EARLY JANUARY

At Earl's Court, Warwick Road, SW5. The largest boat show in Europe and among the most prestigious boat shows in the world. The latest designs in pleasure crafts, yachts and equipment are displayed. Contact: National Boat Shows Ltd.; Meadlake Place, Thorpe Lea Road, Egham, Surrey, TW20 8HE; 017 8447 3377.

OPENING OF THE OLD BAILEY

EARLY JANUARY

An ancient ceremony to open the new court session where the Queen's Justices are in full bottomed wigs and the Mayor of London is in his 19th century robes and ostrich plumed hat.

SERVICE COMMEMORATING CHARLES I

LAST SUNDAY IN JANUARY

Parade at 11:30 at St. James' Palace to mark the beheading of Charles I on

30 January 1649, followed by a service at Banqueting Hall. Write to: Charles I Service; 70 Hailgate, Howden, North Humberside, DN14 7ST. Free of charge.

CHINESE NEW YEAR CELEBRATIONS
LATE JANUARY OR EARLY FEBRUARY
Gerrard Street, W1. Celebrated with a festive march through London's Chinatown. Complete with papier-mâché dragons and extravagant costumes. This is usually on the Sunday nearest the date of the New Year.

FEBRUARY
Reminders:

Early February: Application forms available for submitting work (amateur or professional) to the Royal Academy Summer Exhibition. *See May.*

ACCESSION OF H.M. THE QUEEN
6 FEBRUARY
Anniversary salute of 41 guns in Hyde Park by the King's Troop of the Royal Horse Artillery and a 62-gun salute at the Tower of London by the Honorable Artillery Company. No tickets required.

CLOWN SERVICE
FIRST SUNDAY IN FEBRUARY
In memory of the famous clown Joseph Grimaldi (1778-1837), clowns gather for a church service at Holy Trinity Church; Beechwood Road, E8. The service is attended by many clowns in full costume. No tickets required.

LONDON FASHION WEEK
2ND WEEK IN FEBRUARY
Europe's largest selling exhibition for designer fashion. Visit www. londonfashionweek.co.uk for details.

GREAT SPITALFIELDS PANCAKE DAY RACE
LATE FEBRUARY OR EARLY MARCH (SHROVE TUESDAY)

The tradition dates back to the time when people emptied their pantries of all ingredients and made pancakes before fasting for Lent. Now races are held where teams run for the finish line while flipping pancakes in frying pans. The Old Spitalfields Market; Spitalfields, E1.

MARCH

Reminders:

30 MARCH: Deadline for obtaining application and sponsorship to the Royal Enclosure at Royal Ascot in June (Applies to American Embassy applications).

MOTHERING SUNDAY - BRITISH MOTHER'S DAY
DATE VARIES

BRITISH SUMMER TIME BEGINS
DATE VARIES

Clocks go forward one hour. UK Spring daylight savings takes place a couple of weeks before North America adjusts their clocks.

CAKES AND ALES CEREMONY
ASH WEDNESDAY

Members of the Worshipful Company of Stationers (founded in 1403) proceed from Stationers Hall to St Paul's Cathedral to hear a sermon. Cakes and ale are then dispensed to all.

ORANGES AND LEMONS CHILDREN'S SERVICE
MARCH 28

A church service of thanks for the restoration of the bells of St. Clement Dane (of nursery rhyme fame). Children of the St. Clement's Dane Primary School receive an orange and a lemon each.

HEAD OF THE RIVER RACE

END OF MARCH (USUALLY SATURDAY BEFORE UNIVERSITY BOAT RACE)

A rowing journey from Mortlake to Putney, it is considered to be the largest continuous rowing event in the world. There is a continuous procession of boats throughout the race since; the best view is from the north side of Hammersmith Bridge. Visit www.horr.co.uk for details.

OXFORD AND CAMBRIDGE BOAT RACE

SATURDAY IN MARCH OR APRIL

Held annually since 1829, the race course is from Putney to Mortlake on the Thames. Starting time varies according to the tides. The race can be viewed from many vantage points: bridges, banks, and riverside pubs. For more information, timing and maps visit www.theboatrace.org.

DAILY MAIL IDEAL HOME EXHIBITION

SEVERAL WEEKS IN MARCH

Largest annual consumer home show in the world held at Earl's Court Exhibition Centre, Warwick Road, SW5. Visit www.idealhomeshow.co.uk for details.

BADA ANTIQUES AND FINE ART FAIR

SECOND WEEK OF MARCH

An annual showcase of furniture, paintings, silver, glass, ceramics, jewelry and more. Very high quality and authenticity. Held at the Duke of York's Headquarters; King's Road, Chelsea. Visit www.bada-antiques-fair.co.uk.

RHS LONDON FLOWER SHOW

SECOND WEEK IN MARCH

The Royal Horticultural Society's flower show celebrating spring and the early daffodil competition. Visit www.rhs.org.uk for details.

THE AFFORDABLE ART FAIR, BATTERSEA PARK
SECOND WEEK OF MARCH
Numerous galleries throughout London and other parts of the UK display their various collections of art. A great place to browse, buy and learn about art all under one roof. The event is held bi-annually (the second show is usually in October). Visit www.affordableartfair.co.uk for details.

YONEX ALL ENGLAND BADMINTON CHAMPIONSHIPS
SECOND WEEKEND OF MARCH
Normally held in the National Indoor Arena in Birmingham. Book directly with the NIA (www.necgroup.co.uk/boxoffice) or write to: Badminton Association of England; National Badminton Centre, Bradwell Road, Loughton Lodge, Milton Keynes, MK8 9LA; www.baofe.co.uk.

CHELTENHAM NATIONAL HUNT FESTIVAL, GLOUCESTERSHIRE
SECOND / THIRD WEEK OF MARCH
One of the most important jump racing events of the year; top British and Irish horses competing. Visit www.cheltenham-festival.co.uk or *Chapter 14: Sports and Leisure* for more details.

APRIL
Reminders:
First week of April: Deadline for submitting paintings to the Royal Academy Summer Exhibition. See May.

10 APRIL: Deadline for obtaining application and sponsorship to the Royal Enclosure at Royal Ascot in June (Applies to Canadian High Commission applications).

JOHN STOW'S QUILL PEN MEMORIAL SERVICE
5 APRIL
John Stow wrote The Survey of London in 1598 at the age of 73. This memorial service attended by the Lord Mayor, takes place at St Andrew's

Undershaft Church; Great St. Helens, EC3. As part of the service, the Lord Mayor places a quill in the hand of Stow's statue.

FA CUP FINAL
APRIL OR MAY
Climax of the English football season. See *Chapter 14: Sports and Leisure* for more details.

THE GRAND NATIONAL STEEPLECHASE
Many consider this to be the most famous steeplechase in the world, run at Aintree racecourse, near Liverpool. Visit www.aintree.co.uk or see *Chapter 14: Sports and Leisure* for more details.

MAUNDY THURSDAY
THURSDAY BEFORE GOOD FRIDAY
Held at Westminster Abbey every tenth year and at different cathedrals around the country during the other nine. The Queen distributes purses of specially minted coins to as many poor men and women as the years of her age.

GOOD FRIDAY
FRIDAY BEFORE EASTER SUNDAY – BANK HOLIDAY

HOT CROSS BUNS SERVICE
GOOD FRIDAY
In a ceremony that dates back hundreds of years, 21 widows are given money and hot-cross buns after a church service at St Bartholomew-the-Great in Smithfield.

EASTER SUNDAY SERVICE
Seating at 10:00, St. George's Chapel, Windsor Castle, SL4. The Queen and the Royal Family worship together in St. George's Chapel. Visitors can attend. If you are seated toward the front of the Nave, you may be sitting

with the Royal Family in the choir stalls. The queue is long, so arrive early. Many people do not enter the chapel; so do not be discouraged by the size of the queue. Contact: The Chapel Clerk; Windsor Castle, Windsor, Berkshire, SL4 1NJ.

EASTER SUNDAY PARADE

At Battersea Park; carnival parade with colourful floats and bands and at the Tower of London; Yeomen Warders in state dress.

EASTER MONDAY
MONDAY FOLLOWING EASTER SUNDAY – BANK HOLIDAY

LONDON HARNESS HORSE PARADE
EASTER MONDAY

At Battersea Park. You might not expect to see horse-drawn carriages in the city centre, but this annual Easter Monday event is a huge parade of working horses from giant cart horses to sturdy Shetland ponies, all pulling gorgeous old carts, carriages and engines. A vision of how London must have a looked a century ago. Tickets not required.

THE FLORA LONDON MARATHON
LATE APRIL

The famous London marathon is made up of competitors from around the world: international marathon runners, serious runners, celebrities, disabled runners and those just out for fun. The race winds throughout many areas of London and finishes outside of Buckingham Palace. Visit www.london-marathon.co.uk for details.

H.M. THE QUEEN'S BIRTHDAY
21 APRIL

Hyde Park and Tower of London. A 41-gun salute to mark the actual (not the official) birthday of The Queen, fired by the King's Troop Royal Horse Artillery in Hyde Park (opposite the Dorchester Hotel), and a 62-gun royal salute fired by the Honourable Artillery Company at the Tower of London (on London Wharf). Her official birthday is celebrated at Trooping the Colour; a ceremony held in June.

ST. GEORGE'S DAY
23 APRIL

St. George has been the patron saint of England since the 14th century. On this day, Englishmen wear an English rose in their lapels (St. George's symbol) and the flag of St. George (a red cross on white background) is flown from many buildings throughout England.

SHAKESPEARE'S BIRTHDAY
23 APRIL

Shakespeare's birthday is celebrated in his hometown of Stratford-upon-Avon every year on the weekend closest to the 23rd April. The highlight is the floral procession of dignitaries from all over the world between his birthplace and Holy Trinity Church. Details from Stratford Tourist Information on www.shakespeare-country.co.uk.

CRICKET SEASON BEGINS

MAY
Reminders:
AFTER 1 MAY: Apply for Steward's Enclosure at Henley Regatta. *See June.*

MAY DAY BANK HOLIDAY
FIRST MONDAY IN MAY

THE BADMINTON HORSE TRIALS
EARLY MAY

At Badminton, Avon, Gloucestershire. International equestrian competition. Contact: The Horse Trials Office at www.badminton-horse.co.uk.

POLO SEASON BEGINS
EARLY MAY TO SEPTEMBER

At Windsor Great Park, matches are held most Saturdays and Sundays. Contact: The Guards Polo Club; Smiths Lawn, Windsor Great Park, Englefield Green, Egham, Surrey, TW20 0HP; 017 8443 4212; www. guardspoloclub.com.

GLYNDEBOURNE FESTIVAL
MAY TO AUGUST

International festival of opera. People dress formally, take a picnic and dine on the grass with wine or champagne in hand. The festival is popular so book early for tickets. Special train services run from Victoria Station to Glyndebourne and return from Lewes. Contact: Glyndebourne Festival Opera Box Office; Glyndebourne, Lewes, East Sussex, BN8 5UU; 012 7381 2321; www.glyndebourne.com.

ROYAL WINDSOR HORSE SHOW
MID-MAY

At Windsor, Berkshire. International show with jumping and driving, various displays and trade exhibits. It is possible to become a member for a fee that allows one access to the Members' Enclosure for the week of the show. Contact: The Secretary; Royal Windsor Horse Show Office, Royal Mews, Windsor Castle, Windsor, Berkshire, SL4 14T; 017 5386 0633; www. royal-windsor-horse-show.co.uk.

BATH FESTIVAL
MID-LATE MAY

Festival of music and arts with concerts, exhibitions, tours and lectures. Visit www.bathmusicfest.org.uk for details.

LILIES AND ROSES
21 MAY

Henry VI founded both Eton College and King's College Cambridge.

Every year on the anniversary of Henry's murder in the Tower of London, delegates from the schools place flowers on the spot of the king's death - lilies from Eton and roses from King's.

OAK APPLE DAY
29 MAY

The Chelsea Pensioners honour Charles II, founder of the Royal Hospital in Chelsea, on the anniversary of Charles II's escape after the Battle of Worcester. The king's statue is decorated with oak leaves in memory of the fact that Charles hid in an oak tree to escape his pursuers.

RHS CHELSEA FLOWER SHOW
LATE MAY

Held at the Chelsea Royal Hospital Grounds, this is the world's leading horticultural event; often visited by the Royal Family. Tuesday and Wednesday are reserved for RHS members with admittance to the general public on Thursday, Friday and Saturday. Tickets are limited and all sold in advance. Apply to RHS after 1 January. No children under five are admitted. Visit www.rhs.org.uk/chelsea for details.

TROOPING THE COLOUR
LAST SATURDAY IN MAY, FIRST REHEARSAL

From Buckingham Palace along the Mall to Horse Guards Parade, Whitehall and back again, SW1. The first of two rehearsals (the second held in June) to prepare for the actual Trooping the Colour, the second Saturday in June, in the presence of H.M. the Queen. A magnificent parade of colourful military units celebrates the Queen's official birthday. Tickets required. See June for ticket information.

HAY ON WYE LITERARY FESTIVAL
LATE MAY–EARLY JUNE

For 10 days, this tiny town of 1,300 people and 39 bookshops is overwhelmed with visitors to enjoy a carnival of literature. The program is full of guest speakers, discussion panels renown authors and a full program for children. Visit www.hayfestival.co.uk for details.

REGENT'S PARK OPEN AIR THEATRE SEASON
MAY THROUGH SEPTEMBER

A full programme of plays, both Shakespeare and more modern works. Open Air Theatre; Inner Circle, Regent's Park, NW1; 020 7935 5756; box office: 020 7486 2431; www.openairtheatre.org.uk.

ROYAL ACADEMY SUMMER EXHIBITION
MAY TO AUGUST

At the Royal Academy of Arts, Piccadilly, W1. A juried exhibition of works by contemporary artists. You may purchase tickets on the day or pre-book tickets. Contact: 020 7300 8000 or visit www.royalacademy.org.uk. If you are an amateur or professional artist you can also submit work to the Summer Exhibition.

CHICHESTER FESTIVAL THEATRE SEASON
MAY TO OCTOBER

A rich history of theatre making with an expanded programme of classic plays, musicals and premieres. For information, write to: Chichester Festival Theatre; Oaklands Park, Chichester, West Sussex, PO19 6AP; 012 4378 1312; www.cft.org.uk.

SHAKESPEARE'S GLOBE THEATRE
MAY TO OCTOBER

Enjoy outdoor theatre in the reconstructed Globe Theatre in the heart of London on the bank of the Thames River. Visit www.shakespeares-globe.org for details.

SPRING BANK HOLIDAY
LAST MONDAY IN MAY

JUNE
BEATING THE BOUNDS
EARLY JUNE

Takes place at many churches throughout the UK, one of the most famous is at the Tower of London. The event harkens back to the days when the majority of parishioners were illiterate, and "beating on the boundary marks of the parishes" taught them where the boundaries lay. This event is held on Ascension Day once every three years (last held in 2005).

MEDIEVAL JOUSTING TOURNAMENTS
JUNE TO AUGUST

Jousting tournaments take place at various castles throughout the UK during the summer months. They make for a fun day out; visit the castle, picnic on the grounds and enjoy the jousting tournament in period costume. For more information and the schedule of events/venues, visit: www. knightsroyal.co.uk.

H.R.H. THE DUKE OF EDINBURGH'S BIRTHDAY
10 JUNE

A 41-gun salute fired by the King's Troop, Royal Horse Artillery at noon in Hyde Park (opposite the Dorchester Hotel), and a 62-gun royal salute fired by the Honourable Artillery Company at one o'clock at the Tower of London (on London Wharf). No tickets required.

TROOPING THE COLOUR (THE QUEEN'S BIRTHDAY PARADE)
2ND SATURDAY IN JUNE

Two rehearsals are held before the official event (on the last Saturday in May and the first Saturday in June). The official event is held on the second Saturday in June. Tickets are allocated by lottery. Send a letter requesting tickets along with a self-addressed envelope (s.a.e.) between 1 January and 28 February to: Brigade Major; HQ Household Division, Horse Guards, Whitehall, SW1A 2AX to receive an application. Only two tickets are allocated per successful entry.

Even though tickets are required for the event, anyone can go to St James's Park or in front of Buckingham Palace to get a glimpse of the Queen. The Queen leaves Buckingham Palace at 10:40 and progresses down The Mall to the Horse Guards Parade, arriving at 11:00.

The event is broadcast live on BBC1, and highlights are shown later on the same day on BBC2.

H.M. THE QUEEN'S OFFICIAL BIRTHDAY GUN SALUTE
MID-JUNE; VARIABLE EACH YEAR

A 41-gun salute is fired by the King's Troop, Royal Horse Artillery at 12:52 in Green Park and a 62-gun royal salute fired by the Honourable Artillery Company at one o'clock at the Tower of London (on London Wharf). No tickets required.

STELLA ARTOIS TENNIS TOURNAMENT
MID-JUNE

Men's Tournament held two weeks before Wimbledon. Tickets may be purchased two months prior to the event, but if you register for their mailing list, you will receive priority ticket booking information in January each year. Visit www.stellaartoistennis.com for details.

BEATING RETREAT
EARLY JUNE

This is a musical spectacle of sound and colour held on two successive evenings in the Horse Guards Parade. It has origins to the years of organised warfare when the beating of drums and the parading of Post Guards heralded the closing of camp gates and the lowering of flags at the end of a day of battle. Today, it is a ceremony reserved for special occasions. The event begins at 19:00 with the salute being taken by Her Majesty the Queen or another member of the royal family. Visit www.royalmarinesregimental. co.uk for tickets and details or call 0870 4000 689 (24 hours).

THE DERBY (pronounced "DAR-by")
FIRST WEEKEND IN JUNE

On Epsom Downs. The most famous and prestigious horse race in the world. It covers one and a half miles. Created at a noble dinner party in 1779 and named after one of the diners – Lord Derby. Bookings open 1 January. Visit www.epsomderby.co.uk for details and tickets or call 013 7247 0047.

ORDER OF THE GARTER CEREMONY
LATE JUNE

In June, a special service marks the oldest order of chivalry in England. The Knights of the Garter gather at St. George's Chapel in Windsor Castle, where new knights take the oath and are invested with the insignia. It is attended by the Queen and is preceded by a colourful procession of knights wearing their blue velvet robes and black velvet hats with white plumes. 1,500 people will be admitted at the gate on a first-come, first-served basis.

BIGGIN HILL INTERNATIONAL AIR FAIR
EARLY JUNE

At Biggin Hill Airport, Biggin Hill, Kent. Jet formation aerobatics, historic aircraft rally, modern military jets and extensive ground exhibition. Visit www.militaryairshows.co.uk for details and tickets.

PRINCE WILLIAM'S BIRTHDAY
21 JUNE

KNOLLYS ROSE CEREMONY
24 JUNE

In the 14th century, Sir Robert Knollys was fined for building an unauthorised footbridge across Seething Lane. The fine imposed was one red rose from his garden to be given to the Lord Mayor every year. Today, his descendants along with the churchwardens of All-Hallows-by-the-Tower continue the tradition. Contact: The Clerk to the Company of

Watermen and Lighterman of the River Thames at Watermen's Hall; 16 St. Mary at Hill, EC3R 8EE; 020 7283 2373.

HENLEY ROYAL REGATTA
LATE JUNE OR EARLY JULY
At Henley-on-Thames, Oxfordshire. This international rowing event is also a popular social occasion, with a stringent dress code. Women may only wear a dress (trousers, culottes, and skirts are not permitted), and men must wear a jacket and tie at all times while in the Steward's Enclosure (reserved for members and their guests). The more informal Regatta Enclosure is for the general public and tickets may be purchased in advance after 1 May, or upon arrival. Alternatively, take a picnic and sit alongside the tow path for free. For information visit www.hrr.co.uk or write to: The Secretary; Henley Royal Regatta, Regatta Headquarters, Henley-on-Thames, Oxfordshire, RG9 2LY.

WIMBLEDON TENNIS CHAMPIONSHIPS (WIMBLEDON)
LAST WEEK IN JUNE OR FIRST WEEK IN JULY
See *Chapter 14: Sports and Leisure* for details on applying for tickets. For the public ballot, you must fill out and return the application form postmarked no later than 15 December the year before you want to attend. Note that the tube stop is Southfields, not Wimbledon. Visit www. wimbledon.org for details.

ROYAL ASCOT
USUALLY HELD THIRD WEEK IN JUNE
The world's most famous race meeting dating back to 1711. Tuesday through Friday is attended by the Royal Family. Formal attire, hats and gloves required for ladies and full morning suit for men. To obtain passes for the Royal Enclosure, contact your embassy or high commission for information regarding allocated tickets. For general tickets and information, visit www.royalascot.co.uk.

17

THE QUEEN'S CUP FINAL INTERNATIONAL POLO TOURNAMENT
USUALLY HELD THIRD WEEK IN JUNE

Polo is the fastest growing premium sport in the UK. The Queen's Cup is held at The Guards Polo Club; Royal Windsor Great Park, Windsor. Visit www.guardspoloclub.com for information and details.

HIGHLAND GAMES BEGIN

Many held during the summer all over Scotland. Traditional Scottish games and lots of local colour. Contact: The Scottish Tourist Board; 19 Cockspur Street, SW1Y 5BL; 017 1930 8661; www.holiday.scotland.net.

HOLLAND PARK OPERA SEASON
JUNE THROUGH AUGUST

Featuring the Royal Philharmonic Orchestra, these outdoor concerts offer beautiful music in a fantastic setting. Holland House, one of the oldest houses in Kensington, acts as a backdrop and many people picnic beforehand in the gardens – you can even collect a picnic hamper from the bar. Visit www.operahollandpark.com for details.

OUTDOOR CONCERTS

Summer evening musical concerts are held in July and August on the grounds of several historic houses around London, including 18th century Kenwood House in Hampstead Heath. Arrive early and bring a picnic, a rug, and plenty to drink. Advance booking is advised as most concerts are sellouts. Visit www.picnicconcerts.com for details.

Many other manor houses hold outdoor concerts during the summer. Dates vary each year so contact the individual locations. Some of the most popular are:

- Audley End House, Essex
- Leeds Castle, Maidstone, Kent
- Hampton Court Palace, Surrey
- Hever Castle, Edenbridge, Kent

- Marble Hill, Twickenham
- Pevensey Castle, East Sussex
- Portchester Castle, Hampshire
- Somerset House, London
- Warwick Castle, Warwickshire
- Wrest Park House, Bedfordshire

JULY

ROYAL GARDEN PARTIES AT BUCKINGHAM PALACE

MID-JULY

Three parties are held during the summer; each attended by 10,000 people. A cross section of people are chosen to attend to ensure that all areas of the community are represented. The Queen and the Duke of Edinburgh along with several other members of the royal family circulate among the crowd. Traditional high tea is served. For more information, visit: www.royal.gov.uk.

PROMENADE CONCERTS (THE BBC PROMS)

MID-JULY THROUGH EARLY SEPTEMBER

The world's greatest classical music festival held at the Royal Albert Hall throughout the summer. Visit www.bbc.co.uk/proms for details and ticket information. Guidebooks are available at the end of May including a booking form.

HAMPTON COURT FLOWER SHOW

EARLY JULY

The world's largest flower show presented by the Royal Horticultural Society. Displays from more than 700 exhibitors featuring flowers, plants, accessories, landscape design ideas, the world's largest annual gathering of roses in full bloom and much, much more. Visit www.rhs.org.uk/hamptoncourt for details.

SWAN UPPING
LAST MONDAY IN JULY

Swan Upping is the annual census of the swan population on parts of the River Thames. The Dyers and Vintner's Companies have the right, established in medieval times, to keep swans on the Thames River. So, too, does the Crown. Every year the Queen's Swan Keeper and Swan Markers from the two livery companies row in skiffs along the river to mark the cygnets (baby swans). You can enjoy a view of the proceedings from several pubs along the river. For information on where the boats will be at specific times, telephone: 020 7414 2271 or visit: www.royal.gov.uk (search on swan upping) for details.

DOGGETT'S COAT AND BADGE RACE
LATE JULY OR EARLY AUGUST

Possibly the oldest rowing race in the world, this event was begun by Irish actor Thomas Dogett in 1715 to mark the crowning of George I. Six water boatmen race against the tide from London Bridge to Albert Bridge. The prize is a scarlet livery with a large silver badge. Contact: 020 7283 2373.

GLORIOUS GOODWOOD HORSERACING
LAST TUESDAY TO SATURDAY IN JULY

Horseracing at one of the most beautiful courses in the world, on top of the Sussex Downs. It is one of the highlights of the social summer season – famously described by King Edward VII as 'a garden party with racing tacked on'. Details and tickets at www.goodwood.co.uk.

BRITISH OPEN GOLF CHAMPIONSHIP
MID-JULY

Known for its challenging and always interesting finishes, the British Open is one of the world's favorite and oldest sporting events. Visit www.randa.org for details.

LADIES BRITISH OPEN CHAMPIONSHIPS
MID-JULY

For information, contact: The Ladies' Golf Union; The Scores, St. Andrews, Fife; www.lgu.org.

BRITISH GRAND PRIX
MID-JULY

Premier motor racing event with the world's top drivers in action. Takes place at Silverstone Circuit; Northamptonshire, NN12 8TN; 0870 458 8200. Visit www.silverstone-circuit.co.uk for details.

AUGUST
COWES WEEK
IN LATE JULY OR EARLY AUGUST

On the Isle of Wight. Skandia Cowes Week is the World's premier sailing regatta, with almost 1,000 yachts and 8,000 competitors taking part in some top-class sailing. Sailing races and festival usually attended by Royalty. Visit: www.iwight.com for details.

BUCKINGHAM PALACE OPENS TO VISITORS
EARLY AUGUST TO THE END OF SEPTEMBER

Buckingham Palace is the official London residence of Her Majesty the Queen. The Palace's state rooms and garden are open to visitors while the Queen is on her summer holidays in Scotland. Advance tickets (which will allow you to avoid some of the long queues) go on sale from the last week of July. Book online at www.the-royal-collection.com/royaltickets. You can also purchase tickets on the day of your visit from the Ticket Office at Canada Gate in Green Park between 09:00 and 16:00.

JERSEY BATTLE OF FLOWERS
MID-AUGUST

On the island of Jersey in the Channel Islands. A three-hour parade of floats displaying thousands of flowers, bands, etc. held on Thursday afternoon and Friday evening by moonlight. Crowds gather along the route. Tickets required for the arena. Visit www.battleofflowers.com for details.

EDINBURGH INTERNATIONAL FESTIVAL
MID-AUGUST

The Edinburgh International Festival presents a rich programme of classical music, theatre, opera and dance in six major theatres and concert halls and a number of smaller venues, over a three-week period in late summer each year. It is said to be the largest festival of the arts. For details and information, visit www.eif.co.uk.

EDINBURGH MILITARY TATTOO
THREE WEEKS IN AUGUST

One of the most spectacular shows in the world. A military pageant held on flood lit grounds of Edinburgh Castle. Tickets sell quickly. Bookings can be accepted as early as December of the prior year. Visit www.edinburgh-tattoo.co.uk for details and tickets.

SUMMER BANK HOLIDAY
LAST MONDAY IN AUGUST

NOTTING HILL CARNIVAL
AUGUST BANK HOLIDAY SUNDAY AND MONDAY

This is the largest street festival in Europe involving over one million visitors. An explosion of fun, food, culture and music that began in 1964 when Trinidian immigrants and individuals of Notting Hill brought the people together after the race riots of the 1950s. Visit www.nottinghillcarnival.org.uk for details.

SEPTEMBER
ADMISSION OF SHERIFFS
28 SEPTEMBER OR THE FRIDAY PRECEEDING

The livery companies of the city elect two sheriffs on Midsummer Day.

Today, the new sheriffs march in a colourful procession from Mansion House to the Guildhall to be installed in office. Contact the Guildhall Yard: 020 7606 3030.

ELECTION OF THE LORD MAYOR

29 SEPTEMBER

In a ceremony that dates from 1546, the Lord Mayor is selected at the Guildhall, then rides in state to Mansion House while the city bells ring out. Contact the Guildhall Yard: 020 7606 3030.

OBSERVANCE OF AUTUMN EQUINOX

21 SEPTEMBER

Druids gather at Primrose Hill and Regent's Park.

HORSEMAN'S SUNDAY

18 SEPTEMBER

Church of St. John and St. Michael, Hyde Park Crescent, W2. A morning service dedicated to the horse with mounted vicar and congregation followed by a procession of 100 horses through Hyde Park.

GREAT RIVER RACE

MID-SEPTEMBER

A 22-mile boat race from Richmond, Surrey to Island Gardens, Greenwich involving various types of boats including: Chinese dragon boats, Viking Longboats, whalers, canoes and more. Contact: 020 8398 9057 or visit www.greatriverrace.co.uk for information.

LONDON OPEN HOUSE

MID-SEPTEMBER

Provides the public free access to over 600 buildings (of historical, architectural and/or community interest) throughout London that are normally closed to the public. Takes place over a two-day weekend. An Open House directory is sold listing all sites and details. Visit www.londonopenhouse.org for information.

MAYOR'S THAMES FESTIVAL
MID-SEPTEMBER
Along the banks of the River Thames between Westminster Bridge and Tower Bridge. A spectacular, free, outdoor festival including art exhibitions, shows, street theatre, children's activities and music. Tens of thousands dance in the streets at the festival's climactic event, a spectacular Night Carnival that's a vivid mixture of fireworks, masquerade, dance, music and fantastic costumes. Visit www.thamesfestival.org for details.

OCTOBER
Reminders:
Send for Royal Epiphany Tickets. *See January*.
Send for Cheltenham Hunt Meeting Tickets. *See March*.

PEARLY KINGS AND QUEENS FESTIVAL
FIRST SUNDAY IN OCTOBER
At St. Martin in the Fields Church, Trafalgar Square, WC2. Pearlies are dedicated charity workers who continually assist with fundraising activities for a multitude of organisations. They attend a Harvest Festival Service in traditional full dress of sequined costumes and distinguished pearl-buttoned shirts. Contact the church at 020 7370 7821.

HORSE OF THE YEAR SHOW
EARLY OCTOBER
At the NEC in Birmingham. The climax of national show jumping and showing seasons. For tickets call 0870 010 1052 or book online at www.hoys.co.uk. Tickets usually sell out quickly.

TRAFALGAR PARADE AND SERVICE
21 OCTOBER (OR NEAREST SUNDAY)
At Nelson's Column, Trafalgar Square, WC2. A march to Trafalgar Square remembers the triumph of Lord Nelson at Trafalgar in 1805. Wreaths are laid at the foot of Nelson's Column in the Square.

QUIT-RENTS CEREMONY
LATE OCTOBER

Dating back more than 800 years, the Ceremony is the oldest legal act that is still performed other than the Coronation. It is held to mark the occasion when the City Solicitor pays one of the Queen's officials (the Remembrancer) a token for the rent of properties and land leased long ago. For Shropshire he pays two knives, (one blunt and one sharp) and for the Forge in the Strand he pays sixty-one nails and six horseshoes. For more information, contact: The Chief Clerk to the Queen's Remembrancer; The Queen's Remembrancers' Office, Room E113, Royal Courts of Justice, Strand, WC2A 2LL; 020 7947 6131.

STATE OPENING OF PARLIAMENT
LATE OCTOBER / NOVEMBER

English pageantry at its finest. Her Majesty the Queen rides in the Irish state coach from Buckingham Palace to the House of Lords, where she addresses both houses of Parliament from the Throne in the House of Lords. Viewing along the route. The House of Lords is not open to the public. Check current dates and information at www.parliament.uk.

OPENING OF THE LAW COURTS
LATE OCTOBER / EARLY NOVEMBER

At Westminster Abbey. A closed service is held at Westminster Abbey attended by Her Majesty's Judges and Queen's Counsel dressed in state robes and wigs. Afterwards, the Lord Chancellor leads the procession from the East end of the Abbey to the House of Lords. The first motion of the year constitutes the official opening of the Courts. Contact the House of Lords Information Centre: 020 7219 3000 or visit www.parliament.uk.

BRITISH SUMMERTIME ENDS

Clocks are set back one hour on the Sunday following the fourth Saturday in October.

391

CHELSEA CRAFT FAIR
MID-OCTOBER
Europe's finest craft fair with over 200 exhibitors displaying beautifully made contemporary crafts and applied art. Visit www.craftscouncil.org.uk for details.

NOVEMBER
GUY FAWKES DAY (BONFIRE NIGHT)
5 NOVEMBER
Bonfires, fireworks and burning effigies of Guy Fawkes throughout the UK on the nearest weekend to this date, celebrate his failure to blow up the King and the Houses of Parliament in the Gunpowder Plot of 1605. There is a particularly spectacular event at Leeds Castle in Kent. The Evening Standard and Metro newspapers publish lists of bonfires and fireworks displays in the London area in the week leading up to Guy Fawkes Day.

H.R.H. PRINCE OF WALES' BIRTHDAY
14 NOVEMBER

LONDON TO BRIGHTON RALLY (RAC Veteran Car Run)
1ST SUNDAY IN NOVEMBER
This event is only open to cars built between 1895 and 1904, commemorating the repeal of the "Red Flag Laws" in 1905. With over 500 cars taking part in the 60-mile run to Brighton, it is the largest gathering of old cars in the world. Departures from 08:00 at Hyde Park Corner. Pre-departure festivities and along the route. No tickets required. Contact: The RAC Motor Sports Association Ltd.; Motor Sports House, Riverside Park, Colnbrook, Slough, SL3 OHG; 017 5368 1736.

BOUTIQUE DE NOEL
EARLY NOVEMBER
The Junior League of London's annual Christmas fair features items handcrafted by members as well as unique gifts from selected vendors.

Funds generated by the day and evening event support the community projects of the Junior League of London. For tickets, contact: The Junior League of London at 020 7499 8159.

LORD MAYOR'S PROCESSION AND SHOW
2ND SATURDAY IN NOVEMBER

The new Lord Mayor takes up his post in a colourful procession from Guildhall to the Royal Courts of Justice in his 18th Century Gold State Carriage, escorted by medieval-costumed bodyguards, elaborate floats, acrobats, trumpeters and livery companies. The route is three miles long and features over 6,500 people. No tickets required for viewing along the route. Visit www.lordmayorsshow.org or www.cityoflondon.gov.uk for details.

REMEMBRANCE SUNDAY
ON THE SUNDAY CLOSEST TO 11 NOVEMBER

Around the Cenotaph at Whitehall. A service is held in memory of those killed in battle since 1914. It is attended by the Queen, members of the Royal Family, the Prime Minister, members of the Cabinet and members of the Opposition. Two minutes silence is observed as Big Ben strikes 11:00. During the week which precedes this event, volunteers sell poppies in the streets to raise money for ex-servicemen. Poppy wreaths are placed at many war memorials in village high streets and grave sites.

DECEMBER
Reminders:

15 December – Last day to send in Ballots for Wimbledon. *See June.*

Mid-December – Outdoor skating rinks open for the holiday season around the city: Somerset House, Marble Arch, Natural History Museum, Hampstead Heath, and more. Skates for hire.

CHRISTMAS TREE LIGHTING CEREMONY
MID-DECEMBER
At Trafalgar Square, WC2. Each year an enormous Christmas tree is donated by the people of Oslo, Norway in remembrance and thanks for British assistance during World War II. Carol services are sung every evening beneath the tree until Christmas.

HANDEL'S MESSIAH
At St. Paul's Cathedral. Arrive early for good seats. Contact: The Chapter House; St. Paul's Churchyard, EC4; 020 7236 4128; www.stpauls.co.uk.

CHRISTMAS CONCERTS AND CAROLS
THROUGHOUT DECEMBER
At Royal Albert Hall. Various concerts to cover all tastes and ages including carols by candlelight on Christmas Eve. Visit www.royalalberthall.com for details.

CHILDREN'S PANTOMIMES
Held throughout Britain in local theatres and Town Halls between mid-December and mid-January. Traditional pantomimes with male/female roles reversed, audience participation, sing-along and candy thrown into the audience. Especially popular in London and the seaside resort towns (e.g., Bournemouth). Check theatre listings or local newspapers for information.

WINTER SOLSTICE
21 DECEMBER

CHRISTMAS
25 DECEMBER -- Bank Holiday.
The Queen's Christmas message is broadcast.

CHRISTMAS DAY SWIM
25 DECEMBER

The Peter Pan Cup has taken place every Christmas Day since 1864. While most of us are still tucked up in bed or tearing into a bulging stocking, members of the Serpentine Swimming Club are competing in their annual race across the icy waters of the Serpentine in Hyde Park.

BOXING DAY
26 DECEMBER – Bank Holiday.

NEW YEAR'S EVE
31 DECEMBER

Big Ben tolls at midnight. Enormous crowds gather at Trafalgar Square creating a huge party atmosphere to ring in the New Year.

17

Drawn by Jayden

Organisations

- Government Organisations – Embassies and High Commissions
- Professional Organisations
- Charitable, Social and Service Organisations
- Places of Worship

GOVERNMENT ORGANISATIONS – EMBASSIES AND HIGH COMMISSIONS

In general, your embassy or high commission represents your government and the consular office within every embassy/high commission concerns itself with individual citizens. Therefore, communication with your embassy/high commission will be primarily through the consular office. Consular offices are also located in other cities where there is a high concentration of citizens of a specific nationality.

Consular offices will help you with:

Emergencies

1. Death of a citizen abroad
2. Arrests (the embassy will provide you with the names of lawyers)
3. Financial assistance

Non-emergencies

1. Passports — particular help with stolen or lost passports
2. Registering births and deaths
3. Tax obligations (see *Chapter 3: Money, Banking and Taxation*)
4. Voting — assistance with absentee balloting
5. Notary public

Most foreign states and Commonwealth countries maintain representatives in London. The British Foreign and Commonwealth Office compile an alphabetical listing of such foreign representatives, which can be found at www.fco.gov.uk. It is also available in hard copy from TSO, PO Box 29, Norwich, NR3 1GN. The website provides: the name of the Ambassador or High Commissioner; the address, telephone and fax numbers of the embassy or high commission in London; and, where available, the website and email address for each mission. A complete listing of all European Union Embassies and tourist offices can be found at www.cec. org.uk/info/embassy.htm.

The following is a partial list of embassies in London:

Australian High Commission; Australia House, Strand, WC2; 020 7379 4334; www.australia.org.uk.

Austrian Embassy; 18 Belgrave Mews West, SW1; 020 7235 3731; www.bmaa.gv.at/london.

Belgian Embassy; 103-105 Eaton Square, SW1; 020 7470 3700; www.diplobel.org/uk.

Canadian High Commission; Macdonald House, 38 Grosvenor Street, W1; 020 7258 6600; www.canada.org.uk.

French Embassy; 58 Knightsbridge, SW1; 020 7073 1000; www.ambafrance-uk.org.

Embassy of the Federal Republic of Germany; 23 Belgravia Square, SW1;
020 7824 1300; www.german-embassy.org.uk.

High Commissioner of India; India House, Aldwych, WC2;
020 7836 8484; www.hcilondon.net.

Embassy of Ireland; 17 Grosvenor Place, SW1; 020 7235 2171; Passports
& Visas: 020 7225 7700; www.ireland.embassyhomepage.com.

Italian Embassy; 14 Three Kings Yard, Davies Street, W1; 020 7312 2200;
www.embitaly.org.uk.

Embassy of Japan; 101-104 Piccadilly, W1; 020 7465 6543;
www.uk.emb-japan.go.jp.

Embassy of Luxembourg; 27 Wilton Crescent, London, SW1;
020 7235 6961; www.luxembourg.co.uk.

Royal Netherlands Embassy; 38 Hyde Park Gate, SW7; 020 7590 3200;
www.netherlands-embassy.org.uk.

New Zealand High Commission; New Zealand House, 80 Haymarket,
SW1; 020 7930 8422; www.newzealandhc.org.uk.

High Commission for the Republic of South Africa; South Africa House,
Trafalgar Square, WC2; 0870 005 6974; Visas: 0870 005 6974;
www.southafrica.embassyhomepage.com.

Spanish Embassy; 39 Chesham Place, SW1; 020 7235 5555;
www.spain.embassyhomepage.com.

Embassy of Sweden; 11 Montagu Place, W1; 020 7917 6400; Visas:
020 7917 6415; www.swedish-embassy.org.uk.

18

Embassy of Switzerland; 16-18 Montagu Place, W1; 020 7616 6000; www.swissembassy.org.uk.

Embassy of the United Arab Emirates; 30 Prince's Gate, SW7; 0870 005 6984; Visas: 0870 005 6984; www.unitedarabemirates.embassyhomepage.com.

The Embassy of the United States of America; 24 Grosvenor Square, W1; 020 7499 9000; Visas: 090 4245 0100 / 090 5544 4546; www.usembassy.org.uk.

PROFESSIONAL ORGANISATIONS

Association of MBAs; 25 Hosier Lane, EC1; 020 7246 2686; www.mba.org.uk.

British American Business, Inc.; 75 Brook Street, W1; 020 7467 7400; www.babinc.org.uk.

Independent, non-profit organisation that provides assistance to member companies in the expansion of their activities on both sides of the Atlantic. Services to members include publications, luncheons, lectures and seminars relating to Anglo-American affairs and business.

Institute of Directors; 116 Pall Mall, SW1; 020 7839 1233; www.iod.co.uk.

Institute of Management; 2 Savoy Court, The Strand, WC2; 020 7497 0580; www.managers.org.uk.

CHARITABLE, SOCIAL AND SERVICE ORGANISATIONS

American Women's Club of London; 68 Old Brompton Road, SW7; 020 7589 8292; www.awclondon.org.

Social, recreational and charitable club with facilities for American women living in London.

The American Women of Surrey; P.O. Box 185, Cobham, Surrey KT11 3YG; 079 1026 7962; www.awsurrey.org.
A social club and support group for American women living in Surrey.

Canadian Women's Club; 1 Grosvenor Square, W1; 020 7258 6344; www.canadianwomenlondon.org.
A diverse group of women brought together by their common ties to Canada. Organises various activities, social events, and enables members to undertake projects of interest.

CARE International; 10-13 Rushworth Street, SE1; 020 7934 9334; www.careinternational.org.uk.
Charitable organisation founded in America after World War II. Today it is a confederation of humanitarian organisations that act together to provide emergency responses and assist long-term development to the world's poorest people.

Centre for Creative Communities; Regent's House Business Centre, 24-25 Nutford Place, W1; 020 7569 3005; www.creativecommunities.org.uk.
Charitable organisation for professional artists. The association is geared to strengthening links and increasing opportunities in the arts and arts administration between the United States and the United Kingdom.

Chilterns American Women's Club; P.O. Box 445, Gerrards Cross, Buckinghamshire, SL9 8YU; www.cawc.co.uk.
Operates in the Gerrards Cross and Beaconsfield area.

CTC – The National Cyclists Organisation; 69 Meadrow, Godalming, Surrey GU7 3HS; 0870 873 0060; www.ctc.org.uk.
Britain's national cycling organisation.

Democrats Abroad (UK); Suite 223, 77 Beak Street, W1; 020 7724 9796; www.democratsabroad.org.uk.

The official organisation of the US Democratic Party in the United Kingdom, with the power to organise and elect delegates to the Democratic National Convention.

East Anglia American Club (EAAC); 49 Horsham Close, Haverhill, Suffolk, CB9 7HN; 014 4076 6967; email at Eaacexpats@aol.com.
Social club run as a social, support and information group for American expatriates relocating, either permanently or temporarily, to the East Anglia counties of Cambridgeshire, Essex and Suffolk.

English Heritage; 23 Saville Row, W1; 020 7973 3000; www.english-heritage.org.uk.
Offers exhibitions, museums and guided tours as well as historical re-enactments, displays, concerts and other special events. Funds from the membership help protect and preserve England's historical legacy.

English Speaking Union; Dartmouth House, 37 Charles Street, W1; 020 7529 1550; www.esu.org.
A worldwide registered charity with facilities supported by membership and donations; it aims to promote international understanding through a variety of social and educational activities, including scholarships, lectures, outings and receptions.

Focus Information Services; 13 Prince of Wales Terrace, W8; 020 7937 7799; www.focus-info.org.
Information line: 020 7937 0050. A non-profit organisation that functions as a clearing house of information concerning community services, schools, childcare, organisations, etc. Offers a telephone information line, career and educational services, and seminars and workshops for the international community in the UK.

Hampstead Women's Club (HWC); www.hwcinlondon.co.uk.
Social club for women and their families living in the Hampstead area.

Visit the website for membership and further information.

The Junior League of London (JLL); www.jll.org.uk.

An international organisation of women committed to promoting voluntary service and improving the community through effective action and the leadership of trained volunteers. A registered charity active in the areas of social welfare, the education and welfare of children, the arts and culture.

The Kensington and Chelsea Women's Club (KCWC); Box 567, 28 Old Brompton Road, SW7; 020 7863 7562; www.kcwc.org.uk.

Since 1983 the KCWC has provided social contact and cultural exchange for women in London, both expatriates and British nationals. It is one of the largest women's clubs in London. Monthly meetings with prominent guest speakers.

The Lansdowne Club; 9 Fitzmaurice Place, W1; 020 7629 7200; www.lansdowne-club.co.uk.

A private club that offers a swimming pool, squash courts and fencing as well as a ballroom, a restaurant and regular activities such as Scottish country dancing, chess and bridge.

London Ladies Club; P.O. Box 3870, SW1; 020 7730 4640; www.londonladies.co.uk.

A social club which offers access to the city's top institutions such as museums, colleges, social clubs and societies.

The National Trust; 36 Queen Anne's Gate, SW1; 0870 458 4000; www.nationaltrust.org.uk.

A non-profit organisation and special interest group that purchases or is bequeathed historic properties or places of great natural beauty which are preserved for the nation. Membership entitles you with free entry to properties, various publications, etc. There are also local branches that sponsor activities and trips.

18

Republicans Abroad (UK); www.republicansabroad.org.

Political interest group supporting the US Republican Party with the power to organise and elect delegates to the Republican National Convention.

Rotary Club of London; 6 York Gate, NW1; 020 7847 5429; www.londonrotaryclub.org.uk.

Sport England; 3rd Floor, Victoria House, Bloomsbury Square, WC1; 0845 850 8508; www.sportengland.org.uk.

This organisation works through nine regional offices that can provide a vast array of information on sporting activities throughout England. Visit the Sport England website to research sport opportunities in a specific area.

St. John's Wood Women's Club; www.sjwwc.org.uk.

Social club for women living in the St. John's Wood area.

Oxford and Cambridge Club; 71 Pall Mall, SW1; 020 7930 5151; www.oxfordandcambridgeclub.co.uk.

Telephone for information on club facilities and extensive activities.

University Women's Club; 2 Audley Square, W1; 020 7499 2268; www.universitywomensclub.com.

Social club with facilities for women university graduates or women who are not graduates but are professionally qualified.

Victorian Society; 1 Priory Gardens, W4; 020 8994 1019; www.victorian-society.org.uk.

Special interest group concerned with the preservation and education of Victorian England through trips, seminars and lectures.

Women's Resource Center (WRC); Ground Floor East, 33-41 Dallington Street, EC1; 020 7324 3030; www.wrc.org.uk.

The WRC is a coordinating and support organisation for voluntary and community projects that work for and with women. WRC is a national organisation with a London focus, providing information, training, developmental support, networking opportunities and policy consultation within the non-profit sector.

PLACES OF WORSHIP
Baptist
Bethesda Baptist Church; Kensington Place, W8; 020 7221 7039; www.baptists.net/bethesda.

Buddhist
West London Buddhist Centre; 94 Westbourne Park Villas, W2; 020 7727 9382; www.westlondonbuddhistcentre.com.

The Buddhist Society; 58 Eccleston Square, SW1; 020 7834 5858; thebuddhistsociety.org.

Catholic
Archdiocese of Westminster; www.rcdow.org.uk.
The website contains a list of local parishes.

Brompton Oratory; Brompton Road, SW7; the largest Catholic Church in London.

Holy Cross Catholic Church; Ashington Road, SW6; 020 7736 1068.

St Mary's Catholic Church; 4 Holly Place, NW3; 020 7435 6678.

Church of England
Diocese of London; 36 Causton Street, SW1; 020 7932 1100; www.london.anglican.org. The Diocese website contains a list of churches and a church finder.

Holy Trinity Brompton; Brompton Road, SW7; 0845 644 7533;
www.htb.org.uk.

Evangelical church with contemporary worship style and Sunday school
for children. Located behind Brompton Oratory.

St. Lukes and Christ Church; Sydney Street, SW3; 020 7351 7365.

Traditional-style worship but not High Anglican. Sunday school for
children.

St. Michael's Church; Chester Square, SW1; 020 7730 8889.

Family oriented with children's Sunday school.

Hindu

Shree Swaminarayan Mandir; 105-119 Brentfield Road, Neasden, NW10;
020 8965 2651; www.mandir.org.

Interdenominational

American Church in London (ACL); 79 Tottenham Court Road, W1;
020 7580 2791; www.americanchurchinlondon.org.

An international and interdenominational, Christ-centred community of
faith located in the heart of London.

Islam

Islamic Universal Association; 20 Penzance Place, Holland Park Avenue,
W11; 020 7602 5273; www.salaam.co.uk.

London Central Mosque and Islamic Cultural Centre; 146 Park Road,
NW8; 020 7724 3363; www.iccuk.org.

The largest mosque in London, located in Regent's Park.

Jewish

For a list of London synagogues, go to www.kosherdelight.com.

United Synagogue; 735 High Road, N12; 020 8343 8989; www.unitedsynagogue.org.uk. (Orthodox).

The Movement for Reform Judaism; The Sternberg Centre, 80 East End Road, N3; 020 8349 5700; www.reformjudaism.org.uk.

Contact for information about Reform synagogues in London.

West London Synagogue; 34 Upper Berkeley Street, W1; 020 7723 4404. (Reform).

Methodist

Methodist Central Hall Westminster; Storeys Gate, SW1; 020 7222 8010; www.c-h-w.co.uk.

Mormon

Church of Jesus Christ of Latter Day Saints; 64-68 Exhibition Road, SW7; 020 7584 8685; www.lds.org.uk.

Unitarian-Universalists

Essex Church Congregation; 112 Palace Gardens Terrace, W8; 020 7221 6514; www.unitarian.org.uk.

Rosslyn Hill Unitarian Chapel; Rosslyn Hill, NW3; 020 7433 3267.

Drawn by Saskia

Glossary

for other food related words, see the glossary in *Chapter 10: Cooking, Food and Drink*. For property and real estate terminology, see *Chapter 2: Housing*. For a glossary of words specific to children's items, see *Chapter 8: Children*. the American / British alphabetical glossary follows the British / American listing.

BRITISH	AMERICAN
A	
adjustable spanner	monkey wrench
aerial	antenna
afternoon tea	tea
agony aunt	advice columnist
airing cupboard	linen closet
anorak	parka (lined)
aubergine	eggplant
aussie	australian
B	
bank holiday	legal holiday
banknote, note	bill (money)
barnet	haircut
barrister	lawyer (trial)

BRITISH	AMERICAN
basin	sink
baths	swimming pool
bill	check (restaurant)
biro	ball point pen
biscuit	cookie
blind / roller blind	shade (window)
boiler	furnace / hot water heater
boiler suit	coverall (workmen's)
builder	contractor
bonnet	hood (car)
book	make reservations
boot	trunk (car)
braces	suspenders
break, holiday	recess (school break)
bollie	umbrella
brackets	parentheses
brummie	accent or person from birmingham
bumper	fender (car)
business suit	lounge suit

C

car park	parking lot
caravan	trailer / camper / mobile home
carrier bag	shopping bag
cello tape	scotch tape ®
cheers	thanks
chemist	drugstore / pharmacist
childminder	babysitter
chips	french fries
cinema	movie house / theatre
class / form	grade (school)
cleaner / domestic	maid or janitor

BRITISH	AMERICAN
cling film	saran wrap
cloakroom	checkrooms / half-bath / powder room
clothes peg	clothes pin
coach	tour bus
cockney	accent or person from east end of london
confectioners / sweet shop	candy store
conservatory	porch (enclosed)
continental europe / the continent	europe
cooker	oven / range
cot	crib / baby bed
cotton	thread
cotton reel	spool (thread)
cotton wool	cotton balls
courgette	zucchini
court shoe	pump (shoe)
cowboy builders	swindler (home repair)
cow gum / studio gum	rubber cement
crèche	daycare center / nursery
crisps	potato chips
curling tongs	curling iron
curtains	drapes / draperies
cycle	bicycle

D

decorator	painter
delivery lorry / van	delivery truck
diary	calendar (personal)
directory enquiries	directory assistance
district	precinct
diversion	detour
diy	do-it-yourself
domestic help	cleaning lady

BRITISH	AMERICAN
double number (e.g., double 5)	number used twice (e.g., 55)
drain	sewer pipe (soil pipe)
draper (materials)	dry goods store
draughts	checkers (game)
drawing pin	thumb tack
dress circle	mezzanine
dressing gown	bathrobe
drinks party	cocktail party
dual carriageway	divided highway
dummy	pacifier (for baby)
dustbin / bin	garbage /trash can
duvet	comforter

E

earth wire	ground wire
elastic bands	rubber bands
emulsion	paint (interior house)
engineer	repairman
enquiry	information (phone)
estate agent	real estate agent
estate car	station wagon
extension lead	extension cord

F

face flannel / face cloth	wash cloth
fancy dress	costume
father christmas	santa claus
film	movie
first floor	second floor
fitted carpet	wall-to-wall carpet
fiver	five pound note
flyover	overpass (highway)
football	soccer
fortnight	two weeks

BRITISH	AMERICAN
fringe	bangs
full stop	period (punctuation)

G

BRITISH	AMERICAN
garden	backyard
gateau (cake)	cake
gear lever	gear shift (car)
geordie	accent or person from N.E. England
geyser	water heater (gas)
gin or vodka martini	martini
golf buggy	electric golf cart
grease proof paper	wax paper
grill	broil / broiler
ground floor	first floor

H

BRITISH	AMERICAN
haberdashery	notions
hallmarked	solid sterling (silver)
handbag	purse / pocketbook
hand brake	parking brake
hard shoulder	shoulder (highway)
hardware	housewares / hardware
hard grip / kirby grip	bobbie pin
headmaster / headmistress	principal (school)
high street	main street
hire	rent (goods, car)
hire purchase	time payment
hire purchase plan	instalment payment plan
hob	stove/ cooktop
holiday	vacation
Hoover ®	vacuum cleaner
hose pipe	garden hose

BRITISH	AMERICAN
I	
immersion heater	water heater (electric)
interflora	f.t.d. (florist)
interval	intermission
invoice	bill (account)
ironmonger	hardware store
J	
jab	shot / injection
jacket potato	baked potato
jam	jelly
jelly	jello ® / gelatin
joint	roast (piece of meat)
jug	pitcher
juggernaut	truck (semi)
jumper / heresy	sweater / pullover
jump leads	jumper cables (car)
junior school	elementary school
K	
kagoule	parka (unlined)
kerb	curb (sidewalk)
kit	sports clothes / equipment
kitchen roll	paper towels
kiwi	new zealander
knackered	tired
knickers / pants	underpants / panties
knickerbockers / plus fours	knickers
knock about (tennis)	warm up (tennis)
L	
label	tag
ladder (in tights)	run (in nylons)
larder	pantry

BRITISH	AMERICAN
lavatory / toilet / loo	bathroom
lay-by	pull-off (driving)
lead (dog)	leash (dog)
lead	electric cord /wire
lemon squash	lemonade
lemonade	seven-up® / sprite®
let	rent (real estate)
lift	elevator
limited / ltd	incorporated / inc.
liquidiser	blender
lodger	roomer / boarder
loft	attic
loo	restroom / toilet
lorry	truck
lost property	lost and found

M

macintosh	raincoat
maisonette	duplex / triplex
mate	buddy
methylated spirits	denatured alcohol
milk float	milk truck
mince	hamburger meat / ground beef or other meat
m.o.t.	motor vehicle inspection test
motorbike	motorcycle
motorway	freeway / super highway

N

nappy	diaper
neat	straight (cocktail)
net curtains	sheers (under drapes)
newsagent	news dealer / newsstand
nil / nought	zero

BRITISH	AMERICAN
noughts and crosses	tic-tac-toe
number / registration plate	licence plate

O

off-licence	liquor store
on the pull	on the prowl
oven gloves / mitt	pot holder / gloves
overtake	pass (vehicle)

P

packed lunch	sack or bag lunch
paddle	wade
pants	underwear
paraffin	kerosene
parcel	package
parcel tape	packing tape
pavement	sidewalk
pelmet	valance (drapes)
petrol	gasoline
phone box	pay telephone booth
pillar box (antiquated) post box	mailbox
pinafore dress	jumper
pissed	drunk
plaster / elastoplast	adhesive bandage
point / power point / plug socket	outlet / socket (electrical)
porter	doorman
postal order	money order
post code	zip code
post / postman	mailman
pram	baby carriage / buggy
prep (or homework)	homework
press studs /poppers	snaps (sewing)
public / fee paying school / private	private school
pudding / sweet	dessert

BRITISH	AMERICAN
purse	change purse / wallet
pushchair / buggy	stroller

Q

| quay (pron. 'key') | wharf / pier |
| queue | line (stand in) |

R

removal van	moving van
removal company	moving company
return ticket	round trip ticket
reverse charges	call collect
ring up	call (telephone)
roundabout	traffic circle
rubber	eraser
rubbish / refuse	garbage (trash)

S

s.a.e.	stamped addressed envelope
saloon	sedan (car)
scally	accent or person from liverpool
scribbling pad / book / jotter	scratch pad
serviettes	napkins
shop assistant	sales clerk
sideboards	sideburns
silencer	muffler (car)
single ticket	one way ticket
sitting / reception room / lounge	living room
skip	dumpster (construction)
skipping rope	jump rope
skirting board	baseboard
snog	make out (kiss)
solicitor	lawyer / attorney

BRITISH	AMERICAN
spanner	wrench
spectacles / specs	eyeglasses
spirits	liquor
squaddie	young person in the military (e.g., rotc)
stablisers	training wheels
stand	run (for public office)
stalls	orchestra seats (theatre)
starter	appetiser
state school / grammar school	public school
stone	pit (of fruit) / weight (1 stone = 14 pounds)
stroke / oblique	slash (/)
subway	underground / pedestrian passage
surgery	doctor's / dentist's office
surgical spirit	rubbing alcohol
suspenders	garter belt
sweets / chocolate bar	candy / candy bar
swimming costume	bathing suit

T

BRITISH	AMERICAN
ta	thanks
table tennis bat	ping pong paddle
take-away	take out (food)
tap	faucet
tarmac	pavement
tea	children's supper / dinner
tea trolley	tea cart
teat	nipple (baby bottle)
telly	television
tenner	ten pound note
term (school)	semester
theatre / operating theatre	surgery (medical)

BRITISH	AMERICAN
tights	panty hose
the city	financial district
till	cash register
time-table	schedule
tip (rubbish)	dump (garbage)
tin	can
torch	flashlight
tracksuit bottoms	sweatpants
trainers / plimsolls	sneakers / tennis shoes
traveling rug	blanket (traveling)
treble number (e.g., treble 5)	number used three times (e.g., 555)
trolley	grocery cart
trousers	pants
tube / underground	subway
turn-ups (trousers)	cuffs (pants)
turf	sod (new grass)

U

university	college / university

V

valance	dust ruffle
verge / hard shoulder	soft shoulder (road)
vest	t-shirt / undershirt

W

waistcoat	vest
wardrobe	closet (hanging clothes)
washing up	doing the dishes
washing up liquid	dishwashing liquid (hand)
wash your hands	wash up
wellies (wellington boots)	boots (waterproof)
whinging	whining

white or black (as in coffee)	with or without milk/cream
windcheater	windbreaker
windscreen	windshield
wing mirror	review view mirror (outside)

Z

zebra crossing	crosswalk
'zed' (pron.)	z

AMERICAN	BRITISH

A

antenna	aerial
appetiser	starter
attic	loft
advice column	agony aunt
australian	aussie

B

baby carriage or buggy	pram
baked potato	jacket potato
ball point pen	biro
bandage (adhesive)	plaster
bangs	fringe
baseboard	skirting board
bathrobe	dressing gown
bill (account)	invoice
bill (money)	banknote, note
blanket (travelling)	travelling rug
blender	liquidizer
bobbic pin	hair grip / kirby grip
boots (water proof)	wellies (wellington boots)
broil/broiler	grill
buddy	mate

AMERICAN	BRITISH
C	
cake	gateau (or cake)
calendar	diary
call (telephone)	ring up
call collect	reverse charges
can	tin
candy / candy bar	sweets / chocolate bar
candy shop	confectioners / sweet shop
cash register	till
change purse	purse
check (restaurant)	bill
checkers (game)	draughts
checkroom	cloakroom
cleaning lady	domestic help
closet (hanging clothes)	wardrobe
clothes pin	clothes peg
cocktail party	drinks party
college / university	university
comforter	duvet
contractor	builder
coveralls (workmen's)	boiler suit
cookie	biscuit
costume	fancy dress
cotton balls	cotton wool
crib/baby bed	cot
crosswalk	zebra crossing
cuffs (pants)	turn-ups (trousers)
curb (sidewalk)	kerb (pavement)
curling iron	curling tongs
D	
daycare	crèche
delivery truck	delivery lorry / van
denatured alcohol	methylated spirits

AMERICAN	BRITISH
dessert	pudding / sweet
detour	diversion
diaper	nappy
dime store / five and dime	woolworths / woollies
directory assistance	directory enquiries
dishes (do the)	washing up
dishwashing liquid (hand)	washing up liquid
divided highway	dual carriageway
do-it-yourself	diy
doctor / dentist office	surgery
doorman	porter
drapes / draperies	curtains
drugstore / pharmacy	chemist
drunk	pissed
dry goods store	(materials) draper
dump (garbage)	tip / rubbish
dumpster (construction)	skip
duplex/triplex	maisonette
dust ruffle	valance

E

eggplant	aubergine
electric cord/wire	lead
electric golf cart	golf buggy
elevator	lift
elementary school	junior school
eraser	rubber
europe	continental europe / the continent
extension cord	extension lead

F

faucet	taps
fender (car)	bumper

AMERICAN	BRITISH
first floor	ground floor
fish shop	fishmonger
flashlight	torch
freeway / super highway	motorway
f.t.d. (florist)	interflora
furnace / hot water heater	boiler
french fries	chips

G

garbage (trash)	rubbish / refuse
garbage / trash can	dustbin / bin
garden hose	hose pipe
garter belt	suspenders
gasoline (car)	petrol
gear shift	gear lever
glasses	spectacles / specs
grade (school)	class/form
grocery cart	trolley
ground wire	earth wire / earth

H

half bath / powder room	cloakroom
hamburger meat /ground beef	mince
hardware store	ironmonger
hat check girl	cloakroom attendant
homework	prep (or homework)
hood (car)	bonnet
housewares	hardwares

I

incorporated / inc.	limited / ltd
information (phone)	enquiry
installment payment plan	hire purchase plan
intermission	interval

19

AMERICAN	BRITISH
J	
janitor	cleaner
jello ® / gelatin	jelly
jelly	jam
jump rope	skipping rope
jumper	pinafore dress
jumper cables	jumper leads
K	
kerosene	paraffin
knickers	knickerbockers / plus fours
L	
lawyer / attorney	solicitor
lawyer (trial)	barrister
leash (dog)	lead
legal holiday	bank holiday
lemonade	lemon squash
license plate	number / registration plate
line (stand in)	queue
linen closet	airing cupboard
liquor	spirits
living room	reception room / lounge
lost and found	lost property
lounge suit	business suit
M	
maid	cleaner / domestic help
mail/mailman	post / postman
mailbox	post box
main street	high street
make out (kiss)	snog
make reservations	book

AMERICAN	BRITISH
martini	gin or vodka martini
milk truck	milk float
money order	postal order
monkey wrench	adjustable spanner
motorcycle	motorbike
movie	film
motor vehicle inspection test	m.o.t.
movie house/theatre	cinema
moving van	removal van
moving company	removal company
muffler (car)	silencer

N

napkins	serviettes / napkins
newsdealer / newsstand	newsagent
nipple (baby bottle)	teat
notions	haberdashery
number used twice (e.g., "55")	double number
number used three times	triple number
nursery	crèche

O

on the prowl	on the pull
one way ticket	single ticket
orchestra seats (theatre)	stalls
outlet / socket (electrical)	point / power point / plug socket
oven	cooker
overpass	flyover

P

pacifier (for baby)	dummy
package	parcel
packing tape	parcel tape

AMERICAN	BRITISH
paint (interior house)	emulsion
painter	decorator
panty hose	tights
pantry	larder
pants	trousers
paper towels	kitchen roll
parentheses	brackets
parka (lined)	anorak
parka (unlined)	kagoule
parking brake	hand brake
parking lot	car park
pass (vehicle)	overtake
pavement	tarmac
pay telephone booth	phone box
period (punctuation)	full stop
ping pong paddle	table tennis bat
pit (fruit)	stone
pitcher	jug
porch (enclosed)	conservatory
pot holder / gloves	oven gloves / mitt
potato chips	crisps
precinct	district
principal (school)	headmaster / mistress
private school	public / fee paying / independent
public school	state school / grammar school
pull-off (driving)	lay-by
pump (shoe)	court shoe
purse / pocketbook	handbag

R

AMERICAN	BRITISH
raincoat	mackintosh (mac)

range	cooker
real estate agent	estate agent
rear view mirror (outside)	wing mirror
rent (goods)	hire
rent (real estate)	let
repairman	engineer
restroom / toilet	cloakroom / w.c. / loo / toilet
roast (piece of meat)	joint
roomer / boarder	lodger
round trip ticket	return ticket
rubber bands	elastic bands
rubber cement	cow gum / studio gum
rubbing alcohol	surgical spirit
run (for public office)	stand
run (in nylons)	ladder (in tights)

S

sack lunch	packed lunch
sales clerk	shop assistant
Santa Claus	Father Christmas / Santa Claus
Saran Wrap®	cling film
schedule	time-table
Scotch tape ®	cellotape
scratch pad	scribbling pad / book/ jotter
second floor	first floor
sedan (car)	saloon
semester (school)	term (three yearly)
Seven Up® (Sprite®)	lemonade
sewer pipe / soil pipe	drain
shade (window)	blind / roller blind
sheers (under drapes)	net curtains
shopping bag	carrier bag
shorts (underwear)	pants
shot / injection	jab
shoulder (highway)	hard shoulder

AMERICAN	BRITISH
sideburns	sideboards
sidewalk	pavement
sink	basin
slash (/)	stroke / oblique
snaps (sewing)	press studs / poppers
sneakers / tennis shoes	trainers / plimsolls
soccer	football
sod (new grass)	turf
soft shoulder (road)	verge / hard shoulder
spool (thread)	cotton reel
sports clothes / equipment	kit
stamped addressed envelope	s.a.e.
stand in line	queue
station wagon	estate car
sterling (silver)	hallmarked / solid
stove / cooktop	hob
straight (cocktail)	neat
stroller	pushchair / buggy
subway	tube / underground
supper	tea / supper / dinner
surgery (medical)	theatre / operating theatre
suspenders	braces
sweatpants	tracksuit bottoms
sweater / pullover	jumper / jersey
swimming pool	baths
swindler (home repair)	cowboy builders

T

AMERICAN	BRITISH
thanks	cheers / ta / thanks
take out (food)	take-away
tag	label
tea	afternoon tea
tea cart	tea trolley

AMERICAN	BRITISH

tennis warm-up	knock-about
thread	cotton
thumb tack	drawing pin
tic-tac-toe	noughts and crosses
tired	knackered
time payment	hire-purchase
tour bus	coach
traffic circle	roundabout
trailer / camper / mobile home	caravan
training wheels	stabilisers
truck	lorry
truck (semi)	juggernaut
trunk (car)	boot
t-shirt	vest
t.v.	telly
two weeks	fortnight

U

umbrella	brollie
underground / pedestrian passage	subway
underpants / panties	knickers / pants
undershirt	vest

V

vacation	holiday
vacuum (cleaner)	Hoover ®
valance (drapes)	pelmet
vest	waistcoat

W

wade	paddle
wall street (financial industry)	the city
wall-to-wall carpet	fitted carpet
wallet	purse
wash cloth	face flannel / face cloth

19

AMERICAN	BRITISH
wash up	wash your hands
water heater (electric)	immersion heater
water heater (gas)	geyser
wax paper	grease proof paper
wharf / pier	quay (pron. 'key')
whining	whinging
windbreaker	windcheater / kagoul
windshield	windscreen
with or without? (milk / cream in coffee)	white or black?
wrench	spanner

Y

yard	garden

Z

z	'zed' (pron.)
zero	nil / nought / zero
zip code	post code
zucchini	courgette

NOTES

NOTES

MEASUREMENT CONVERSIONS

Liquid Measures		
	UK (Imperial / Metric)	US Imperial
Teaspoon	5 ml	$1/6$ oz
Dessertspoon	10 ml	$1/3$ oz
Tablespoon	15 ml	½ oz
Gill	150 ml	5 oz
Cup	10 oz / 290 ml	8 oz / 250 ml
Pint	20 oz / 585 ml	16 oz / 470 ml

Dry Measures			
	UK Imperial	UK Metric	US Imperial
Flour	5 oz	140 g	1 cup
Sugar	1 oz	25 g	2 tbsp
	8 oz	225 g	1 cup
Brown sugar	6 oz	170 g	1 cup
Breadcrumbs or nuts	4 oz	115 g	1 cup
Yeast	1/4 oz	7 g	2 ½ tsp
Butter	1 oz	25 g	2 tbsp
	8 oz	225 g	1 cup
	4 oz	100 g	1 stick (8 tbsp)

When measuring dry ingredients such as flour or sugar for a British recipe, remember to weigh the items as the ingredients will be listed in ounces or grams. (Remember, eight ounces of two different ingredients may have distinctly different volumes.)

Further Conversions

Grams to Ounces	Multiply grams by 0.03527
Ounces to Grams	Multiply ounces by 28.35
Quarts to Litres	Multiply quarts by 0.95
Pounds to Grams	Multiply pounds by 453.6
Pounds to Kilograms	Multiply pounds by 0.4536
Kilograms to Pounds	Multiply kilograms by 2.205
Stones to Pounds	Multiply stones by 14
Centigrade to Fahrenheit	Multiply C by 1.8 and add 32
Fahrenheit to Centigrade	Multiply F by 5, subtract 32 and then divide by 9

Cooking Temperatures

Celsius	Fahrenheit	Gas Mark	Description
110	225	1/4	Very slow
125	250	1/2	Very slow
140	275	1	Slow
150	300	2	Slow
165	325	3	Moderate
180	350	4	Moderate
190	375	5	Moderate / Hot
200	400	6	Moderate / Hot
220	425	7	Hot
230	450	8	Hot
240	475	9	Very hot

For fan-assisted ovens you should either turn the heat down slightly or decrease the cooking time.